Ralph E. Hutchinson (California):

A contributor to *Great Vineyards and Wine-makers, Wines of the World, Serena Sutcliffe's Handbook of Wine,* as well as an occasional contributor to *Wines and Vines* and *The Wine Spectator,* Ralph E. Hutchinson is a professor of economics who acts as a consultant to wineries. Charter member of the Society of Wine Educators, he belongs to the American Society of Enology and Viticulture, Les Amis du Vin, and Southern California Wine Writers. Professor Hutchinson lives in Claremont, California.

Richard Figiel (East of the Rockies):

Editor of *International Wine Review,* Richard Figiel was editor of *Eastern Grape Grower & Winery News* for vineyardists and winemakers. He has written about American wines for several magazines and books, most recently *A Price Guide to Good Wine* (Addison-Wesley, 1983). After working in several of the vineyards and wine cellars of New York's Finger Lakes district, he established his own Silver Thread Vineyard on Seneca Lake near his home in Ithaca.

Ted Jordan Meredith (The Northwest):

A resident of Washington state, Ted Jordan Meredith has been writing about the wines of the northwest for more than a decade. He is the author of the widely praised *Northwest Wines* (Nexus Press). He lives in Kirkland.

A DICTIONARY OF

OF

AMERICAN WINES

A DICTIONARY OF AMERICAN WINES

RALPH E. HUTCHINSON

RICHARD FIGIEL

TED JORDAN MEREDITH

BTB
BEECH TREE BOOKS
WILLIAM MORROW
New York

Library of Congress Catalog Card Number: 85-70575

ISBN: 0-688-02833-0

Printed in the United States

First Edition

1   2   3   4   5   6   7   8   9   10

Designed by Keith Sheridan Associates, Inc.

Produced by Smallwood & Stewart 156 Fifth Avenue New York 10010

Maps: Ed Lipinski

BTB

The word "book" is said to derive from *boka*, or beech.
The beech tree has been the patron tree of writers since ancient times and
represents the flowering of literature and knowledge.

INTRODUCTION

If there is any constancy in the American wine industry it is
the persistence of change and dynamic growth. But change
is not so much a product of the youthfulness of the industry
as fundamental to its spirit. During the late 19th century
wines from regions such as California, New York, and Ohio
enjoyed a worldwide reputation — by the time Prohibition
ended in 1933 both the reputation and the industry had been
virtually destroyed. Today wine is produced in over 40
states and in a range of geographic conditions and climates
as diverse as any in the world: not just in select California
valleys or the shores of New York's Finger Lakes, but in the
foothills of Oregon, the farmland of West Virginia, the
plains of Texas. From staggering quantities of everyday table
wines to premium varietals that equal the best from Europe,
America has proved itself to be an innovative, enthusiastic
and, above all, supremely benign home to winemaking.

One beneficial result of Prohibition was that it freed
winemakers from tradition and fostered a spirit of experimentation, exemplified today in the work of institutions
such as the University of California at Davis, in developing
virus-free rootstocks, breeding new grape varietals, and
matching varietals to regions. In the remarkable renaissance
of American winemaking over the last two decades,
winemakers have taken a more scientific approach to their
art than their European equivalents. The wooden and con-
crete fermenters of an earlier period have been replaced by
refrigerated stainless steel tanks which permit more precise
control of fermentation. Centrifuges have been added for
the clarification of musts and wines, resulting in cleaner vintages, and many wineries have built their own laboratories.

At the same time the domestic audience for wine has
grown and also become more sophisticated. At the beginning of the 1980s sales of domestic table wine reached 290
million gallons, six times the figure of 1960.

Beyond the task of encompassing this continuing
change and unique diversity, any writer on American

wine has to cope with the sheer quantitative changes. During the writing of this book nearly 100 new wineries came into being, some merged and changed their names, a few stopped producing wine. But it is this vitality that makes American wine such an absorbing subject.

By far the greatest difficulty has been what to leave out. Almost by definition a book on American winemaking has to be selective, and the authors have tried to be as judicious in their choice of what wineries are included as in their descriptions. The size of a winery is always a consideration for inclusion but is not the overriding factor. In order to create the most representative picture of diverse winemaking across the country we have also taken into account the quality of their wines and their originality.

The entries that follow are arranged alphabetically, covering wineries, major growing regions, grape varieties, and wine terms.

Wineries: The location (town) and region or state follow every winery entry. Where the winery is located in a significant winegrowing region, the region is indicated. Alongside each winery entry is an estimate of recent output and a list of its leading wines. Wineries that produce only in bulk or for distribution through restricted outlets have generally been omitted.

Regions: The regional descriptions in this book are selected to cover the most significant, cohesive areas for winemaking, and sometimes incorporate several of the recently introduced BATF Viticultural Areas. Where appropriate, recent vintage evaluations follow the entry.

Grape Varieties: Brief descriptions are given of the major vinifera, hybrid, and native American grapes.

Wine Terms: Several definitions are given of grape-growing, winemaking, and tasting terms as well as those commonly used on the labels of American wines.

Ralph Hutchinson, California
Richard Figiel, East of the Rocky Mountains
Ted Jordan Meredith, Idaho, Oregon, Washington

ACACIA WINERY
Napa, San Francisco Bay North

Output: 22,000 cases

*Leading Wines:
Vineyard-designated
Chardonnays, Pinot Noirs*

Founded in 1979 by Jerry Goldstein and Mike Richmond (who was formerly with Freemark Abbey), Acacia specializes in vineyard-designated Chardonnays and Pinot Noirs. The winery owns 50 acres of Chardonnay covering the gentle undulations of the hills behind the winery in the cooler Carneros district of the Napa Valley. Some Chardonnay and all Pinot Noir grapes are purchased from selected vineyards.

Altogether, Acacia produces five different Chardonnays and five different Pinot Noirs, each labeled to indicate geographic origin of the grapes. The Chardonnays include two vineyard-designated wines. The Marina Estate wine is made from Acacia's own grapes and reflects the influence of its cool marine climate in its leaner style. The second vineyard-designated wine is made from grapes grown in the famous Winery Lake Vineyard, located a short distance from the winery in the heart of the Carneros district. Located further inland than Acacia's Marina Vineyard, Winery Lake's growing season temperatures are warmer and the wine is fuller with a spicey-fruity character.

Acacia's Pinot Noirs are all vineyard-designated and all five vineyards are located within a mile of the winery in Carneros. The coolness of the district benefits the grapes and their wines with enhanced color, flavor, and acidity. However, each wine is unique, reflecting differences in solar exposure, soil composition, clones, and rootstock. In particular, those from Iund, Madonna, and Winery Lake show intense varietal character.

Acetic (Acetic acid)

A sharp, offensive taste (and component) of wine, often associated with vinegar. It is produced when the wine is exposed to air and winemakers prevent it by using air-tight tanks and keeping equipment sanitary. But a trace of acetification is present in many wines and even a slightly perceptible amount can add to the complexity of some wines, particularly full-bodied reds. This stylistic use of acetic acid is more common in French wine (particularly Burgundies) than in American wines.

A

Acidity

The tart component in the taste of wine. Novices often find the acidity in wine disagreeably sour, but experience reveals its importance to add freshness, accent flavors, and enhance wine's affinity with food. White wines are usually made with higher acidity than reds, to complement fruity flavors and balance any sweetness. Wines low in acidity tend to taste flat, and their sweetness can become cloying; wines high in acid tend to taste sharp.

Grapes lose their natural acidity as they ripen, a process accelerated in warmer climates. In the chemistry of grapes and wine, acids play a key role in flavor development and improvement with aging: higher acid wines are generally better keepers. "Total Acidity" is the winemaker's term for a measurement of various types of acid in wine.

ADELAIDA CELLARS
Paso Robles, Central Coast

Output: 7,500 cases

*Leading Wines:
Blanc de Blancs,
Cabernet Sauvignon,
Chardonnay*

Although Adelaida Cellars is relatively young (it received a bonded number only in August of 1983), two wines are already available: a 1981 Cabernet Sauvignon and a 1982 Chardonnay—the specialties of this small 10-acre winery.

Adelaida—with some European backing—is also responsible for the Tonio Conti label. This is a line of *méthode champenoise* sparkling wines. The first release was of 1,700 cases of Blanc de Blancs from Chardonnay grapes harvested in 1982 at the Estrella River vineyard. Subsequent production has been about twice this figure.

ADELSHEIM VINEYARD
Newberg, Oregon

Output: 14,000 cases

*Leading Wines:
Chardonnay, Merlot,
Pinot Gris, Pinot Noir,
Riesling, Semillon*

David and Ginny Adelsheim planted their 18-acre vineyard in the northern Willamette Valley in 1971, and crushed their first commercial vintage in 1978. One of the wineries most attentive to European viticultural and winemaking methods, David Adelsheim researched French and German texts and worked at the Lycée Viticole in Beaune. He has also conducted detailed research on the organoleptic effects of different oak sources and species, the differences in bending the staves by steaming or toasting by fire, and their varied contributions to the character of different wines.

Although very much committed to making Oregon wines from Burgundian grape varieties, Adelsheim also makes Semillon and Merlot from Washington grapes, two wines he began making prior to the availability of Oregon grapes and continues to make by popular demand. Washington winemakers tend to emphasize Semillon's intense, grassy fruit qualities. Adelsheim's Semillon from Washington grapes moderates the fresh fruit character in favor of the alternate complexities of a more restrained style. Of the Oregon varieties, Adelsheim's Chardonnay is richly flavored with soft acidity. The Pinot Noirs are delicate, with moderate tannins, and spicy varietal fruit enhanced by aging in heavily toasted Allier oak barrels.

ADLER FELS
Santa Rosa, San Francisco Bay North

Output: 6,000 cases

Leading Wines:
Cabernet Sauvignon,
Chardonnay,
Gewurztraminer,
Johannisberg Riesling,
Mélange à Deux,
Pinot Noir,
Sauvignon Blanc

Adler Fels is German for "Eagle Rock"—the name of the nearby crest that overlooks this winery. Sitting precariously 1,500 feet above the valley floor, the main building looks as if it could have been transplanted from the banks of the Rhine to the Sonoma Valley.

The winery was founded in 1980 by graphic artist David Coleman, his wife Ann Ryan, and Pat Heck, and has five variable-capacity tanks to accommodate very small lots. Equipped with floating tops that adjust to the amount of wine in the tank, they eliminate the need for a layer of inert gas—the usual protection from oxidation. This equipment reflects the winery's specialty: production of numerous small lots of vineyard-designated wine made from selected Sonoma County locations, frequently in lots no larger than 400 cases.

This approach has paid dividends in the form of awards in five California wine competitions in 1983 and 1984, and Adler Fels is particularly proud of its 1982 Fumé Blanc from the Salzbeger/Chan Vineyards, which won more awards than any other 1982 Sauvignon Blanc.

Mélange à Deux, a sparkling wine made from a blend of Johannisberg Riesling and Gewurztraminer, uses a slight variation on the *méthode champenoise*. The grapes are harvested when fully ripe (23 degrees Brix, against 18 or 19 degrees Brix) and fermentation is allowed to proceed until about 3 percent residual sugar is left unfermented. It is the fermentation of this residual sugar after bottling that provides the effervescence in Mélange à Deux; no dosage sugar is added after disgorging to remove sediment so the wine is very dry but intensely fruity.

AHERN WINERY
San Fernando, South Coast

Output: 6,000 cases

Leading Wines:
Cabernet Sauvignon,
Chardonnay,
Napa Gamay Blanc,
Sauvignon Blanc,
Zinfandel

Like many other winery owners in the Los Angeles area, Jim and Joyce Ahern were home winemakers for several years before founding Ahern in 1978.

Ahern has a reputation for seeking out small lots of good fruit from the best vineyards, notably those in the cooler Edna Valley south of San Luis Obispo, and—in the best tradition of home winemakers turned professional—laboring over these small lots to assure a quality product. Their work has already paid dividends; their barrel-fermented Edna Valley Chardonnay has done well in competitions throughout the state.

A

Alcohol

One of the products of fermentation, ethyl alcohol or ethanol adds a 'volatile' dimension to wine that enhances its sensory potential. The presence of alcohol permits greater complexity by allowing more substances into solution. Alcohol is also a natural preservative, but this function has become less important as the technology of winemaking has improved. Today, wines with low alcohol (10 percent or less) can be as stable as high alcohol wines. The standard range is 9-14 percent for table wines; 18-21 percent for sherry and other fortified wines. Increasing levels of alcohol give wine more body and viscosity. Too much alcohol, especially in relation to other components, produces a hot sensation and obscures other attributes.

ALDERBROOK VINEYARDS
Healdsburg, San Francisco Bay North

Output: 10,000 cases

Leading Wines:
Cabernet Sauvignon,
Chardonnay,
Gewurztraminer,
Johannisberg Riesling

Founded in 1982, this small winery has now crushed grapes in only three harvests, but has already made its mark in California wine competitions, winning a good reputation for its Sauvignon Blanc in particular.

Alderbrook owns 63 acres of vineyards located in Dry Creek Valley Viticultural Area which should come to maturity in the next few years and has 30,000 gallons of storage capacity.

ALEXANDER VALLEY VINEYARDS
Healdsburg, San Francisco Bay North

Output: 18,000 cases

Leading Wines:
Cabernet Sauvignon,
Chardonnay,
Chenin Blanc,
Gewurztraminer,
Johannisberg Riesling

The Wetzel family purchased the old Cyrus Alexander estate in the valley that bears the name of this pioneer, and in 1964 began planting grapes and constructing a 65,000-gallon winery. Their first wines were not produced until 1975, the year after Hank Wetzel's graduation from U.C. Davis with a degree in enology.

Currently, 120 acres are planted to Chardonnay, Gewurztraminer, Chenin Blanc, Johannisberg Riesling, Merlot, Cabernet Sauvignon, and a small amount of Pinot Noir, all of which are produced as estate wines. Particularly noteworthy are their Chenin Blanc, which often achieves an almost Chardonnay-like character; their Cabernet Sauvignon, which is blended in classic Bordeaux style with a little Merlot; and their Pinot Noir. Alexander Valley Vineyards is one of the largest wineries in California producing a wide range of varietals solely from estate-grown grapes.

Alicante Bouschet

One of the few teinturier (red juice) grapes planted in commercial vineyards in California. It was highly favored during Prohibition because of its deeply colored juice and its thick-skin which enabled it to withstand cross-country shipping. Although it is not generally highly regarded by commercial winemakers, except as a blending grape to add color to generic blends, a few California wineries produce a robust varietal from it. There are about 3,500 acres planted in California, most of them in the Central Valley.

ALLEGRO VINEYARDS
Brogue, Mid-Atlantic Coast

Founded in 1981, Allegro quickly established the northern outpost of an emerging Cabernet Sauvignon district that stretches from Pennsylvania's York County through Maryland into Virginia. Allegro's most successful wines have been its reds, a rarity among eastern wineries. In the excellent vintages of the early 1980s, the Cabernet has been a rich wine with firm acid structure and elegant nuances of Cabernet Franc and Merlot in the blend. Three dry white varietals — Seyval, Chardonnay, and Vidal — and Allegro's generic blends have also been consistently well-made, often distinctive wines. Opus 1, an inspired blend of peach wine and Seyval, brought national attention to the tiny winery when the Mondavi-Rothschild collaboration chose the same name for its Napa Valley red. Two-thirds of the 15-acre vineyard grows French-American varieties, one-third vinifera.

Output: 2,000 cases

Leading Wines:
Cabernet Sauvignon,
Chardonnay, Opus 1,
Seyval Blanc,
Late-Harvest Seyval
Vidal Blanc, Vin Blanc,
Vin Rouge

ALMADEN VINEYARDS
San Jose, San Francisco Bay South

Founded by Charles LeFranc in 1852, Almadén lays claim to being the second oldest winery in California. Now surrounded by housing developments, its Blossom Hill Road headquarters is on the site of LeFranc's original winery, and it was here that he planted cuttings from his native France and became one of the first to cultivate *Vitis vinifera* successfully in California.

The modern history of the winery begins in 1941, when Louis Benoist bought the idle LeFranc property and decided to return it to production. He hired Frank Schoonmaker as an adviser, and under his expert guidance Almadén was one of the first to begin extensive plantings in Monterey and San Benito counties with a view to making fine varietal wines. In 1967 Benoist sold Almadén to National Distillers and Chemical, which continued and expanded the winery's growth.

Today Almadén has 40 million gallons of storage in four winery locations and its annual sales make it the tenth largest winery in the United States. Only sparkling wines are still produced at Blossom Hill Road, but all other Almadén wines are finished and bottled here by modern bottling lines that can fill 40,000 cases a day. (The fastest of these lines is capable of filling, corking, labeling, boxing a bottle, and loading a case onto a pallet for shipping in 6 minutes.)

Almadén owns 5,700 acres of vineyards, just over 4,000 of which are in San Benito County. Contracts with growers give the winery control over

Output. 9.6 million cases

Leading Wines:
Cabernet Sauvignon,
Chardonnay,
Gamay Beaujolais,
Gewurztraminer,
Johannisberg Riesling
Merlot, Pinot Noir,
Sauvignon Blanc;
Charles Le Franc:
Cabernet Sauvignon,
Chardonnay, Fumé Blanc,
Late-Harvest
Johannisberg Riesling
Pinot St. George,
Royale, Zinfandel;
Almadén Mountain:
Burgundy, Chablis,
Chianti, Claret,
Grenache Rosé,

A

Nectar, Rhine,
Vin Rosé; Almadén:
Blancs de Blancs,
sparkling Chardonnay
Nature,
Eye of the Partridge;
La Domaine:
Brut, Cold Duck,
Extra Dry, Pink Sparkling
Burgundy; Various dessert
and aperitif wines

a further 12,000 acres, more than 90 percent of the grapes grown in the San Benito region. Plantings are diverse; more than 20 varieties are grown in the San Benito vineyards alone.

The more than 50 table, dessert, and aperitif wines and brandies, which run the full range from generic jugs to vintage-dated varietals, are produced at wineries and distilleries in Hollister, Kingsburg, McFarland, and Pacines in the Central Coast region. (Almadén's 40,000-barrel cellar at Cienega for red wine aging is possibly the largest of its kind in the world.)

The best of each year's vintage is bottled under the Charles LeFranc label, and recent LeFranc Fumé Blancs and Cabernet Sauvignons have been impressive. Other labels include Almadén, Almadén Mountain, La Domaine, and generics.

In 1982 a Chardonnay was introduced under the Caves Laurent Perrier label. Part of a joint venture with Laurent Perrier of France, it is produced in the crisp, highly acidic style of the still, *coteaux champenois* wines of France.

Among Almadén's line of sparkling wines, top rank must be accorded to the Chardonnay Nature, which is made from Chardonnay grapes with little or no sugar in the dosage.

ALPINE VINEYARDS
Corvallis, Oregon

Output: 3,500 cases

Leading Wines:
Cabernet Sauvignon,
Chardonnay,
Pinot Noir,
Riesling

First planted in 1976 on a hillside site in the southern Willamette Valley, Dan and Christine Jepsen's 20 acre-estate vineyard includes Cabernet Sauvignon as well as the more traditional Willamette Valley varietals.

In cooler years, the Cabernet yields a very pleasant light wine, but warmer years bring out the best from the grape. Alpine's Cabernet grapes have moderate acidity, and the Jepsens do not further reduce the acid level by putting it through malolactic fermentation. Alpine's red wines undergo a relatively long cool fermentation at 70° to 75°F. The cooler fermentation temperature captures more of the inherent fruitiness of the grape. Alpine's Riesling is fermented at a cool 45°F six to eight weeks to preserve the delicate fruit esters. The Riesling is often bottled cool so that the entrapped carbon dioxide is released in the glass as a refreshing spritz.

AMADOR FOOTHILL WINERY
Plymouth, Sierra Foothills

Output: 7,500 cases

Leading Wines:
Cabernet Sauvignon,
Fumé Blanc,
White Zinfandel,
Zinfandel

This small winery was founded in 1980 by a former home winemaker, Ben Zeitman, and his wife in response to the growing demand for Amador Zinfandels. Currently they have 10.5 acres of vineyards mainly planted to Zinfandel and 18,000 gallons of storage.

AMITY VINEYARDS
Amity, Oregon

Amity was founded in 1974 when Myron Redford purchased a 15-acre vineyard, in the northern Willamette Valley. Redford's Riesling and Gewurztraminer are full-flavored and nearly dry, bearing Amity's stylistic trademark, but Redford is best-known for Pinot Noir.

Amity was the first Oregon winery to release a carbonic maceration Pinot Noir Nouveau. But barrel-aged Pinot Noir is clearly Amity's major focus. Believing that blending is an important part of the winemaker's art, Redford purchases Pinot Noir grapes from several vineyards, ferments the wines separately, and tastes them in varying proportions and combinations before determining the final blends for bottling.

Amity usually releases two barrel-aged Pinot Noirs each vintage, one made for early consumption and a Winemaker's Reserve' selection. Typically, Redford's finest Pinot Noirs are higher in tannin and acidity than most, and this acidity, in conjunction with concentrated varietal fruit, gives them the balance and depth for rewarding development in the cellar. Cellaring times vary according to the character of the vintage, but some of the reserve bottlings, such as the 1977 Wadenswil, will readily develop in the bottle for a decade or more.

Output: 10,000 cases

Leading Wines:
Chardonnay,
Gerwurztraminer,
Pinot Noir, Riesling

S. ANDERSON VINEYARD
Napa, San Francisco Bay North

The Andersons own 49 acres of Chardonnay vineyards and specialize in estate-bottled Chardonnay and vintage-dated Blanc de Noirs sparkling wines made exclusively from purchased Pinot Noir grapes. Carol Anderson, who studied at U.C. Davis, is the winemaker, and all of her sparkling wines are made by *méthode champenoise*. To facilitate this, dramatic 16-foot-high tunnels have been dug into the hillside above the winery, which give nearly 7,000 square feet for riddling and aging.

First vintage of the Chardonnay was in 1979, and a 1980 sparkling wine was released in 1983; the success of the Anderson's experiment was confirmed in record prices for both wines in the 1984 Napa Wine Auction.

Output: 6,000 cases

Leading Wines:
Blanc de Noirs
sparkling wine,
Chardonnay

ARBOR CREST
Spokane, Washington

One of three wineries in the Spokane metropolitan area of eastern Washington, Arbor Crest was founded in 1982 by Dave and Harry Mielke, farmers and orchardists. The winemaker is Scott Harris, a U.C. Davis graduate in enology and formerly assistant winemaker at California's Davis Bynum winery.

Although Riesling comprises most of the production for the majority of new Washington wineries, Arbor Crest is focusing on Chardonnay and Sauvignon Blanc, and nearly half of the production is in these two

Output: 20,000 cases

Leading Wines:
Cabernet Sauvignon,
Chardonnay,
Gewurztraminer,
Merlot, Riesling,
Sauvignon Blanc,

A

varieties. Both are aged in French oak barrels. The Sauvignon Blanc is finished with slight residual sugar.

Arbor Crest has been very successful with a diverse range of wines, including semisweet Muscat Canelli and late-harvest Riesling and Gewurztraminer. The red wines emphasize the clarion fruit of the grape coupled with a structure and extract for longer aging.

ARTERBERRY
McMinnville, Oregon

Output: 2,500 cases

Leading Wines: Chardonnay, Pinot Noir, Riesling, Sparkling cider, Sparkling wine

Oregon's first sparkling wine from Chardonnay, a traditional Champagne grape variety, was produced by Arterberry in 1979. Subsequent releases have included blends with Pinot Noir.

A winemaking graduate from U.C. Davis, Fred Arterberry uses wine grapes from his family's vineyard in the Red Hills of the northern Willamette Valley. Because grapes grown in cooler climates ripen at lower sugar levels, Arterberry believes that the Willamette Valley is ideal for sparkling wine grapes, which must be harvested at low sugars. Recent releases of sparkling wines show additional refinement and balance.

Aurora (Aurore)

When New York wineries began to turn from native American to French-American hybrid varieties in the 1960s, the major white grape planted was Seibel hybrid 5279 — Aurora. It remains the most extensively planted French hybrid in New York State (1,800 acres in 1980). But other hybrid varieties have eclipsed Aurora's record of performance in the vineyard and the bottle.

A very early ripener, often the first grape to reach eastern American winepresses, Aurora is best suited to cool climates, where maturity comes after the hottest days of summer. More wineries are pressing Aurora at relatively low Brix levels for light, appley, country wines. Early Auroras also play an important role in the cuvées for many eastern sparkling wines. The grapes tend to break down when fully ripe, producing strong, wild flavors in full-bodied wine. In either style, Aurora almost always finishes semisweet.

AUSTIN CELLARS
Solvang, Central Coast

Output: 18,000 cases

Leading Wines: Chardonnay, Gewurztraminer, Pinot Noir, Sauvignon Blanc, Seyval Blanc, White Riesling

Anthony Austin began his winery in 1981 with 100 acres of his own and 25 leased acres of vineyards in the cool, Region II Santa Maria Viticultural Area. Although six wines are produced, it is the Pinot Noir and botrytised Sauvignon Blanc that are specialties of this 48,000-gallon winery. Both benefit from the cool coastal climate, and in the Pinot Noirs Austin is continuing the reputation for this wine he built during his tenure as winemaker at Firestone Vineyards.

B

WILLIAM BACCALA WINERY
Ukiah, San Francisco Bay North

Output: 12,000 cases

*Leading Wines:
Chardonnay, Sanel,
Sauvignon Blanc*

Founded in 1981, this Russian River winery produces three wines for sale under their own label of Estate William Baccala and does custom crushing for other labels.

Wine production techniques are an unusual blend of old and new at William Baccala. In a more traditional vein, sulphur dioxide is not added to the grapes at the press or to the must, and the young wine is left on the lees for an additional six to eight weeks, before being transferred to small French oak barrels for further development. But after only 4-6 months the wine is returned to modern stainless steel tanks for blending, fining, and cold stabilization, and finally filtration.

Baco Noir

Baco was the first red French-American variety to be planted extensively in the United States. Following World War II it opened the door to a new generation of eastern red wines — dry, ungrapey, French-style wines. Baco makes a relatively austere, herbaceous wine with light to medium body, similar to a light, regional Bordeaux. When very ripe, it can develop muscle without filling out into a big wine. Other varieties are often blended in to smooth and round it out, and ameliorate Baco's characteristic green, stemmy nose and bitter edge. With 600 acres (1980), New York probably accounts for over three-quarters of United States acreage.

BAINBRIDGE ISLAND WINERY
Bainbridge Island, Washington

Output: 2,000 cases

*Leading Wines:
Chardonnay,
Madeleine Sylvaner,
Muller-Thurgau*

The first vines in this tiny 2-acre vineyard were planted in 1978 by Gerard and JoAnn Bentryn. The winery and vineyard are on Bainbridge Island, a 30-minute ferry ride from Seattle. The Bentryns specialize in vinifera varieties suited to the cool western Washington climate. The wines are Germanic in style: low alcohol, crisp, slightly sweet. Chardonnay is pro-

B

duced in several styles from dry to soft and late-harvest versions. Grapes from other local growers supplement the production and some wine, including the Chardonnay, is made from Columbia Valley grapes.

BALDINELLI VINEYARDS
Plymouth, Sierra Foothills

Output: 11,000 cases

Leading Wines:
Cabernet Sauvignon,
White Zinfandel,
Zinfandel

This winery, founded in 1979 by Kaiser engineer Edward Baldinelli, has about 50,000 gallons of storage capacity and 70 acres of vineyards in the Amador region, which is prized for its powerful Zinfandels. The cachet of Baldinelli, however, is the tamer style of Zinfandel that it coaxes out of its 60-year-old vines.

BALDWIN VINEYARDS
Pine Bush, Hudson River Valley

Output: 2,500 cases

Leading Wines:
Landot Noir,
Ravat (Vignoles), Riesling,
Seyval Blanc, Vidal

Grapes were purchased for the first vintage at Baldwin in 1982, the same year the vineyard was planted. Baldwin's location, in the hilly interior of the Hudson region away from the river, promises wines with high acidity and fruit. The early vintages, from some of the same French-American varieties planted, use American and French Limousin oak to soften and broaden the wines. Vinifera wines are being added as the small vineyard comes into bearing.

BALVERNE WINERY AND VINEYARDS
Windsor, San Francisco Bay North

Output: 25,000 cases

Leading Wines:
Chardonnay,
Gewurztraminer,
Healdsburger,
Johannisberg Riesling,
Sauvignon Blanc,
Scheurebe, Zinfandel

The 710 acres of the Balverne estate are situated in the Chalk Hill Viticultural Area on the site of a dormant volcano. Over 250 acres of the vines are planted on 35 separate plots, some so steep that they are terraced.

Scheurebe, the most unusual of Balverne's seven wines, is made from a cool-ripening Sylvaner Riesling cross-developed in Germany and produced in very limited amounts in the United States. Twelve acres are planted to this rare variety. The winery, which was founded in 1973, also produces a proprietary blend called Healdsburger, made from Gewurztraminer, Scheurebe, and Johannisberg Riesling. A Cabernet Sauvignon is planned for 1985. Seven different vineyards are designated on the labels of this 228,000-gallon winery: Stone Crest, Stone Ridge, Annaberg, Deer Hill, Oak Creek, Pepperwood, and Quartz Hill.

Barbera

Transplanted from northern Italy's Piedmont where it is produced as a varietal, Barbera makes red wines of high acidity, full body, and good color. There are over 16,000 acres planted to Barbera in California, nearly all in the Central Valley. A few wineries make Barbera as a varietal.

BARBOURSVILLE VINEYARDS
Barboursville, Virginia

Barboursville was the first significant European venture into American winemaking outside California. Attracted by similarities to growing conditions in Italy, the Zonin family — one of Italy's largest wine producers — bought an 800-acre plantation near Charlottesville, Virginia, in 1976 to develop a 50-acre American wine property within an Italian-style, diversified farm.

The wines are influenced but not dominated by Italian winemaking styles. Cabernet Sauvignon and Chardonnay are the principal varietals (all Barboursville wines are varietals), followed by White Riesling, Gewurztraminer, Merlot, and a white Pinot Noir. The two reds are supple, middle-weights emphasizing fruit and texture over wood and early maturing — not unlike their counterparts in Friuli or Trentino. After difficult early vintages (1978 was the first), the Chardonnay has also been a successful, European-style wine.

The estate once belonged to James Barbour, governor of Virginia in the early 19th century. Evocative ruins of his mansion, designed by Barbour's friend Thomas Jefferson, grace the label.

Output: 6,000 cases

Leading Wines:
Cabernet Sauvignon,
Chardonnay, Merlot

BARGETTO WINERY
Soquel, San Francisco Bay South

Founded in 1933, Bargetto has long been known for high quality fruit and berry wines that retain the clear tastes of the fruits from which they are made. The Olallieberry is possibly the star of Bargetto's line, but seven grape wines have been introduced and are also receiving favorable attention, in particular a white Riesling.

Bargetto buys most of its grapes from Tepusquet Vineyard in Santa Barbara County and features the name of the vineyard on wines made from those grapes.

Output: 25,000 cases

Leading Wines:
Apricot, Cabernet
Sauvignon, Chardonnay,
Chenin Blanc,
Gewurztraminer,
Johannisberg Riesling,
Olallieberry, Petite Sainte
Marie, Pomegranate,
Raspberry, Zinfandel

BARNARD-GRIFFIN WINERY
Kennewick, Washington

This small winery is owned and operated by Rob Griffin and Deborah Barnard, his wife. Griffin, formerly winemaker at Washington's Preston Wine Cellars, is now winemaker for the Hogue Cellars, and will continue making wine for Hogue as well as his own winery. The very successful Barnard-Griffin Chardonnay and Sauvignon Blanc, barrel-fermented in French oak, are less angular and more rounded than many Washington renditions of these grapes. The first Barnard-Griffin wines, from the 1983 vintage, were released in 1984.

Output: 1,500 cases

Leading Wines:
Chardonnay, Riesling,
Sauvignon Blanc

Barrel-fermented

Wines fermented in barrels tend to develop earthy, woody or vanilla flavors. Some winemakers believe fermenting in barrels integrates these flavors into the character of the wine better than simply aging it in barrels. Barrel fermentation is a stylistic technique used with many red wines and few whites (notably Chardonnay).

BEAULIEU VINEYARD
Rutherford, San Francisco Bay North

Output: 350,000 cases

Leading Wines:
Beau Tour,
Cabernet Sauvignon
Private Reserve,
Rutherford Cabernet
Sauvignon, Chablis, Brut
Champagne, Champagne
de Chardonnay,
Chardonnay, Gamay
Beaujolais, Johannisberg
Riesling, Pinot Noir,
Sauvignon Blanc

BEAU TOUR.
NAPA VALLEY
CABERNET SAUVIGNON
PRODUCED AND BOTTLED BY BEAULIEU VINEYARD
AT RUTHERFORD, NAPA COUNTY, CALIFORNIA
ALCOHOL 12.5% BY VOLUME

One of the historic names in the Napa Valley, Beaulieu was founded in 1900 by Georges de Latour, a Frenchman who, having failed to discover gold in the Sierra Foothills, turned to winemaking. The original vineyard was planted with cuttings Latour brought back from France, and because the winery had been able to remain open during Prohibition making sacramental wines, it emerged with an enviable cellar of aged wines.

During the late 1930s Beaulieu gained international respect for its Cabernet Sauvignon, sold under the more marketable name of Burgundy. From 1938, however, Beaulieu wines—and in particular their Cabernet Sauvignon—came to be associated with André Tchelistcheff who became winemaker in 1938 and remained for 35 years. Born in Russia and educated in Czechoslovakia before studying at the Institut National Agronomique in Paris, where Latour discovered him, Tchelistcheff is legendary in the development of California wine. Almost single-handedly he placed the Napa Valley on the world's enological map, while the list of the winemakers he has taught or influenced reads almost like a Who's Who of California winemaking.

At Beaulieu, Tchelistcheff concentrated on Cabernet Sauvignon, introducing the practice of aging the wine in small barrels before release, generally two to three years for the Beaulieu Private Reserve, which under his guidance became the benchmark for this varietal for several decades. Private Reserve is still one of California's most sought-after Cabernets, prized for its subtlety and Bordeaux-like elegance. Paradoxically, this French-style Napa claret is one of the only major California Cabernets to be aged exclusively in American oak.

Beaulieu has been owned since 1969 by Heublein Wine and Spirits, which has doubled the size of the winery and initiated a move toward a more extensive line of wines. (Tchelistcheff had already pioneered the planting of Pinot Noir in the cooler Carneros region.) Tchelistcheff retired in 1973, but his son Dimitri continues his tradition at Beaulieu, flying in from Hawaii to act as consulting enologist.

Currently, Beaulieu has 1,300,000 gallons of storage and owns 745 acres of vineyards. More than 15 wines—generics, sparkling wines, dessert wines, and varietals—are produced by the winery. Aside from Beaulieu's two Cabernet Sauvignons (the Private Reserve and a less expensive wine called Rutherford), a Cabernet-Merlot blend labeled Beau Tour, a Pinot Noir, Sauvignon Blanc, and a Johannisberg Riesling are of interest.

BELLEROSE VINEYARD
Healdsburg, San Francisco Bay North

Bellerose has specialized in Bordeaux-style red wines since its founding in 1979. This preference is reflected in the varietal composition of the 52-acre vineyard, which is planted to Cabernet Sauvignon, Merlot, Cabernet Franc, Petit Verdot, and Malbec.

Wines are fermented in specially designed stainless steel tanks that allow for the traditional practice of punching down of the cap; following fermentation, the young wines are left in contact with the skins for up to two weeks to maximize the color and complexity. They are then aged 14 months in oak barrels. Only two wines are produced: Cuvée Bellerose Cabernet Sauvignon (a Cabernet-Merlot blend with a little Cabernet Franc, Petit Verdot, and Malbec), and Rosé du Val (a Merlot-Riesling blend).

Output: 5,000 cases

Leading Wines:
Cabernet Sauvignon,
Rosé du Val

BELVEDERE WINE COMPANY
Healdsburg, San Francisco Bay North

Belvedere is the brainchild of Peter S. Friedman, who had been one of the forces in establishing the highly successful mail-order and personalized label programs at Windsor Vineyards. Friedman resigned from Sonoma Vineyards, the parent company of Windsor, in 1977, and in 1979 began the two Belvedere programs.

The Grapemaker series is a highly unusual arrangement in which Belvedere makes wines from grapes grown by a select group of Sonoma vineyards, and then labels the wines with only the name of those vineyards. Friedman describes the Grapemaker series as a vineyard program with a winery designation—the reverse of the more ususal winery program with vineyard designations. One parent company—Belvedere—is responsible for the wines presented under a variety of labels.

Cabernet Sauvignon and Merlot come from Robert Young Vineyards; Chardonnay and Pinot Noir from Bacigalupi Vineyards; a Cabernet Sauvignon from York Creek Vineyards; and a Chardonnay and Pinot Noir from Winery Lake Vineyards.

It is noteworthy that Friedman has selected vineyards of the highest prestige and quality for this series. Winery Lake Vineyards has perennially grown prize-winning grapes, Robert Young Vineyards has achieved great fame in its arrangement with Chateau St. Jean, and Bacigalupi Vineyards is famous for having grown the grapes from which Mike Grgrich produced the 1973 Chardonnay that won the historic Paris tasting of 1976.

The second program, begun in 1980, is the Wine Discovery series under which Belvedere acts as a *négociant* in bottling wines purchased in bulk. In 1983, 40,000 cases of varietals were released in the Wine Discovery series.

Leading Wines:
Robert Young:
Cabernet Sauvignon,
Merlot;
Bacigalupi:
Chardonnay, Pinot Noir;
York Creek:
Cabernet Sauvignon;
Winery Lake:
Chardonnay, Pinot Noir

BENMARL WINE COMPANY
Marlboro, Hudson River Valley

Output: 10,000 cases

Leading Wines:
Champagne, Chancellor,
Chardonnay,
Estate Reserve
Red and White;
Marlboro Village Red,
White, Seyval Blanc,
Nouveau, Spring Wine

1980
BENMARL
Hudson River Region Red Table Wine
MARLBORO VILLAGE

PRODUCED AND BOTTLED BY THE BENMARL WINE CO LTD · MARLBORO N.Y.

Benmarl has blended classicism and innovation to build one of the East's premier wine estates. The classicism comes from a village in the French Côte d'Or, where the Miller family lived and breathed Burgundy wine before opening their own Hudson Valley winery. This experience is reflected in a commitment to barrel-aged, dry table wines with full, soft fruit — a distinctly Burgundian winemaking style that put the Hudson Valley back on the wine map with Benmarl's first vintage in 1971. Their Marlboro Village blends have the rounded, dry-fruit character of the *village* wines of Burgundy.

These and most of Benmarl's 20-odd other wines are not made from the classic grape varieties of Burgundy, as might be expected, but from French-American hybrids. Mark Miller was one of the early champions of the hybrids, believing that the Hudson Valley's slate soil, hard winters, and long summers combine to bring out excellence that cannot be achieved with these varieties in Europe. Although he makes a few varietals, Miller favors blending and has developed a skill for structuring wines that gives Benmarl's cuvées a characteristic harmony and complexity. These marriages are often aged in oak barrels, but some reds and whites are kept out of wood for fresher, lighter character, including a dry rosé and raspberryish-Nouveau. Limited amounts of vinifera varietals are also produced, notably a mellow, well-aged Chardonnay.

Benmarl's 75-acre vineyard is one of the oldest continuously operating vineyards in America, although it has been completely replanted. The most innovative aspect of Benmarl is its marketing scheme. About 85 percent of the wine is sold under a Cuvée du Vigneron label to more than a thousand subscribers nationwide.

BERINGER VINEYARDS
St. Helena, San Francisco Bay North

Output: 800,000 cases

Leading Wines:
Burgundy,
Cabernet Sauvignon,
Chablis, Chardonnay,
Chenin Blanc,
French Colombard,
Fumé Blanc, Gamay
Blanc, Gamay Rosé,
Gewurztraminer,
Grey Riesling,
Johannisberg Riesling,
Petite Syrah, Pinot Noir,
Zinfandel, White
Zinfandel;

Beringer is one of the oldest vineyards in the Napa Valley: it has operated continuously since Jacob and Frederick Beringer founded it in 1876. In that year they purchased 97 acres just north of St. Helena, and later built an elegant 17-room mansion, the Rhinehaus, which now serves as a visitors' center. During Prohibition the winery stayed in operation making sacramental wines.

In 1970 the picturesque mansion and winery were purchased by Nestlé, the Swiss food company, and since then has been a division of its Wine World Inc. Myron Nightingale, formerly at Cresta Blanca, was hired as winemaker shortly after the purchase and began an ambitious program of expansion. Several thousand feet of tunnels, dug into the hillside in the 19th century behind the Rhinehaus, were rehabilitated and a new 2.25 million-gallon winery was built directly across Highway 20 from the visitors' center.

Nightingale established himself as one of California's most innovative winemakers — and Beringer honored him and his wife, Alice, by naming a wine after them. It is made from Semillon grapes, treated with botrytis mold to concentrate their sugar and flavor constituents. Alice developed a technique called single sporing to purify botrytis and assure the absence of other molds. Cultures grown from single spores were then utilized in the treatment of Semillon grapes. The finished Nightingale wine is full of complex fruit and honeylike aromas and flavors, and is like liqueur on the palate. Unfortunately, output has been very limited.

Other wines of merit are Cabernet Sauvignon, Fumé Blanc, and Chardonnay. The last has restraint and balance without sacrificing the exuberance of California fruit. This style is evident in all three Chardonnay bottlings: estate-bottled Napa, Gamble Ranch, and Private Reserve. Beringer controls through outright ownership or by lease 2,800 acres of vineyards in Sonoma County and the Napa Valley.

Beringer's second label, Los Hermanos, appears on both 750-ml packages as well as on 1.5-liter magnums. They are some of the best bargains of the Napa Valley.

Los Hermanos:
Burgundy,
Cabernet Sauvignon,
Chablis, Light Chablis,
Chardonnay,
Chenin Blanc,
Light Chenin Blanc,
French Colombard,
Light French Colombard,
Light Rhine, Light Rosé,
Rosé Rhine,
Zinfandel,
White Zinfandel,

BILTMORE ESTATE WINERY
Asheville, North Carolina

Biltmore Winery began as an experimental vineyard established at the old Vanderbilt estate in the early 1970s. The early planting of French-American hybrids (totaling 11 acres) soon shifted to vinifera varieties as the location in North Carolina's western foothills proved suitable. To move to the next stage was relatively easy as a winery fit well into Biltmore's concept of a working estate in the European tradition. The first vintages, beginning in 1978, were complex, hybrid-vinifera blends in a dry, restrained style. In the early 1980s the estate's dairy complex was converted into a modern, 100,000-case winery, and a skilled enologist was brought in from France.

Two labels, Biltmore Estate and Biltmore, are used to designate premier and second-level bottlings as in the chateaux of Medoc. One hundred and twenty acres of vineyards surrounding the 250-room Vanderbilt chateau give the stunning impression of a classic French wine estate. As the vineyards and wines mature, this is a new producer to follow closely.

Output: 35,000 cases

Leading Wines:
Biltmore Estate Red,
Biltmore Estate White,
Biltmore Champagne

BJELLAND VINEYARDS
Roseburg, Oregon

Paul Bjelland's 19-acre vineyard was first planted in 1967 when he moved from California to Oregon's Umpqua Valley. Unlike most Oregon winegrowers, Bjelland produces a significant portion of his production as berry wines. Bjelland berry wines are intensely fruity and finished with some residual sugar.

Output: 1,000 cases

Leading Wines:
Blackberry, Boysenberry,
Brambleberry,
Chardonnay,
Gewurztraminer,
Riesling, Semillon

B

BLACKWOOD CANYON VINTNERS
Prosser, Washington

Output: 5,000 cases

Leading Wines:
Cabernet Sauvignon,
Chardonnay, Semillon,
Select late-harvest wines

M. Taylor Moore, manager of the Ciel du Cheval vineyard on Red Mountain, at the far eastern end of the Yakima Valley, is developing his own 180-acre vineyard and winery nearby. Until his own Blackwood Canyon estate vineyards mature, Moore is purchasing grapes from Ciel du Cheval and from other Columbia Valley growers. All the dry white wines undergo malolactic fermentation and are left on the lees for about nine months. The Cabernet is left on the skins for about two weeks after fermentation is completed. These traditional methods contribute to the complexity and refinement of Blackwood Canyon wines.

BLANC VINEYARDS
Redwood Valley, San Francisco Bay North

Output: 1,500 cases

Leading Wines:
Cabernet Sauvignon,
White Cabernet
Sauvignon,
Sauvignon Blanc

Blanc Vineyards was started in 1973, when the Blanc family purchased a 100-acre ranch on the benchland of Redwood Valley in the northern limits of Mendocino County.

Most of the grapes produced from these vineyards are sold to local wineries. But in 1983 the Blancs completed a small 6,000 gallon winery and made their first commercial release of a Cabernet Sauvignon.

BOEGER WINERY
Placerville, Sierra Foothills

Output: 10,000 cases

Leading Wines:
Cabernet Sauvignon,
Chenin Blanc, Hangtown
Red and Gold, Merlot,
Riesling, Sauvignon Blanc,
Sierra Blanc, Zinfandel,
White Zinfandel

The Boegers own 32 acres of vineyards and lease a further 20 acres. Founded in 1973, the winery has 40,000 gallons of storage capacity and produces seven wines including Cabernet Sauvignon, Merlot, Chenin Blanc, Sauvignon Blanc, and Riesling. The winery is part of a trend in this Zinfandel-heavy area toward greater varietal diversification and Boeger's Merlot has won a lot of interest. Perhaps the best known wine is a blend called Hangtown Red, after the Gold Rush era name for Placerville.

BOGLE VINEYARDS
Clarksburg, Sacramento Valley

Output: 16,000 cases

Leading Wines:
Chenin Blanc,
Grey Riesling,
Petite Sirah,
Sauvignon Blanc

Founded in 1979, this small winery is situated in one of California's newest, officially approved Viticultural Areas. Grapes were planted in Clarksburg prior to Prohibition, but the area has only recently been making a viticultural comeback. Bogle has 300 acres of vineyards planted to Chenin Blanc, Grey Riesling, Semillon, Sauvignon Blanc, Petite Sirah, and Cabernet Sauvignon, and is a technologically advanced winery. Harvesting is done by machine and grapes are field crushed. Fermentation at cold temperatures requires up to two weeks for completion, yielding wines of intense fruitiness.

B

JEAN CLAUDE BOISSET VINEYARDS
St. Helena, San Francisco Bay North

A wine producer and shipper of major importance in Burgundy, Jean Claude Boisset purchased 57 acres of mature vineyards in the Napa Valley in 1980. For the 1980 and 1981 vintages, Boisset utilized the facilities of Conn Creek to crush Cabernet Sauvignon and Chardonnay. Since then three varietals have been made from grapes in Rombauer Vineyard Winery. Construction of a 40,000-case winery is planned.

Output: 5,000 cases

Leading Wines:
Cabernet Sauvignon,
Chardonnay,
Sauvignon Blanc

BONNY DOON VINEYARDS
Santa Cruz, San Francisco Bay South

Founded in 1983, Bonny Doon has 29 acres of vineyards mainly planted to Pinot Noir and Cabernet Sauvignon. In addition, approximately one acre is devoted to each of the three main white varieties of the Rhône Valley—Marsanne, Rousanne, and Viognier. The limited quantities of these varietals are unique to Bonny Doon in the United States. Storage capacity is only 15,000 gallons.

Output: 4,500 cases

Leading Wines:
Chardonnay, Claret,
Marsanne, Pinot Noir,
Rousanne, Syrah,
Viognier

BOOKWALTER WINERY
Pasco, Washington

For many years, Jerry Bookwalter managed the Sagemoor Farms vineyards, the largest independent vineyard operation in the Northwest. In 1983, Bookwalter left Sagemoor to operate his own vineyard-management business and to start his own winery. Grapes for Bookwalter's wines come from vineyards near Pasco, and from the Wahluke Slope, one of the Columbia Valley's most important new growing areas. The first wines released by Bookwalter emphasize the crisp, fresh fruit of the grape.

Output: 3,800 cases

Leading Wines:
Chardonnay,
Chenin Blanc,
Riesling

BOORDY VINEYARDS
Hydes, Mid-Atlantic Coast

Philip and Jocelyn Wagner, pioneers of modern eastern American winegrowing, established Boordy in 1945, introducing the commercial production of French-American hybrid grapevines to the United States. First with their nursery and then with the winery, they inspired a number of vineyards in Maryland and influenced dozens of other eastern winemakers. After the Wagners retired from commercial winemaking, one of the local Maryland vineyards became the winery's new home.

Boordy has preserved the original style and commitment of the first new generation winery in the East: a commitment to the blending of hybrid varieties with the best of French country table wines in mind. The style is dry, food-oriented, and understated. A Beaujolais-like Nouveau Red continues to play an important role in the product line; and the fresh, fruity youthful qualities of Beaujolais have much to do with the inspira-

Output: 6,000 cases

Leading Wines:
Cedar Point Red,
Nouveau Red,
Premium Red, White,
and Rosé, Seyval Blanc,
Vidal Blanc, Vin Gris

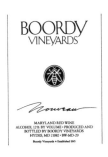

tion of Boordy wines. Vidal and Seyval Blanc have earned places as varietals, the latter now left *sur lie* ("on the lees") to give up some fruit for the earthy character associated with French Burgundies.

The new managers have also added vinifera wines to the Boordy line. The 14-acre estate vineyard supplies less than half the grapes used; the rest come from several other Maryland vineyards, including the original property in Riderwood.

BORRA'S CELLAR
Lodi, Central Valley

Output: 1,000 cases

Leading Wines:
Barbera, Barbera Blanc,
Zinfandel

The Borra family has owned vineyards in the Lodi area since 1915, but there was no family winery until 1975, when Stephen and Beverly Borra established a cellar under the family home.

The Borras own 30 acres of vineyards and lease another 20. Hand picking at Borra is followed by fermentation in open-top redwood fermenters, a practice no longer in widespread use in the California wine industry. After fermentation, Borra wines receive 24 months of aging in 50-gallon American oak barrels.

BOSKYDEL VINEYARD
Lake Leelanau, Michigan

Output: 2,500 cases

Leading Wines:
Boskydel Red, White,
and Rosé,
De Chaunac,
Seyval Blanc,
Vignoles

Boskydel planted the first wine grapes on northern Michigan's Leelanau Peninsula in the mid-1960s. Of 35 varieties tested, it selected six French-American hybrids for commercial wine production begun in 1976. All wines are vintage-dated and estate-grown from the 25-acre vineyard overlooking Lake Leelanau. French country wines serve as Boskydel's model. Vignoles is the best wine.

Botrytis Cinerea

Sometimes called the "noble mold" or "noble rot," botrytis is a fungus that is scrupulously avoided in most vineyards. In a few varieties — notably Riesling, Sauvignon Blanc, and Ravat (Vignoles) — and in favorable weather during ripening, botrytis is sometimes permitted to infect the grapes and concentrate their flavors and sugars through dehydration. Botrytised grapes produce small amounts of rich, sweet wine that have a scent and flavor introduced by the mold which suggests honey and apricots. Greatly reduced yields and increased risks of crop spoilage mean that "botrytised" wines fetch very high prices.

Bottle-Fermented

The best sparkling wines undergo their secondary fermentation (the one that produces effervescence) in their bottles, rather than in pressurized tanks. This allows intimate contact with the yeast, producing more complex, creamy flavors and a finer "bead" (bubbles). But the words "Bottle Fermented" on a label invariably mean the wine was made by the transfer process rather than the classic and superior *méthode champenoise*.

BOUCHAINE VINEYARDS
Napa, San Francisco Bay North

This winery has been developed by Jerry Luper, formerly winemaker at Freemark Abbey and Chateau Montelena, and now in charge of wine-making at Bouchaine. Thirty-five acres of vineyards were planted in 1982 and more acreage has been added, principally Chardonnay and Pinot Noir, two specialities. The large 170,000 gallons of French oak and stainless steel storage are used for the production of Chateau Bouchaine wines and for custom crushing for other wine labels, such as Jerry Luper's Private Reserve Cabernet Sauvignon.

Output: 25,000 cases

Leading Wines:
Chardonnay, Pinot Noir,
Sauvignon Blanc

THE BRANDER VINEYARD
Los Olivos, Central Coast

In this small winery of 40 acres of vineyards and 15,000-gallon capacity, owner/winemaker Fred Brander specializes in Sauvignon Blanc. The wine made from this variety has developed a fine reputation for its Bordeaux-style complexity, achieved through the addition of Semillon and a degree of oak-aging. Brander is also the winemaker and part-owner of Santa Ynez Valley Winery.

Output: 6,500 cases

Leading Wines:
Cabernet Blanc, Cabernet
Franc, Chardonnay,
Merlot Blanc, Sauvignon
Blanc, Semillon

BRAREN PAULI WINERY
Petaluma, San Francisco Bay North

In this partnership between Larry Braren and Bill Pauli, geologist Braren is the winemaker and Pauli manages the 135 acres of vineyards. When it was founded in 1980 Braren Pauli was the first winery to be established in the Potter Valley close to the northern limits of winegrowing in Mendocino County. Today there are 7,000 gallons of storage capacity in the former dairy barn which houses the winemaking equipment.

Grapes for Braren Pauli wines come from vineyards in the Potter and Redwood valleys near the winery in Mendocino County, and the Alexander Valley in Sonoma County.

Output: 4,000 cases

Leading Wines:
Cabernet Sauvignon,
Chardonnay, Merlot,
Sauvignon Blanc,
Zinfandel

BRIDGEHAMPTON WINERY
Bridgehampton, Long Island

The only winery on Long Island's South Fork has a strong sense of stylistic distinction from North Fork wines, based on differences in growing seasons. Somewhat shorter, cooler summers contribute to Bridgehampton's early-maturing, lively, full-fruit style. White wines dominate the line, particularly a rich but medium-bodied, mouth-filling Chardonnay with but-

Output: 6,000 cases

Leading Wines:
Chardonnay,
Premiere Cuvée Blanc

B

Fumé Blanc, Merlot-Cabernet Sauvignon, Pinot Noir, Riesling

tery oak tones, and an elegantly balanced, off-dry Riesling. Bridgehampton's Merlot-Cabernet blend plays up the texture and soft fruit of Merlot. Approximately half the grapes used are purchased from other South Fork vineyards.

Brix

The measurement of sugar in grapes and in fermenting must, used to determine when to harvest and to track the course of fermentation. Measured in degrees, Brix corresponds to the percentage of sugar in solution; for example, 20° Brix indicates 20 grams of sugar in 100 grams of liquid. Grapes are usually harvested between 18° and 25° Brix, depending on variety, growing conditions, characteristics of the fruit, style of wine desired, and so on. Since sugar is converted into alcohol in fermentation, higher Brix grapes, fermented dry, produce higher alcohol wine. Multiplying the degrees Brix of grapes by 0.55 gives the approximate alcohol content if wine is fermented dry.

Output: 100,000 cases

Leading Wines: Burgundy, Chablis, Flor Sherry, Holiday, May Wine, Rosario, Ruby Port, Tawny Port

BROTHERHOOD WINERY
Washingtonville, Hudson River Valley

The only survivor of the Hudson Valley's 19th-century heyday as wine country, Brotherhood has not missed a vintage since the first bottle of sacramental wine was made in 1839, making it the oldest continuously existing winery in the United States. At the turn of the century, Brotherhood wines were sold throughout the nation and in Europe and Africa.

Distribution has shrunk and the winery concentrates today on a thriving tourist business, reflected in a product line that leans toward sweet specialty wines. One such is the delicate, woodruff-scented May Wine, which rivals its German namesake. But Brotherhood's venerable, ivied stone compound and vaulted cellars seem to suggest its best wines: dark, rich Port and solera sherries. Its dry Flor Sherry colors the austere bite of a Spanish fino with a delicate suggestion of native American fruit.

Output: 18,000 cases

Leading Wines: Cabernet Sauvignon, Chardonnay, Pinot Noir, Riesling, Zinfandel

DAVID BRUCE WINERY
Saratoga, San Francisco Bay South

David Bruce is a dermatologist who practices in San Jose and follows his avocation at a hillside winery in nearby Saratoga. He terraced the hillside in 1961, planted 25 acres of vines, and founded a winery in 1964. His first commercial wines went on sale in 1967.

All of Bruce's wines—whites and reds—are known for a strength and varietal intensity which was the virtual trademark of California wines in the mid-70s. But Bruce has kept up with the times, and recent bottlings have shown a movement toward lighter, more elegant wines.

Brut

The term indicating relative dryness in a sparkling wine. On the label of American sparkling wines, it can mean anything from bone dry to over 1.5 percent residual sugar, a perceptible level of sweetness that is somewhat masked by the effervescence. Brut style wines are the major category of high-quality sparkling wines. They are made to complement food and are often the best in a producer's line.

BUCKINGHAM VALLEY VINEYARDS
Buckingham, Mid-Atlantic Coast

About 20 miles north of Philadelphia, in Bucks County, Kathy and Jerry Forest started one of the first of Pennsylvania's new generation of wineries in 1966. The family grows 15 acres of French-American hybrids immediately around the winery for a selection of red, white, and rosé wines, principally vintage varietals. Well-aged reds are a specialty, receiving up to three years in oak, which nicely rounds out varieties well-chosen for this treatment. A dry Vidal Blanc is the headliner among a half dozen whites. Some grapes are purchased for sweet, native American wines.

Output: 8,000 cases

Leading Wines:
Baco Noir, Cayuga White, Chelois, De Chaunac, Niagara, Rosette, Seyval Blanc, Vidal Blanc

BUEHLER VINEYARDS
St. Helena, San Francisco Bay North

Located in the hills east of the Napa Valley, Buehler's vineyards overlook Lake Hennessy. Sixty acres of vines were planted to only three varieties, Cabernet Sauvignon, Zinfandel, and Pinot Blanc, in 1972. The cultivar Pinot Blanc is the true Pinot Blanc of Burgundy, a white fruited member of the Pinot Noir family.

A winery was completed on the property in time for production of the first Buehler estate wines, a Cabernet Sauvignon and a Zinfandel, in 1978. Storage capacity, of stainless steel and small French oak barrels, totals 60,000 gallons.

Output: 10,000 cases

Leading Wines:
Cabernet Sauvignon, Muscat Blanc, Pinot Blanc Vrai, Zinfandel

BUENA VISTA WINERY AND VINEYARDS
Sonoma, San Francisco Bay North

Buena Vista was founded in 1857 by the flamboyant Agoston Haraszthy, the Hungarian immigrant who is generally recognized as the father of modern viticulture and winemaking in California. Haraszthy bought vineyard land from the Vallejo family—Mariano Vallejo was the last Mexican governor of the region of California that includes what is now the town of Sonoma.

In characteristic style, Haraszthy built a grand villa on the land, surrounded by formal gardens and extensive aging tunnels. Over the following years, he traveled extensively and wrote numerous pamphlets promoting California wine and winemaking. In 1861 he was appointed by the state to visit Europe to study winemaking and bring back grape varieties.

Output: 80,000 cases

Leading Wines:
Burgundy, Cabernet Sauvignon, Carneros Spiceling, Chablis, Chardonnay, Fumé Blanc,

Gamay Beaujolais,
Gewurztraminer,
Johannisberg Riesling,
Zinfandel,
various sherries

He returned with 100,000 cuttings from some 300 varieties, which were scattered randomly among local vineyards.

Haraszthy's wines at Buena Vista won several awards, but, plagued by financial troubles, the winery began to decline and Haraszthy's interest turned to other projects. *Phylloxera* devastated the vines in the 1870s, and by the time of the 1906 earthquake, which destroyed the tunnels, the property had long since been abandoned.

When Frank Bartholomew, a San Franciscan who was head of United Press International, bought the property at auction in 1941, he was unaware that he had acquired a historical landmark in California wine. When he learned the story from Leon Adams, he set about restoring the winery buildings, reopening the tunnels, and replanting the vineyards. Within 10 years he had a new generation of Buena Vista wines on the market.

In 1968 Bartholomew sold Buena Vista to Vernon Underwood and Young's Market Company, which bought 700 acres of former grazing land in the Carneros region (now an official Viticultural Area), planted it to vineyards, and built a modern winery for Buena Vista.

In 1976 Buena Vista was acquired once again, by a West German family, the Moller-Rackes, who enlarged the new winery's capacity to 900,000 gallons. The original winery, six miles away, serves as a visitors' center and tasting room.

Jill Davis, a graduate of the enology program at U.C. Davis, is the winemaker, and solely responsible for making the 16 wines produced at Buena Vista. Her Chardonnays and Gewurztraminers are highly regarded, while with her Cabernet Sauvignon she has demonstrated that this grape can do well in the cooler conditions of the Caneros region. Most unusual of Buena Vista's wines is Spiceling, a proprietary blend of Gewurztraminer and Johannisberg Riesling.

An additional 1,000 acres of land in the Carneros region were acquired in 1984, making Buena Vista the largest owner of vineyard land in that region; planting will begin in 1985.

Bulk Process, See Charmat Process

BULLY HILL VINEYARDS
Hammondsport, Finger Lakes

Output: 100,000 cases

Leading Wines:
Baco Noir,
Champagne Brut,
Chancellor,
Marechal Foch,
Seyval Blanc,
Vidal Blanc

Founded by members of the Taylor wine family who were unhappy with the way the state's largest winery was being run, in the mid-1960s, Bully Hill was at the forefront of the New York state wine industry. Bully Hill was dedicated to the French-American hybrid varieties, which were then new, and their capacity to make refined, European-style wine without blending with California wine or ameliorating with water. This was the first of a new generation of farm wineries in the Finger Lakes area seeking a regional style of dry table wines from strictly local grapes. In its first decade, Bully Hill explored the range of hybrid varieties, focusing on some of the most promising: Seyval Blanc, Baco Noir, Aurora, and Chancellor. In the hands of winemaker Hermann Wiemer, they were good country wines. With the promotion of Walter S. Taylor, owner and master marketer, they brought national recognition to the new hybrid varieties of New York State.

In its third decade, Bully Hill remains the champion of the hybrids and only the hybrids, while its neighbors turn more of their attention to viniferas. The loss of several talented winemakers has plagued recent vintages and made it difficult to peg the best labels. But Bully Hill is breaking ground again with the Finger Lakes' first brandy.

Burger

This white variety produces neutral wines of no great varietal character and in the past its chief use has been in generic blends. But some producers of sparkling wines have shown interest in this variety in recent years. There are about 2,000 acres planted in California.

BURGESS CELLARS
St. Helena, San Francisco Bay North

Output: 28,000 cases

Leading Wines:
Cabernet Sauvignon,
Chardonnay, Zinfandel

Tom and Linda Burgess acquired the Souverain Winery facilities of J. Leland Stewart in the early 1970s, after the Souverain name had been bought by Pillsbury. Their Howell Mountain site has been used as a winery since 1880. Winemaker Bill Sorenson makes a small list of varietals, highlighted by rich Cabernet Sauvignons, Zinfandels, and Chardonnays. Recent vintages of these wines have shown a lighter style, making Burgess part of a statewide trend toward easier, less-intense wines. The winery also has a fine reputation for consistency and value.

A second label — Bell Canyon Cellars — offers Cabernet Sauvignon that is purchased as wine, raised in the Burgess cellars, and then bottled. Sixty acres of vineyards are owned and 25 are leased.

BURGESS

1981
Napa Valley
Zinfandel

Output: 20,000 cases

Leading Wines:
Cabernet Sauvignon,
Chardonnay,
Fumé Blanc,
Gewurztraminer,
Pinot Noir,
Zinfandel

DAVIS BYNUM WINERY
Healdsburg, San Francisco Bay North

Originally in Albany, across the bay from San Francisco, this winery relocated to Healdsburg in 1973. Its wines are produced from grapes grown on the gravelly benchland along the Russian River as well as in the Dry Creek and Alexander valleys. Davis Bynum has had more success with its reds than its whites, and its Pinot Noir was one of the first to demonstrate that a sound, reasonably priced wine could be produced from this grape in Sonoma.

B

BYRD VINEYARDS
Myersville, Mid-Atlantic Coast

Output: 7,000 cases

Leading Wines:
Cabernet Sauvignon,
Chardonnay,
Gewurztraminer,
Riesling, Sauvignon Blanc,
Seyval Blanc

After a cautious start in 1976 with simple, fruity French-American vari-etals and blends, Byrd has shifted to a strategy of direct combat with the leading names of Napa Valley and Bordeaux. Cabernet Sauvignon has led the assault. Blended with Merlot and Cabernet Franc in the good vintages of the early 1980s, it is loaded with fruit and spice; an intense, fairly tannic wine made for aging to complexity. Chardonnay and Sauvignon Blanc are similarly intense, ripe wines, relying on eastern acid levels to hold them together. All Byrd wines are estate-bottled and all are dry except Riesling, which is made in a lighter style.

Cabernet Franc

The 413 acres of this red variety planted in California are mostly in the San Francisco Bay North region, where it is used primarily as a blending grape with other Bordeaux varieties, mainly Cabernet Sauvignon, which it closely resembles. Acreage in other states is minimal. On the rare occasions it is used to make a varietal, the result is a wine of appealing aroma and refreshing fruitiness.

Cabernet Sauvignon

Cabernet Sauvignon achieved fame and immortality hundreds of years ago as the principal grape in red Bordeaux wines. But more recently, it has found a home in California, where it is generally considered to make the best red wine in the state.

A classic Cabernet Sauvignon wine exhibits delicious fruit in its youth, along with very hard tannins. As the wine develops, the fruit recedes, and the tannins soften.

In a departure from Bordeaux practice, American winemakers have usually made wines from 100 percent Cabernet Sauvignon grapes. In the climate of California, where Cabernet can get very ripe, this has led to a perception of them as particularly hard, "monster" wines. Lately, the Bordeaux influence has grown; more Merlot and Cabernet Franc are being blended into American Cabernet Sauvignon in an effort to soften the wines and to add complexity. Several other regions have recently demonstrated their abilities with this grape in their own style, such as Washington, Virginia, and Long Island.

CAIN CELLARS
St. Helena, San Francisco Bay North

This small 60,000-gallon winery, founded in 1981, is located in the Spring Mountain area at the northern end of the Napa Valley, an area populated with small boutique wineries. Although the estate contains 542 acres only 70 acres are planted to grapes.

Output: 12,000 cases

Leading Wines:
Cabernet Sauvignon,
Chardonnay, Merlot,
Sauvignon Blanc

CAKEBREAD CELLARS
Rutherford, San Francisco Bay North

Output: 35,000 cases

Leading Wines:
Cabernet Sauvignon,
Chardonnay,
Sauvignon Blanc

Cakebread Cellars

NAPA VALLEY

Sauvignon Blanc

1984

•

PRODUCED AND BOTTLED BY CAKEBREAD CELLARS
RUTHERFORD, NAPA VALLEY, CALIFORNIA, USA
ALCOHOL 12.5% BY VOLUME

The Cakebreads became interested in making wine when Jack was on an assignment in the early 1970s to photograph vineyards and wineries for a wine book. Thirty-five acres were planted and a dramatic wooden winery was built that won an award for its design.

Jack's son Bruce became the winemaker after completing the enology program at U.C. Davis. Cakebread is best known for Sauvignon Blanc, which is full of varietal character. Excellent Cabernet Sauvignons and Chardonnays have been made, as well as an unusual Zinfandel, full of black pepper spiciness. Unfortunately, the Zinfandel is no longer available; the old vines that produced the grapes for this wine have been replanted.

CALERA WINE COMPANY
Hollister, Central Coast

Output: 12,000 cases

Leading Wines:
Chardonnay, Pinot Noir,
Zinfandel

Calera (the Spanish word for lime kiln) is the creation of Josh Jensen, whose goal is to produce great Burgundy-style Pinot Noirs in California.

Jensen's first vintage of Pinot Noir was produced in 1978; since then he has been receiving plaudits for his wines. He is indeed one of the most Burgundian of Pinot Noir stylists in California and owes much of his success to his efforts in matching the right vines to the right soils and microclimates. His vineyard designation program has produced a range of individual — but consistently excellent — Pinot Noirs: the more accessible Jensen Vineyard Pinot Noir, and the longer-aging Reed Vineyard and Selleck Vineyard Pinot Noirs. The winery is small, with only 40,000 gallons of storage capacity.

CALIFORNIA

As a wine region, California is a relatively large area (158,693 square miles). Its 700–mile length from north to south encompasses numerous, varied growing conditions: microclimates, solar exposures, and soils. It has been said that somewhere within its length are to be found conditions analogous to all the microclimates of European vineyards. Statewide generalizations are therefore misleading at best. But this does not mean that it's impossible to outline certain factors, principally climate and soil, that will organize California's staggering viticultural diversity into something more manageable.

California's climate is dominated by three major geographic features: the Pacific Ocean; the great, inland Central Valley; and the mountains that surround this valley. A marine influence occurs in those vineyard areas nearest the Pacific Ocean. Cool ocean air is a great friend to coastal vineyards, moderating California's high temperatures. In addition, it is not uncommon for morning fog to roll in from the Pacific Ocean, shielding the grapes for half the day from the scorching rays of the sun. Grapes like the sun, but moderation is the key word in viticulture; too much sun means too much sugar, which leads to too much alcohol, and ultimately to awkward wines.

The second geographic influence on climate — the Central Valley — stretches from Mount Shasta in the north to the Tehachipi Mountains in the south. It is bordered on the east by the Sierra Nevada Mountains, and on the west by a lower coastal range of mountains. It does not benefit from the influence of the Pacific Ocean; thus growing season temperatures are significantly higher. In the Central Valley, growing conditions are unfavorable to the great wine grapes, which prefer cool regions. But here is located the great wine-shed of California that yields millions upon millions of gallons of "jug" wines.

The mountains of California comprise the third major geographic influence on climate. To the east of the Central Valley are the Sierra Nevada Mountains, rising gently at first, then steeply, to 15,000 feet at Mount Whitney (the highest point in the nation outside Alaska). These mountains form a great barrier running nearly the full length of the state, and insulate California from much of the weather pattern of the mid-sections of the United States. The tallest peaks are generally covered with snow throughout the entire year, and it is the melting of this snow that provides a gigantic irrigation system without which the Central Valley would not thrive. Of at least equal importance, viticulturally speaking, are the coastal mountains found on the western side of the Central Valley. These mountains help to create the favorable growing conditions — and the great diversity — of California's finest winemaking regions. The folds of the mountains create valleys with microclimates ideal for fine wine grapes (valleys such as Napa and Sonoma in the north and Salinas and Santa Maria in the Central Coast). The mountains provide well-drained soil at steep elevations that, due to the coolness of the growing season, yield grapes of great intensity. Finally, the gaps between these mountains sometimes act as wind tunnels, drawing in cool ocean air which moderates temperatures in the inland valleys.

As for the influence of soil on California's wine, a similar diversity frustrates generalizations. Soils are extremely varied within each region, and no great reaches of identical soil are to be found anywhere in the state as they frequently are in Europe (the chalk of Chablis and Champagne and the slate of the Mosel come to mind). But this means little to many of California's winemakers. One of the chief divisions between the European and Californian visions of winemaking is over the importance of soil. To the Europeans, the soil is perhaps the most important factor in the character of the wine; to Californians, the weather and the skill of the winemaker are more significant factors.

For this reason, California vineyards plant grape varieties in specific areas with climate rather than soil in mind. Such early-ripening varieties as Chardonnay and Pinot Noir are concentrated in the cooler regions. Varieties that appear to prefer more heat (such as Zinfandel) or ripen later (Cabernet Sauvignon) are planted in warmer regions. These heat-loving

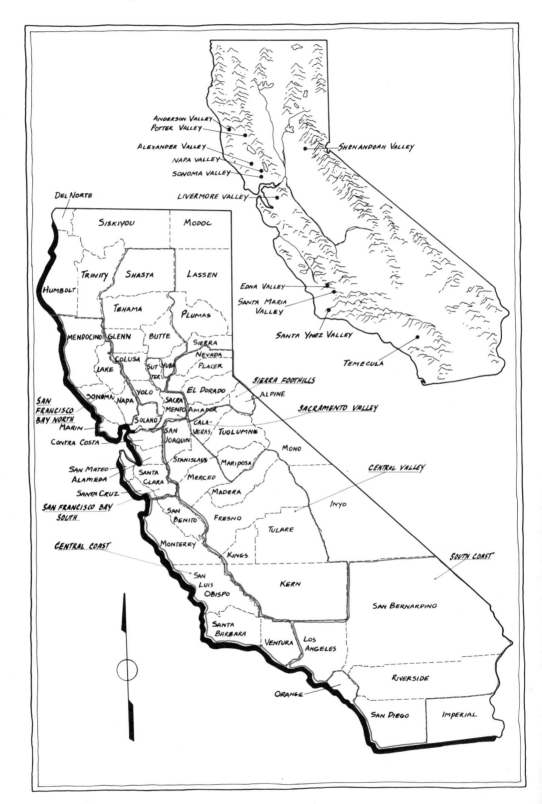

varieties do well in the interior valley and in the inland areas of the southern part of the state.

But California's great length and varied growing conditions—from Mosel coolness to Jerez heat—call for division of the state into smaller areas within which geographic features, microclimates, and growing conditions are similar, for the purpose of discussions of winegrowing. Any such division must be somewhat arbitrary in nature, particularly in California, where the process of identifying similarities and differences in growing conditions throughout the state was begun only recently. Nevertheless, for our purposes, the state is divided into seven regions, mainly on the basis of geographic location, but partly also on the basis of viticultural considerations and differences in growing conditions. These regions are San Francisco Bay North, San Francisco Bay South, Central Coast, South Coast, Sacramento Valley, Central Valley, and Sierra Foothills.

Because each vineyard area and sometimes a single vineyard is planted to several varieties, in contrast to the European practice of planting only one or a few varieties in a region, California vintages are difficult to generalize. This is further complicated by the wide variety of growing conditions within the state's 700-mile length. Therefore, any meaningful evaluations of California vintages must be specific to individual regions and assessments of leading varieties follow each regional entry.

CALLAWAY VINEYARDS AND WINERY
Temecula, South Coast

Output: 100,000 cases

*Leading Wines:
Chardonnay,
Chenin Blanc,
Fumé Blanc,
White Riesling,
Sauvignon Blanc,
Sweet Nancy*

Callaway had a rare opportunity at its inception in 1969: it was the first vineyard to be established in the Temecula area (not far from Los Angeles), where there was no history of the vine-louse *phylloxera*. Most of the world's vineyards were almost destroyed by this louse in the late 19th century, and vineyards ever since have had to graft their vines onto a hardier rootstock to guard against the pest. Some say that the world's wines have never been the same—that the hardier rootstock yields wines of diminished character and complexity. As many California wineries lie in areas that produced wine during the 19th century plague, not many of them have been able to avoid the grafting. But Callaway's 105 acres of vinifera wines are planted on their own rootstocks, and afford wine lovers a chance to see what pre-*phylloxera* viticulture might have been like.

In 1981 Callaway sold the vineyards and winery to Hiram Walker and Sons, but he remained as chairman of the board. The winery's capacity has been expanded several times and had reached a total of 575,000 gallons in 1983. The vineyards have also been expanded to 150 acres.

With the 1984 crush, Callaway's managerial team implemented a decision to produce only white wines, and the winery now specializes in six white wines made from four grape varieties including a notable Chardonnay, fresh and unusual because of the absence of oak aging. Fumé Blanc is made from Sauvignon Blanc grapes. Sweet Nancy is a specialty product of Callaway Winery since its introduction almost by accident in 1973. Callaway was on the verge of discarding the entire crop of moldy Chenin

CALLAWAY
Vineyard & Winery®

Vintage 1983

TEMECULA, CALIFORNIA
Fumé Blanc

VINIFIED & BOTTLED BY CALLAWAY VINEYARD & WINERY®
TEMECULA, CALIFORNIA   ALCOHOL 13.1% BY VOLUME

C

Blanc grapes when it was discovered that the mold was *Botrytis cinerea*, the mold that is responsible for the great sweet wines of Sauternes and the late-harvest wines of Germany. The crop was made into wine by a northern California winery with great success, and the wine has been produced in subsequent vintages when weather conditions have produced the mold.

CAMBIASO WINERY AND VINEYARDS
Healdsburg, San Francisco Bay North

Output: 80,000 cases

Leading Wines: Cabernet Sauvignon, Chardonnay, Chenin Blanc, Petite Sirah, Sauvignon Blanc, White Zinfandel, Red, White, Rosé

Founded at Repeal in 1934 by Giovanni and Maria Cambiaso, the winery was operated by their son Joseph and daughters Rita and Theresa from the 1940s until 1972, when it was sold to the Likitprakong family, distillers from Thailand. The new owners added stainless steel tanks to the numerous small redwood tanks and small oak barrels for aging. They have converted Cambiaso from a small winery producing jug wines to an active modern enterprise specializing in premium wines. Storage capacity is now 1,000,000 gallons. Fifty-two acres of vineyards are owned.

CANANDAIGUA WINE
Canandaigua, Finger Lakes

Output: 2 million cases

Leading Wines: Chateau Martin, Mother Vineyard Scuppernong, Richards Wild Irish Rose, J. Roget Champagne, Virginia Dare

Richards Wild Irish Rose, a fortified blend of grapey, high-acid labrusca varieties and mellow, neutral California wine, is the flagship label and the symbol of Canandaigua's style. With production facilities in the Finger Lakes region, North Carolina, Virginia and California's Central Valley, the company has created wine recipes with uncanny marksmanship for mass American tastes since 1945. The lengthy product line includes native American and French hybrid table wines, fortified specialties, flavored, and sparkling wines. There are virtually no estate vineyards, on the premise that a distressed grape market provides ample cheap supplies. J. Roget sparkling wine is a successful eastern challenge to Gallo's Andre champagne. Mother Vineyard Scuppernong has a lightly oxidized, sherry character that works well with the Muscadine flavor for an aperitif.

CAPARONE VINEYARD
Paso Robles, Central Coast

Output: 3,000 cases

Leading Wines: Cabernet Sauvignon, Merlot

The goal of this small 10,000-gallon winery, founded in 1979, is to produce California wines from the Nebbiolo grape that match the greatness of some of the wines of the Piedmonte of northern Italy. To this end, the owners, M.D. and M.E. Caparone, have planted 8 acres of their 60-acre vineyard to this variety. Only two other wineries are currently producing wine from Nebbiolo.

Carbonic Maceration

A specialized method for fermenting whole, uncrushed grapes in a pressurized atmosphere of carbon dioxide. Typically, it produces a distinctive type of red wine: fresh, tart, berryish, and short lived. These are the first wines released from each vintage, usually in November, and are intended for consumption within a few months, while their fragile, youthful charm is in full flower. American wines made by carbonic maceration are normally labelled "Nouveau," echoing the wines of French Beaujolais that popularized this technique. (Nouveau on the label, however, does not guarantee that the wine was made by carbonic maceration.)

Carignane

Spanish in origin, Carignane is also grown in southern France. In California it has been used commercially mainly as a blending grape. However, it is now sometimes made as a varietal by a few California wineries. Typically it is heavy, tannic, and rather simple.

CARMENET VINEYARD
Sonoma, San Francisco Bay North

Output: 25,000 cases

Leading Wines:
Cabernet Sauvignon,
Sauvignon Blanc

Carmenet is the Northern California outpost of Chalone, one of California's most important wineries. In recent years, Chalone has spread in two directions: it now owns a part of Edna Valley Vineyard to the south of Monterey, and is complete owner of Carmenet, a new winery in Sonoma's Valley of the Moon.

The winery is an interesting addition to the Burgundian-oriented Chalone operations, for Carmenet specializes in Bordeaux-style wines — both Cabernet Sauvignon and Sauvignon Blanc.

Carnelian

A new red variety created by Dr. Harold Olmo at U.C. Davis by crossing Carignane with Cabernet Sauvignon then crossing the result with Grenache. Most of the 2,000 acres planted in California are in the Central Valley, where it is used primarily as a blending grape. Past efforts to produce Carnelian as a varietal have been discontinued in California. However, the Tedeschi Vineyard on Maui, Hawaii, has been experimenting with Carnelian as a sparkling blanc de noirs.

CARNEROS CREEK WINERY
Napa, San Francisco Bay North

Output: 23,000 cases

Leading Wines:
Cabernet Sauvignon,
Chardonnay,

Carneros Creek specializes in Pinot Noirs produced from 21 acres of vineyards planted solely to this variety. Francis Mahoney, winemaker and one of the owners, has been experimenting for several years with 20

C

Pinot Noir,
Sauvignon Blanc

clones of the grape in a selection program designed to reveal which of these clones appears to be best suited for the region. Many feel that proper clonal selection is the key to producing quality Pinot Noir — so far mainly a failure-laden quest in California. Others hold that the key is microclimate, and the cool Carneros region has recently been cited as likely to produce breakthrough California Pinot Noirs.

In addition to Pinot Noir made from Carneros Creek grapes, Chardonnay and Sauvignon Blanc are produced. A second specialty of the winery is Cabernet Sauvignon made from grapes purchased from Fay Vineyard, famous locally and in California for the high quality of its grapes.

CASA LARGA VINEYARDS
Fairport, Finger Lakes

Output: 6,500 cases

Leading Wines:
Aurora, Cabernet
Sauvignon, De Chaunac,
Delaware,
Gewurztraminer,
Johannisberg Riesling,
Pinot Noir, White and
Red Table Wine

Casa Larga's name indicates the Italian roots of this small family winery near Lake Ontario, founded in 1978. True to those roots, Casa Larga works hard to produce red wines with some measure of richness and spice, from Pinot Noir and Cabernet Sauvignon to the less demanding French-American hybrids. The red viniferas are utterly dependent on vintage. Johannisberg Riesling and Gewurztraminer are clearly the best white wines, notable for their delicacy and finesse in the finish. Riesling is the drier wine of the two, more compatible with light meals than most New York Rieslings.

Cascade

Cascade was one of the first French-American hybrid varieties brought to this country from France. When the vine proved winter hardy and relatively disease resistant, it was widely planted around the East. But Cascade's potential for red wine was soon eclipsed by newer selections and it is now used only for rosés or to lighten blends. Although the berries are almost black, the wine is light in body and color. There are less than a few hundred acres planted to Cascade, and this acreage is declining.

CASCADE MOUNTAIN VINEYARDS
Amenia, Hudson River Valley

Output: 8,500 cases

Leading Wines:
Aurora, Chancellor,
Le Hamburger Red,
New Harvest Red,
Reserved Red,
Spring White,
Little White Wine

Cascade Mountain takes its winemaking cues from its location in the Berkshire foothills near the New York-Connecticut border. The high elevation of the home vineyard at the winery (14 acres) favors hardy, early-ripening French–American hybrid varieties. Cool, sunny growing seasons produce wines with prominent fruit, acid, and color. William Wetmore, owner and winemaker, likens his area to the French region of Beaujolais, emphasizing freshness and fruit and, unlike most other New York wineries, turning much of his attention to reds. Cascade's New Harvest Red blends free-run and skin-fermented Foch and Leon Millot for a wine with bright, forceful flavors. Since the first vintage in 1977 Wetmore's aim has been to provide local markets with wines made to be consumed young and full of fruity charm.

A second vineyard (40 acres) was established a mile from the winery, but several hundred feet lower in elevation, broadening Cascade Mountain's repertoire to include Vidal, Seyval, and Vignoles.

CASSAYRE-FORNI CELLARS
Rutherford, San Francisco Bay North

Cassayre-Forni is run by three engineers, all formerly home winemakers. Jim and Paul Cassayre and Mike Forni designed many of the new Napa Valley wineries which have been built during the wine boom. Its first wine, a 1976 Cabernet Sauvignon, was made in leased space at Carneros Creek Winery (one the owners designed). The 1977 and the superb 1978 vintages were fermented in a barn behind winemaker Forni's home and barrel-aged in his basement. Finally, the winery which the three designed and built themselves on Forni's property was completed and the 1979 wines were made in the new facility.

The partners own no vineyards, but buy grapes from selected vineyards in the Napa Valley and in Dry Creek and Alexander valleys in Sonoma County. All wines are aged in French Nevers or American oak cooperage.

Output: 7,000 cases

Leading Wines:
Cabernet Sauvignon,
Chardonnay,
Chenin Blanc,
Zinfandel

CASWELL VINEYARDS
Sebastopol, San Francisco Bay North

Situated in Sonoma's cool Green Valley (Region I), an approved Viticultural Area, Caswell puts major emphasis on cool climate Burgundian grapes: Chardonnay and Pinot Noir. A Zinfandel and Rosé of Zinfandel are also made in small quantities as is an apple wine.

Founded in 1982, Caswell owns 64 acres of vineyards and produces 5,000 gallons of storage capacity. Plans are for expansion eventually to 10,000 cases annually.

Output: 1,500 cases

Leading Wines:
Apple Wine, Chardonnay,
Pinot Noir,
Rosé of Zinfandel,
Zinfandel

Catawba

Catawba originated as a chance hybrid on the Catawba River of North Carolina and was the first native American grape to establish itself as a commercial wine variety. Indeed it was the foundation of America's first major winery, established by Nicholas Longworth in Cincinnati in the 1820s. Longworth's still and sparkling Catawba sold across the country and abroad, inspiring the famous Longfellow poem "Ode to Catawba Wine".

Although the grape is red, Catawba's pale juice is used to make rosé or white wine. It has the pronounced grapey scent and flavor of labrusca, but with a spicy overlay that adds interest. Without exception, this is a wine to drink young and in the spirit of simple refreshment. Since Longworth's day, Catawba has been the basis of cuvées for many of the East's most successful sparkling wines; effervescence provides a brisk, attenuating context for its fresh, spicy fruit. Vineyard acreage (about 7,000) is concentrated in New York, Ohio, and Missouri.

CATOCTIN VINEYARDS
Brookerville, Mid-Atlantic Coast

Output: 3,000 cases

Leading Wines:
Cabernet Sauvignon,
Chardonnay,
Eye of the Oriole (rosé),
Johannisberg Riesling,
Roger's Big Red, Seyval

A new winery in Maryland hill country with particular promise, Catoctin specializes in Chardonnay and Cabernet Sauvignon. Grapes from Catoctin's two partner vineyards have, in earlier years at other wineries, helped reveal this region's potential for fine wines from these varieties. The first crush in 1983 produced a full-bodied Chardonnay with prominent, mature fruit and restrained oak overtones. The cellar strategy relies on estate vineyard control to let the grapes hang to advanced ripeness, then to work with well-settled, low-solids juice for very clean but generous, rich wines.

CAYMUS VINEYARDS
Rutherford, San Francisco Bay North

Output: 30,000 cases

Leading Wines:
Cabernet Sauvignon,
Chardonnay,
Johannisberg Riesling,
Late-Harvest Riesling,
Pinot Noir,
Pinot Noir Blanc (called
Oeil de Perdrix),
Sauvignon Blanc

Charles Wagner, the proprietor of Caymus Vineyards, began as a grape grower and had developed a reputation as a viticulturist who knew how to produce fine Pinot Noir grapes before he opened his winery. The 70 acres in his vineyards are planted to Cabernet Sauvignon and Johannisberg Riesling as well as to Pinot Noir, from all of which fine estate-bottled wines bearing the Caymus label are produced.

Wines are also made from purchased grapes, including a much lauded Zinfandel. Purchased Cabernet Sauvignon and Chardonnay are sold under the Liberty School label, which bears a picture of the one-room schoolhouse of Charles Wagner's childhood.

The winemaker, Randall Dunn, also owns vineyards and his own winery on Howell Mountain where he specializes in estate-grown Cabernet Sauvignon.

Cayuga White

The first of a new generation of European-American hybrid grape varieties, Cayuga White was released by the New York State Agricultural Experiment Station (Geneva) breeding program in 1972, from a cross of Seyval with the little-known Schuyler variety.

Mainly grown around the Finger Lakes, Cayuga is the eastern counterpart of Chenin Blanc. The vine is vigorous and productive. From fully ripe grapes, the wine has assertive, fruit-salad flavors, uncomplicated, occasionally recalling its labrusca ancestry, and almost always finished with some sweetness. The acreage planted to Cayuga White, currently a few hundred, is increasing.

CEDAR HILL WINE COMPANY
Cleveland Heights, Lake Erie

Output: 2,000 cases

Leading Wines:
Brut Sparkling Wine,
Chardonnay, Chelois,
Seyval

The cellar of one of Cleveland's best French restaurants, Au Provence, is packed with barrels and small tanks of regional wine. Both restaurant and winery are under the same ownership. Cedar Hill shops for small lots of grapes along the Lake Erie grape belt and on to the Finger Lakes, bringing back whatever looks promising from each harvest, mostly French-American hybrids, some vinifera and labruscas. The wines typically have firm acidity and the aromatic signature of wooden cooperage, but there is little concern here for consistency. This is a freewheeling, experimental cellar calling for the same in consumers. Chateau Lagniappe is the first label, and Seyval, Chardonnay, Chelois, and Brut Sparkling Wine have been individual standouts.

Cellared and Bottled by

Use of the word "cellared" indicates that the wine was purchased in bulk from another winery, a procedure not associated with the best American wines, and may have been blended, aged, or otherwise finished before bottling by the winery on the label. This kind of arrangement has been upgraded by some California firms in recent years, modeled after the highly respected *négociants* of France, to facilitate the selecting and blending of superior wines.

CENTRAL COAST

This long, narrow region in California encompasses a series of coastal valleys that harbor vineyards. Included in this region are the counties of Monterey, San Benito, San Luis Obispo, Santa Barbara, and Ventura.

Rainfall in Monterey County is low, perhaps as low as 10 inches per year, necessitating irrigation of the vineyards planted there; and vineyards east of Paso Robles in San Luis Obispo county also require irrigation to compensate for inadequate winter rainfall. But in other areas of the Central Coast, winter rainfall is adequate.

Temperatures during the growing season in the Central Coast counties vary from a very cool Region I, in those areas nearest the coast, to Region III, in those further inland or sheltered from the onshore flow of ocean air. Those vineyards north of the city of Salinas are in the coolest grape-growing region in the United States: harvest dates in the northern Salinas Valley are usually a month or more behind those even in the vineyards around San Francisco Bay. Further south, however, temperatures are warmer and harvest dates coincide more closely with those to the north.

Vineyards in the Central Coast are planted in a wide range of topographical conditions—on the valley floors, on the benchlands of these valleys, and even on mountainsides.

In the northern, and cooler, climes early ripening varieties such as

White Riesling and Chardonnay are planted. In the warmer, inland areas Cabernet Sauvignon and Zinfandel do well. Sound Pinot Noirs have been produced in the northern Salinas Valley as well as from the hillside vineyards in the mountains west of Paso Robles and in the Santa Ynez Valley in northern Santa Barbara County.

Seven varieties account for nearly 60 percent of the vineyard acreage in the Central Coast. Chardonnay is the leading variety with over 7,000 acres, followed closely by Cabernet Sauvignon and White Riesling, with approximately 6,600 acres of each planted in the five county area. Chenin Blanc, Pinot Noir, Zinfandel, and Sauvignon Blanc are also important, and Pinot Blanc acreage is increasing.

Nearly two-thirds of the vineyards growing in the Central Coast are planted in Monterey County — about 32,000 acres out of a total of 51,000. (Santa Barbara County is second, with approximately one-third as many vines planted there as in Monterey County.) In Monterey, the great Salinas Valley, long famous as the 'Lettuce Capital of the World' has now become known for its vineyards and wines. Until the planting boom of the late 1960s and early 1970s there were few vines planted in the county.

Growing season temperatures in the Salinas valley range from Region I north of Salinas to Region III near King City at the southern end of the valley. Ocean breezes off the Pacific provide a cooling influence in the north which lessens as the distance from Monterey Bay grows. Grape varieties have been matched more carefully to growing conditions in Monterey than in any other vineyard area in California. Early ripening varieties such as Pinot Noir and Chardonnay are planted in the north and later-ripening, more heat-tolerant varieties such as Cabernet Sauvignon and Zinfandel are planted to the south.

The most heavily planted varieties in Monterey are Cabernet Sauvignon, which leads the other varieties in acreage, Chenin Blanc, White Riesling, Chardonnay, Pinot Noir, and Sauvignon Blanc. These six varieties account for nearly 60 percent of the vineyard acreage in Monterey.

In the early years of vineyard development, Monterey wines, particularly the reds, suffered from a characteristic dubbed 'Monterey veggies' — an aroma and flavor of bell peppers or asparagus. Experiments were made with controlled irrigation, metering water to the vines instead of flooding the fields, and late harvesting; and the 'veggies' are no longer present in Monterey wines.

Monterey Wine Country Associates has secured BATF approval for the use of the name 'Monterey' on wine labels (without the 'County'). Contained within the boundaries of the Monterey Viticultural Area are two others with official standing: Arroyo Seco and Carmel Valley.

The Santa Ynez Valley in northern Santa Barbara County is becoming known for Pinot Noir and Sauvignon Blanc. The Edna Valley, located a few miles south of San Luis Obispo, is developing a reputation for its Chardonnay wines.

An interesting feature of Monterey and San Benito counties is that the vines planted there are growing on their own rootstock. With no previous

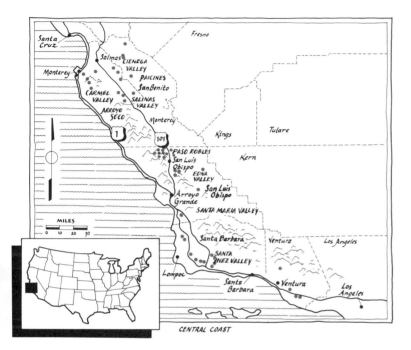

CENTRAL COAST

plantings of grape vines and no evidence of the presence of phylloxera, it was not necessary to graft vinifera to resistant American rootstock. How long this will remain the case is coming into question as there now appears to be some evidence of the disease in these regions.

1980   Cool weather produced a very light crop. Chardonnay was light in body, high in acidity, and somewhat lacking in flavor. Cabernet Sauvignon showed good acid/sugar ratios, but the wines are still fairly hard. Contrary to usual experience, there was almost no botrytis.

1981   A June heat wave resulted in some severe losses in the whites. The grapes that survived produced wines of generally average quality, although some examples are excellent. Cabernet Sauvignon and Zinfandel fared better and there are one or two exciting examples in this vintage. Some good late-harvest Rieslings and Gewurztraminers were produced.

1982   Despite storm damage, Chardonnay and Sauvignon Blanc appear well-balanced, with some varietal character, particularly for the latter. Harvest dates were late, extending into December in Monterey. Cabernet Sauvignons and Zinfandels show good fruit and are very good quality.

1983   Crop damage among certain varieties. Some excellent botrytised Sauvignon Blancs were made in Monterey, and Chardonnays from San Luis Obispo and Santa Barbara harvested before the rains began are also good. Cabernet Sauvignon and Zinfandel were harvested early in Monterey but were not of outstanding quality; the Zinfandel crop was lost in Santa Barbara and San Luis Obispo.

1984   The heat wave produced high sugar levels resulting in high alcohol. Acidity remained good and wines will be full-flavored and full-bodied. Some full-flavored Cabernet Sauvignon, and Zinfandel. Chardonnay and Sauvignon Blanc may have alcohol levels as high as 14 percent.

C

CENTRAL VALLEY

The southern section of California's great interior valley is variously known as the Central Valley or the San Joaquin Valley. This vast area includes the counties of Fresno, Kern, Kings, Madera, Merced, San Joaquin, Stanislaus, and Tulare. Approximately 60 percent of the state's wine grapes are growing here together with nearly all California's raisin grapes—mainly Thompson Seedless. The Central Valley is home to the enormous wineries that produce millions of gallons of everyday "jug" wines each year: 75 percent of the wine produced in California.

Growing season temperatures in the cooler northern portion of the valley place it in Region IV. But temperatures increase progressively further south, and the vineyards near Bakersfield are in Region V. The intense heat throughout the valley necessitates extensive irrigation: a system of canals carries water from the Sierra Nevada runoff to the eastern side of the Valley. The western half of the valley is irrigated by the California Water Project which brings water from the Sacramento and San Joaquin rivers.

The combination of intense heat, abundant irrigation, and fertile soils results generally in high yields per acre. But in the past, Central Valley wines have been thin and "overcooked." The development of new hybrids by U.C. Davis and extensive planting of varieties such as French Colombard that are high in acidity have raised the standards and produced highly drinkable, if straightforward table wines.

Agriculture in the Central Valley is highly diversified and, although grapes are the most important agricultural product, fruit and nut trees and cotton, among other crops, are also significant. Much of the soil in the long flat valley is deep and fertile. There are, however, areas especially along the west side in which soils lack fertility and productivity of any crop is limited.

The single most important variety planted in the Central Valley is Thompson Seedless, a raisin grape, with in excess of 270,000 acres. The total acreage planted to all wine varieties is now approaching 350,000 acres. French Colombard leads wine grape acreage with approximately 51,000 acres; Chenin Blanc has approximately 31,000 acres; and there are 15,000 acres of Grenache, and 13,000 acres of Barbera.

CHADDSFORD WINERY
Chaddsford, Mid-Atlantic Coast

Output: 8,750 cases

Leading Wines:
Cabernet Sauvignon,
Chambourcin,
Chardonnay,
Johannisberg Riesling,
Nouveau Seyval Blanc,
Steuben Rosé,
Country Rouge and White

The location of Chaddsford Winery, southwest of Philadelphia, was chosen to meet the viticultural demands of Chardonnay, Seyval Blanc, Cabernet Sauvignon, Riesling, Chambourcin—varieties the owners believe have shown best in the East. The search for a vineyard site was still underway when wine production began in 1982 with grapes purchased locally and in western Pennsylvania.

There are two wine styles at Chaddsford. Light, crisp, fruity wines for early consumption include a delicate Steuben rosé, various country

C

blends, and a tart, berryish Nouveau Chambourcin made by carbonic maceration. High-acid fruit and cold fermentation are key production elements for most of these. By contrast, Cabernet Sauvignon and Reserve Chambourcin are given plenty of skin contact and fermented warm to increase tannin and body, then well-aged for earthy-woody character. Cabernet and Chardonnay are finished in French Nevers oak; Chambourcin in American barrels.

Output: 10,000 cases

Leading Wines:
Burgundy, Chablis,
Cracker Ridge White Cat,
Ridge Rosé, Seyval Blanc,
Spring Wine, Vidal Blanc,
V.S.R

CHADWICK BAY WINE COMPANY
Fredonia, Lake Erie

A partnership of Chautauqua County grape growers formed this winery in 1980 to build a trade in regional, everyday wines from abundant local sources. Chadwick's line of about 10 wines favors blends rather than varietals, and presents a continuum of dry to sweet table wines from varying proportions of French-American hybrids and labrusca grapes. The reds, notably V.S.R. (Very Special Red), have been most successful, with medium body and soft texture. Chadwick's barrel-aged Seyval trades fruit for aroma and body. Inexpensive, picnic-style labrusca wines account for much of the production.

CHALET DEBONNE VINEYARDS
Madison, Lake Erie

The Debevc family's Concord-Niagara grape farm was typical of Lake Erie fresh-juice vineyards when they built their winery in 1970. Wines from those two original varieties can still be found with a line of 20 native American, French-American hybrid, and vinifera varietals and blends. A well-managed, prosperous first decade provided Chalet Debonne with one of the best-equipped small cellars in the East.

Chalet Debonne whites are most successful. The regular Chalet Debonne label relies on blends and well-established varietals for reasonable price and consistency from vintage to vintage. A Debevc Vineyards label is used for limited production, vintage varietals treated more experimentally from year to year. Cold-fermented Johannisberg Riesling has a floral, Mosel character. Vignoles is harvested late, often botrytised, for a concentrated dessert wine. Cabernet Sauvignon made an impressive entry in 1982. Chalet Debonne puts a light oak finish on most of its wines. It has a 30,000-gallon capacity of small oak cooperage.

Output: 15,000 cases

Leading Wines:
Chardonnay,
Debonne White,
Delaware,
Johannisberg Riesling,
Vidal Blanc, Vignoles

CHALONE VINEYARD
Soledad, Central Coast

Set in the Chalone region, Chalone Vineyard's international reputation for the quality of its wines, particularly for its Pinot Noir and Chardonnay, is due to the winemaking skills of Dick Graff, who acquired the property in 1965. Grapevines had been planted on the Chalone

Output: 15,000 cases

Leading Wines:
Chardonnay,
Chenin Blanc,
Pinot Blanc, Pinot Noir

benchlands above the Salinas Valley as early as 1920, and in 1982 it was officially approved as a Viticultural Area.

The area around the winery is arid and vineyard yields are low; its 960 acres of vineyards produce only 15,000 cases of wine annually (winery storage capacity is 50,000 gallons). Grapegrowing and winemaking techniques are rigorously Burgundian, and Graff's Chardonnays and Pinot Noirs demonstrate this clearly. The former are sometimes thought of as California Montrachet: enormous wines with great complexity and subtlety. The Pinot Noirs have been at the forefront of this varietal's development in California and are among the few in the state to attain a truly Burgundian character. Because of the high quality and consistency of these wines, they are often hard to find in retail outlets; much of the output is purchased through the winery's mailing list.

Graff's younger brothers have joined him in Gavilan Vineyards, which now owns Chalone and is involved with two sister companies, Edna Valley Vineyards and Carmenet.

Chambourcin

A red French-American hybrid variety that develops more body than most, when grown in relatively warm districts. Most of the acreage is in southeastern Pennsylvania and Virginia, where varietal Chambourcins have a light nose but medium body and a good mouth feel, and are likely candidates for extractive fermentations and wood aging (and blending) to flesh out the wine. Chambourcin is somewhat reminiscent of Cabernet Franc, and similarly grown in the Loire Valley of France. In northern states, it tends to produce thin, austere wine. Chambourcin acreage, currently a few hundred, is increasing.

CHAMISAL VINEYARDS
San Luis Obispo, Central Coast

Output: 3,000 cases

Wine: Chardonnay

After Norman Goss sold a chain of restaurants in southern California, he bought land in the up-and-coming Edna Valley Viticultural Area. A small winery was built in 1980 and Chamisal ferments Chardonnays in stainless steel and ages them in French oak barrels just long enough to provide a hint of oak to complement the fruit without masking it. Chamisal has 12,000 gallons of storage capacity.

CHAMPS DE BRIONNE WINERY
George, Washington

Output: 10,000 cases

Leading Wines: Gewurztraminer, Riesling, Semillon

Situated on a bluff overlooking the Columbia River, in a new growing area near George, Champs de Brionne is a new winery owned by Vince and Carol Bryan. Michael B. Hoffman, formerly winemaker at California's HMR winery, is winemaker. In addition to the varieties already released, Champs de Brionne is developing Chardonnay,

C

Cabernet Sauvignon, and Pinot Noir—a variety that has not yet proved
very successful in other growing areas in the Columbia Valley. The Bryans
believe that the microclimate and the vineyard's alkaline, gravelly, lime
soil will be particularly suited to the Burgundian varieties. The 124-acre
vineyard is not yet fully developed (1983 was the first vintage for the
young winery) but Semillon, a highly successful Washington variety, has
shown particularly well. It is distinctly varietal, yet does not exhibit the
overly grassy characteristics that can sometimes become wearisome
through the course of a meal or tasting.

Chancellor

With Marechal Foch, Chancellor is one of the most respected red French-
American hybrids. It is relatively easy to grow, productive, and cooperative in the wine cellar, virtues that have established it in many vineyard
districts not only around the eastern United States, but also in France.
French acreage still far exceeds American (a few hundred acres) mainly in
the Finger Lakes, Hudson River Valley, southeastern Pennsylvania, and
Virginia.

As a pure varietal, the wine has simple, clean fruit flavor, sometimes
with a piney herbaceous accent, but little of the sharp stemminess that
crops up in other red hybrids. It is usually blended with other varieties to
add some depth and complexity.

CHANDON
Yountville, San Francisco Bay North

Output: 270,000 cases

*Leading Wines:
Blanc de Noirs,
Napa Valley Brut,
Panache*

Domaine Chandon is the first venture by a French wine firm into
California, initiating a trend that has been followed by most major French
Champagne houses. In 1973 Moët-Hennessy, the parent company of Moët
et Chandon in Epernay and Hennessy Cognac, hired John Wright (now
president of Domaine Chandon) to develop vineyards and build a winery
to produce sparkling wine in the Napa Valley. Wright bought a total of
1,200 acres in three locations—Carneros, Mount Veeder, and
Yountville—and built the winery at Yountvile.

The first cuvées were blended with wines made from purchased grapes
that had been vinified in leased space at Trefethen Vineyards, so that the
winery had sparkling wines for sale when it first started production in
1977. Dawnine Dyer is the winemaker in residence, but Edmond
Maudière, *chef du cave* at Moët Chandon, flies in from France several
times a year to act as consultant on the blends.

Chandon's techniques are a blend of traditional French methods,
modern technology, and adaptation to the slighter warmer conditions of
the Napa Valley, combined to achieve grapes of high acid and low sugar
used in Champagne. Grapes are picked at low Brix, 18° or 19°, as they are
in Champagne, but many are harvested at night by machine, a technique
impossible in France because the vines are too closely spaced and generally

47

grow on hillsides too steep for mechanical harvesters. Chandon's wines are generally the traditional blends of Champagne—Pinot Noir and Chardonnay—but Maudière and Dyer add a little Pinot Blanc to bring the Napa Chardonnay closer to that of Champagne.

Domaine Chandon makes two styles of sparkling wine which are, in deference to the French parentage, not called Champagne. One, Napa Valley Brut, is a blend of Pinot Noir and Chardonnay, the traditional grapes of Champagne, with a small amount of Pinot Blanc. The label does indicate, however, that *méthode champenoise* was employed in its production. The second sparkling wine is Blanc de Noirs. Made of 100 percent Pinot Noir grapes, which impart an attractive salmon pink color, the wine is fruitier than the Napa Valley Brut and tastes sweeter, although both contain exactly the same amount of dosage sugar.

A third product of importance in the Chandon repertoire is Panache, a California version of the ratafia of Champagne: an aperitif made from lightly fermented Pinot Noir juice obtained from later pressings of the grapes. Brandy is added to stop fermentation, with about half the sugar of the juice unfermented.

CHAPPELLET WINERY
St. Helena, San Francisco Bay North

Output: 20,000 cases

Leading Wines:
Cabernet Sauvignon,
Chardonnay,
Chenin Blanc,
White Riesling

Chappellet Winery, founded by Donn Chappellet in 1969, produces only four varietal wines. Chappellet's Cabernet Sauvignons have drawn much attention and an almost cult-like following. Austere wines with firm structure but immense fruit, they are designed to age at least 10-15 years. These wines have fetched record prices at auction—their first offering in 1969 made over $1,000 a bottle. Since Cathy Corison became winemaker at Chappellet, in 1981, its Cabernets have been made in a lighter style and are often blended with 10 percent Merlot.

Perhaps the most unusual of Chappellet's other wines is a Chenin Blanc. This wine differs from the usual Napa Valley style by spending a month in small French oak barrels before being bottled completely dry. This treatment adds complexity and a lingering finish without overwhelming the varietal character of Chenin Blanc.

Charbono

Acreage planted to this red vinifera in California is relatively small: of the 90 acres growing in the state, 80 are in the Napa Valley. Long thought to be Italian in origin, current thinking places its European home as France. When Charbonos are young they are harsh and tannic, but with age—up to ten years and more—they become smooth and pleasant, though remaining robust.

Chardonnay

This white vinifera achieved fame in the Burgundy region of France, where for centuries it has produced complex and intensely-flavored dry white wines. California has become a second home for Chardonnay; the state's best white wines, often capable of challenging the finest of Burgundy, are invariably produced from this grape. There are 24,000 acres planted to Chardonnay in California, reflecting an increase of 23 percent in just two years. Half California's Chardonnay grapes are found in Napa and Sonoma counties, but recent plantings in some southerly areas such as Edna Valley and Santa Maria Valley have been tremendously successsful. In the last decade Chardonnay has been planted in the northeast and eastern states as far afield as Idaho and Long Island.

Chardonnay in both France and America is made in a bewildering variety of styles. The classic Chablis style — steely, lean, and acidic — is encountered in eastern states and Oregon more often than in California. But Chardonnays with rich texture, mouth-filling flavor, and intense aromas, something like the great Burgundies of Montrachet, are more common in California. Most American Chardonnays are somewhere on a continuum between the Chablis and the Montrachet styles, though American Chardonnays of all types are usually richer and less acidic than their French counterparts.

Charmat Process

A shortcut procedure for cutting the cost of sparkling wine production by inducing the secondary fermentation in pressurized tanks rather than in the bottle. The effervescent wine is then bottled under pressure. Also called Bulk Process or Bulk Fermented.

Charmat wines have coarser bubbles, are generally not aged on yeast sediment, and hence are less complex than bottle-fermented wines.

CHATEAU BENOIT WINERY
McMinnville, Oregon

Fred and Mary Benoit planted their first vineyard in the southern end of the Willamette Valley in 1972, later adding a second vineyard in the northern part of the valley.

In addition to the typical repertoire of Oregon wines, Benoit produces a carbonic maceration Pinot Noir Nouveau and a bottle-fermented sparkling wine from a blend of Pinot Noir and Chardonnay. Of these, the Washington Sauvignon Blanc is released with a noticeable residual sugar in an off-dry style.

Output: 10,000 cases

Leading Wines:
Chardonnay,
Pinot Noir,
Riesling,
Sauvignon Blanc,
Sparkling wine

CHATEAU CHEVALIER
St. Helena, San Francisco Bay North

Output: 10,000 cases

Leading Wines:
Cabernet Sauvignon,
Chardonnay,
Pinot Noir

Chateau Chevalier was revived by the Bissonette family in 1969, when they moved from San Francisco into the 19th-century stone house halfway up Spring Mountain in the Napa Valley. They cleared the surrounding hillsides, planted 60 acres of Chardonnay and Cabernet Sauvignon, and installed winery equipment. Although the first wines from their own grapes were not released until 1976, they made wine from purchased grapes in 1972, under the Mountainside Vineyard Label.

Gil Nickel, owner of Far Niente, and his brother John brought Chateau Chevalier from the Bissonettes in 1983 and are operating it as a separate entity, producing Pinot Noir as well as Cabernet Sauvignon and Chardonnay. All are made in a traditional European style and see some aging in small French oak barrels.

CHATEAU DE LEU WINERY
Suisun, San Francisco Bay North

Output: 10,000 cases

Leading Wines:
Chardonnay,
French Colombard,
Fumé Blanc, Gamay

Situated in Green Valley (Solano), approved as a Viticultural Area in 1982, Chateau de Leu is one of several small new wineries that are reviving grapegrowing and winemaking in Solano County. The winery owns 75 acres of vineyards and has 38,000 gallons of storage capacity. Field crushing is employed to insure the freshness of the must.

CHATEAU DU LAC
Lakeport, San Francisco Bay North

Output: 60,000 cases

Leading Wines:
Chardonnay,
Cabernet Sauvignon,
Chevelot du Lac
(Semillon),
Johannisberg Riesling,
Sauvignon Blanc,
Zinfandel

North of the Napa Valley, Lake County is an area that grew grapes in the pre-Prohibition era and is now making a comeback. One of the new wineries contributing to the revival is Chateau du Lac, founded in 1981 with 85 acres of grapes and a storage capacity of 112,000 gallons. Most wines are sold under the Kendall-Jackson label (the co-owners are Jess and Kendall Jackson); other wines are labeled Chateau du Lac or Jackson Vineyards. Kendall-Jackson Chardonnays — flavorful, well-balanced, and very reasonably priced — have already developed a devoted following.

CHATEAU ESPERANZA
Bluff Point, Finger Lakes

Output: 7,000 cases

Leading Wines:
Chancellor,
Johannisberg Riesling,
Late-Harvest Ravat,
Seyval Blanc

The Chateau Esperanza name refers to the 150-year-old, Georgian mansion that was adapted into this winery, one of the most iconoclastic in the Finger Lakes region. In Esperanza's early years, following the first vintage of 1979, wine was made in barrels that fit into the low-ceilinged cellar. In these small lots consistency took a backseat to experimentation. One premise of that experimentation was the belief that grapes were picked too early in the Finger Lakes. Most of Esperanza's grapes have been purchased on loose contracts, and sometimes were late culls from vineyards already picked for bigger wineries. The result—for better or worse—has been wines more intense in varietal character than most. The style was racy and risky, as odd flavors and volatile acidity tend to creep into wines from very ripe fruit.

This style has been modified in recent years under a succession of new winemakers. Larger tanks have replaced the barrels. A small estate vineyard has been developed, but Esperanza's chilly location at the north end of Keuka Lake will keep it buying the grapes, especially for the vinifera wines that are becoming a more important part of the product line. Vineyard names often appear on labels.

Riesling has been a specialty from the first vintage, fitting well into the late-harvest style with more extract and color than other Finger Lakes versions. Esperanza's Late-Harvest Ravat consistently ranks among the best of this French hybrid variety, an almost liquorous wine, layered with almond-apricot-mandarin flavors. Seyval and Chancellor have also fared well. The latter represents a continuing commitment to red wine, and is one of the best from the Finger Lakes.

CHATEAU GRAND TRAVERS
Traverse City, Michigan

Output: 15,000 cases

Leading Wines: Chardonnay, Merlot, Riesling

A Riesling specialist tucked under one of Lake Michigan's northern wings, Chateau Grand Travers makes a flowery, semidry, Kabinett-Mosel version of the variety and two sweeter, late-harvest bottlings. Warm water surrounding the vineyard on a finger of land sticking into Grand Traverse Bay delays fall frosts into November, permitting grape sugars to accumulate. During the summer, the same water sends cooling breezes through the vineyard to preserve acids vital for late-harvest wines, and to keep infections of the botrytis mold pure and "noble." But very cold winters keep the crop small and variable.

Chardonnay is still marginal in this location, and is made here with and without oak aging. Grand Travers prides itself on growing and producing only vinifera wines, but most of the rest of their line originates in California.

CHATEAU MONTELENA
Calistoga, San Francisco Bay North

Output: 25,000 cases

Leading Wines: Cabernet Sauvignon, Napa and California Chardonnay, Johannisberg Riesling, Zinfandel

The old stone building housing Chateau Montelena was built by State Senator Alfred Tubbs in 1882 and was used only sporadically for winemaking until it was closed during Prohibition. After a brief revival following Repeal, the property was sold in 1947 to a Chinese couple who created the beautiful Oriental water gardens east of the main building.

The wine boom was just beginning when the property was acquired in 1968 by Lee and Helen Paschich. A thoroughly modern winery was designed by Miljenko Grgich, who left the Robert Mondavi Winery to

C

become the winemaker at Montelena. Grgich also oversaw the replanting of 100 acres of vineyards, even doing some of the replanting himself, using only red varieties, mostly Cabernet Sauvignon and Zinfandel. White grapes are purchased.

It was at Chateau Montelena that Miljenko (Mike) Grgich became world renowned as a winemaker and in the process demonstrated that California was capable of producing world-class wines. His 1973 Chardonnay, his first vintage at Montelena, was one of the original full, rich Napa Valley versions of this varietal, setting a style that has been widely imitated. That vintage won the controversial tasting at L'Académie du Vin in 1976, surpassing several top-rated white Burgundies from France.

Mike left Chateau Montelena to found his own winery, Grgich Hills Cellars, and was succeeded by another well-known winemaker, Jerry Luper, who has since gone to Chateau Bouchaine. But Chateau Montelena's Chardonnays have remained first-rate since that victory. Two varieties are produced: Napa, and a slightly less oaky California.

CHATEAU ST. JEAN
Kenwood, San Francisco Bay North

Output: 170,000 cases

Leading Wines:
Chardonnay, Fumé Blanc,
Gewurztraminer,
Johannisberg Riesling,
Pinot Blanc, Brut
Sparkling Wine, Blanc de
Blanc sparkling wine

When Robert and Edward Merzoian and Kenneth Sheffield founded Chateau St. Jean in 1974, naming it after Jean Merzoian, Edward's wife, they gave Dick Arrowood carte blanche to design the winery he wanted. Arrowood created an extremely modern facility capable of accommodating small lots of grapes, so that each vineyard lot could be vinified differently and credited on the Chateau St. Jean labels.

Individual designations continue; there may be as many as four Rieslings and six Chardonnays from the same vintage in the market at the same time. A close working relationship with the grape growers assures that the grapes will be up to Chateau St. Jean's specifications. The winery also owns 124 acres of vineyards, and a limited amount of wine is produced from grapes grown on this land.

Chardonnay from the Robert Young Vineyard, for example, always fetches the highest price for its rich, buttery concentration—though some Chateau St. Jean aficionados prefer the lower-priced, sometimes better-balanced Chardonnays from other vineyards.

Although some remarkably good Cabernet Sauvignons and Zinfandels were made by Arrowood in the first few years, red wine production was discontinued after 1980. Now only white wines are made in the 500,000-gallon Kenwood facility. The winery is especially noted for its sweeter, late-harvest versions of Johannisberg Riesling and Gewurztraminer and plans to reduce production of drier wines from these grapes.

Chateau St. Jean was sold to Suntory, Japan's largest producer of whiskey, in August 1984 for a reported $40 million. Suntory has pledged to stay out of aesthetic decisions at the winery; it likes the wines being produced at Chateau St. Jean, and has no plans to change them.

C

CHATEAU STE. MICHELLE
Woodinville, Washington

By far the Northwest's largest winery, Chateau Ste. Michelle owns roughly one-quarter of the state's vinifera vineyards, and is one of America's major premium wineries.

Ste. Michelle's roots go back to the founding of Nawico and Pommerelle wineries in Washington, immediately following repeal of Prohibition. In 1954 these two wineries merged to form American Wine Growers and, except for an incidental bottling of Grenache, most of their wines were generic or sometimes fortified blends primarily of labrusca grapes. But in 1967, American Wine Growers released its first premium vinifera wines under a new label, Ste. Michelle. A group of local investors purchased the winery in 1973, and the following year Chateau Ste. Michelle became a wholly-owned subsidiary of the United States Tobacco Company.

With this powerful new backing Chateau Ste. Michelle's growth has been dramatic. It produced a mere 6,000 cases in 1967, but by 1990 expects to produce nearly 800,000 cases a year from its three wineries. The Woodinville winery, built in 1976 on an 87-acre estate near Seattle, has been outgrown but continues to house the corporate offices and be the principal showcase winery. It remains the center for all Ste. Michelle's oak-aged wines.

In 1983, Chateau Ste. Michelle completed construction of River Ridge, a modern $26 million facility overlooking the Columbia River near its vineyards in Paterson. This major investment reflects the parent company's commitment to the wine industry, and to Washington as a winegrowing region. Nearly three times the size of the Woodinville winery, River Ridge handles the majority of the harvest crush. The largest tanks at River Ridge, however, have no more than a 12,000-gallon capacity, allowing for more individual control of separate wine batches for special releases or later blending.

While River Ridge crushes and clarifies Chardonnay and Sauvignon Blanc, the juice is sent to Woodinville for fermentation and wood aging. Red wine grapes are processed at the refurbished Nawico winery in Grandview, in the Yakima Valley. After the must is fermented, the red wine is sent to Woodinville to spend time in oak barrels.

Chateau Ste. Michelle purchases grapes from various locations in the Columbia Valley, but it has been expanding its own vineyards to achieve greater control over its grape supply. Its principal vineyards include 68 acres in the Yakima Valley, 580 acres in the Cold Creek Valley — a warm growing site near the Columbia River that averages 3,300 heat units a year during a 210-day growing season — and 1,780 acres surrounding the River Ridge winery at Paterson.

Chateau Ste. Michelle's whites are made in a clean, crisp style. Prior to fermentation the must is clarified to remove excess solids. The first wine to gain national attention and recognition for Ste. Michelle, Riesling continues to be its leading wine and is produced in two versions: a semidry

Output: 500,000 cases

Leading Wines:
Cabernet Sauvignon,
Chardonnay, Fumé Blanc,
Merlot, Riesling,
Semillon Blanc

WASHINGTON
JOHANNISBERG RIESLING
1982

PRODUCED AND BOTTLED BY CHATEAU STE. MICHELLE
WOODINVILLE, WASHINGTON · USA · ALCOHOL 11.3% BY VOLUME

labeled Johannisberg Riesling, and a sweeter, richer rendition labeled White Riesling.

With the maturation of the Washington wine industry and the certainty that the Columbia Valley growing climate is well-suited to other grape varieties, Chateau Ste. Michelle's drier wines — Chardonnay, Fumé Blanc, and Semillon Blanc — are rapidly gaining in importance. Chardonnay is partly fermented in small French oak barrels. At about 8° Brix, the Chardonnay must is transferred to the oak barrels to finish fermentation. The fruit of the grape is emphasized, and the Chardonnay and Sauvignon Blanc receive only brief aging in French oak tanks and barrels. The Chardonnays often seem understated in their youth, but age and develop very well. Semillon is receiving increasing attention at Chateau Ste. Michelle. The standard release sees no oak and is finished with slight residual sugar. A reserve bottling is finished dry and aged in French oak. Other whites include Chenin Blanc, Gewurztraminer, and Muscat Canelli. Farron Ridge White, Red, and Rosé are blends available in larger bottle sizes.

With few exceptions, the red wines have not achieved the same immediate high level of success as the whites, but recent releases, and wines yet to be released, bode well for the future. While the first Merlot and Cabernet wines were aged in American oak, French oak is increasingly becoming the predominant cooperage, and the reserve Cabernet Sauvignon is aged entirely in French oak. Special releases have included botrytised Chenin Blanc, Riesling Ice Wine, bottle-fermented sparkling wine, and a continuing series of reserve wines.

Ste. Michelle has done much to bring attention and recognition to one of America's most important new winegrowing regions.

Chelois

A red French-American hybrid variety, Chelois has a herbaceous fruit character that lends itself to the style of red French Burgundy, accenting soft, mature fruitiness. It does not require aging but generally puts it to good use, except for unstable color that tends to leach out and brown, and this has led some wineries to use Chelois for rosés. Acreage is small, only a few hundred acres, but increasing; it is scattered through the East and Midwest.

Chenin Blanc

The white grape of the Loire Valley, and particularly of Vouvray, Chenin Blanc is heavily planted in the Central Valley of California, with over 30,000 acres of the state's total of about 45,000 acres. As a varietal, California Chenin Blanc is typically light in body, fruity, and slightly sweet. But it is also used as a blending grape in generic whites and as a base wine for inexpensive sparkling wines.

CHICAMA VINEYARDS
West Tisbury, New England

The island of Martha's Vineyard, off Cape Cod, was named in 1602 for its mantle of wild grapevines but it didn't actually have a vineyard until Chicama was founded in 1971. With one of the longer growing seasons (averaging 30 days longer than the nearby New England coast), and insulated by the ocean from winter freezes, Chicama not only grows vinifera varieties exclusively, but also can sustain and ripen such exotics (for the East) as Zinfandel, Ruby Cabernet, and Chenin Blanc. The Zinfandel and Chicama's Cabernet Sauvignon are particularly successful New England anomalies—middle-weight wines with good balance and varietal character. All wines are estate-bottled from the 46-acre vineyard.

Output: 5,000 cases

Leading Wines:
Cabernet Sauvignon,
Ruby Cabernet,
Chardonnay,
Gewurztraminer, Seamist
Sparkling Wine, Zinfandel

THE CHRISTIAN BROTHERS
San Francisco Bay North and Central Valley

The Christian Brothers teaching order of the Catholic Church was founded in 1680 by St. Jean Baptiste de La Salle. Properly known as "Fratres Scholarum Christianarum," (Brothers of the Christian Schools) they are not priests, but a religious teaching order whose members take vows of chastity, obedience, and poverty.

The Brothers first came to California in 1868 to take charge of St. Mary's College, but did not begin to make wine commercially until 1882. In 1879, they had bought land in Martinez, east of Oakland, to build a novitiate. When they discovered 12 acres of grapes growing on the property, they began to turn those grapes into wines, producing their first vintage in 1881 for sacramental use and at their own table. Within a few years they were selling wines to the public and today income from wine sales helps to support thirteen schools in the western United States.

The expansion of the city of Martinez, encroaching upon their privacy and property, prompted the Brothers to look for another site for their novitiate, which they found in the Giersberger Winery near the city of Napa. By 1932, their new monastery was completed and they moved both novitiate and winery to Mont La Salle on the lower slopes of the Mayacamas Mountains.

The Christian Brothers continued to produce wines throughout Prohibition, making sacramental and medicinal wines. (The latter appears to have been anything a physician would prescribe and would have been purchased at a pharmacy.)

Today the Christian Brothers operate three wineries in the Napa Valley. In addition to the winery next to the monastery on Mont La Salle, the Brothers occupy a large 19th-century stone winery, formerly known as Greystone Cellars, north of St. Helena, and a large, modern winemaking and storage facility just south of St. Helena.

In addition to the three Napa Valley wineries, the Brothers also produce ports and sherries in their Mount Tivy Winery at Reedley in the Central Valley, and brandy at a fifth location in Fresno.

Output: 2.25 million cases

Leading Wines:
Burgundy, Cabernet
Sauvignon, Chablis,
Chateau La Salle, Chenin
Blanc, Claret, Fumé Blanc,
Gamay Noir,
Gewurztraminer,
La Salle Rosé,
Napa Rosé,
Pineau de la Loire, Pinot
Noir, Pinot St. George,
Rhine, Riesling, Sauterne,
Sauvignon Blanc,
Zinfandel, Vin Rosé,
Ports, Sherries,
Vermouths, Brandies,
sparkling wines

C

Christian Brothers' five wineries have a combined storage capacity of nearly 40 million gallons, which makes them one of the largest wine-making operations in California. They are the largest winery and biggest grapegrowers in the Napa Valley. Christian Brothers brandy, introduced in the 1940s, now accounts for approximately one-third of the brandy sold in the United States. The 1,600 acres of vineyards owned by the Christian Brothers makes them one of the largest vineyard owners in the state.

Until the mid-1970s, the Christian Brothers did not vintage date their wines, preferring to blend different vintages to assure consistency and continuity. However, with the release of a special lot of 1976 Gewurz-traminer in 1977, they began a selected list of limited quantities of varietals and dessert wines.

Cellarmaster and the most visible symbol of Christian Brothers wines and brandies is Brother Timothy, who in 1984 celebrated his fiftieth year in the wine industry.

CILURZO VINEYARD AND WINERY
Temecula, South Coast

Output: 8,000 cases

Leading Wines: Beaujolais, Cabernet Sauvignon, Chardonnay, Chenin Blanc, Fumé Blanc, Gamay, Petite Sirah

The Cilurzos, Vincenzo and Audrey, pioneered Temecula, planting the first vineyard in the region in 1967. They have since been followed by several other wineries and vineyards that have discovered that the warm climate of this region is tempered by cool breezes off the ocean. Cilurzo owns 10 acres and has 44,000 gallons of storage capacity.

CLINTON VINEYARDS
Clinton Corners, Hudson River Valley

Output: 2,500 cases

Leading Wines: Seyval Blanc, Seyval Blanc Reserve, Seyval Naturel

Clinton specializes in Seyval Blanc, the most prominent of French-American hybrids. In this rolling, eastern fringe of the Hudson Valley, the Seyval vine (which tends to produce too much fruit with too little character) seems to find a good balance of winter stress and summer sustenance. Modest crops ripen consistently well (high sugar, high acid) into wines with clean, bright fruit in a dry but not quite bone-dry style. Clinton's is clearly one of the benchmark Seyvals. A limited-edition, Yugoslavian-oak-aged version carries the Reserve label; and a still more limited *méthode champenoise* sparkling Seyval Naturel retains its fresh fruit with yeasty overtones.

Clone

A naturally occurring variant or mutant strain within a grape variety. In some varieties, such as Pinot Noir and Riesling, many clones have been carefully selected, propagated, and identified with particular viticultural districts for the production of wine with superior attributes. Clonal selection has only recently become important in American wine districts.

CLOS DU BOIS
Healdsburg, San Francisco Bay North

Clos du Bois began when three graduates of Cornell University, Frank M. Woods, Thomas C. Reed, and Dennis Malone, began buying vineyards in Sonoma County in 1962. By the mid-1970s, they had acquired 1,000 acres in the Alexander and Dry Creek valleys and in 1974 they leased space at a Sonoma County winery and began making wine, releasing their first vintages in 1976 under the Clos Du Bois label.

A 450,000-gallon winery has since been constructed so that the partners now control production from vineyard to bottle, and seven varietals are produced from their own grapes.

Clos du Bois' Gewurztraminer is a consistent award-winner, and its early harvest Gewurztraminer is one of the most food-worthy versions of that variety produced in the state. The winery also puts great stress on viticultural origins and six vineyard-designated wines are produced: Briarcrest and Woodleaf are 100 percent Cabernet Sauvignon; Alcaire and Flintwood are Chardonnays; Cherry Hill is Pinot Noir; and Marlstone is a Cabernet Sauvignon/Merlot blend, the Marlstone vineyard being planted to both of these grape varieties.

In some years the Marlstone wine is nearly 50 percent Merlot; in others a much higher proportion of Cabernet Sauvignon is used. The wine is a good example of Frank Wood's intention to get away from what he considers an unhealthy focus on varietal labeling. In this he is one of the leaders in a state-wide trend toward wines that are blends of varieties, following a European approach rather than intense examples of single varieties.

Clos du Bois has a sister winery, River Oaks, whose wines are produced from acreage in Alexander Valley, receive less cellar aging, and are less complex than the Clos Du Bois wines. Comprising about 60 percent of the annual output, they are priced below Clos Du Bois wines and usually constitute good value.

Output: 250,000 cases

Leading Wines:
Cabernet Sauvignon,
Chardonnay,
Gewurztraminer,
Johannisberg Riesling,
Marlstone,
Merlot, Pinot Noir,
Sauvignon Blanc;
River Oaks Vineyards:
Cabernet Sauvignon,
Chardonnay,
Johannisberg Riesling,
Zinfandel, Red and White
table wines

CLOS DU VAL
Napa, San Francisco Bay North

Beginning with its first vintage in 1972, Clos Du Val has been well-known for a consistent string of complex, long-lived Cabernet Sauvignons. Winemaker Bernard Portet grew up at Chateau Lafite-Rothschild, where his father was *regisseur* for many years. He attended the wine school at Montpellier and worked in wineries in southern France and South Africa before coming to the United States in 1968 to found Clos Du Val. His French background is certainly evident in Clos du Val's elegant Cabernet Sauvignon, and in its exemplary claret-like Zinfandel.

Clos Du Val had an established reputation for these two wines before Bernard turned his attention to white wines. His first Chardonnay was produced 10 years after the winery's first red wines. But recent releases have also included Sauvignon Blanc and a much-praised Semillon. Never-

Output: 32,000 cases

Leading Wines:
Cabernet Sauvignon,
Chardonnay,
Merlot, Sauvignon Blanc,
Semillon, Zinfandel

theless, the Clos de Val reputation remains strongest for red wines.

Clos Du Val owns 120 acres planted to Cabernet Sauvignon, Merlot, and Zinfandel near the winery, giving it control over all these grapes, and an estate-bottled designation has been carried on its labels from the first vintage. An additional 150 acres in the Carneros region are being developed for Chardonnay and Pinot Noir and the winery now has 100,000 gallons of storage capacity.

A second label called Gran Val has been developed for lower-priced and less complex wines.

Cold Stabilization

Cold stablization follows fermentation. The wine is typically chilled below 32°F to aid clarification and precipitate tartrates that are in unstable solution. These tartrates sometimes turn up as crystal deposits in bottles that have been chilled.

COLUMBIA WINERY
Bellevue, Washington

Output: 40,000 cases

Leading Wines:
Cabernet Sauvignon,
Chardonnay,
Gewurztraminer,
Grenache, Merlot,
Riesling, Semillon

Formerly Associated Vintners, Columbia is Washington's oldest continuing premium vinifera winery. It was begun in the late 1950s, when a group of University of Washington professors led by Lloyd Woodburne began making wine at home from some of the few vinifera grapes then grown in the state. Early successes encouraged the group to purchase a grape crusher and, to avoid violating legal strictures, they formed a corporation. In 1962, they established themselves as a bonded winery—Associated Vintners.

The turning point, however, came in 1966 when Leon Adams, the noted wine authority, impressed by one of Woodburne's Grenaches, suggested that Associated Vintners should become a commercial winery. Further critical encouragement came in the following year from André Tchelistcheff, one of the most famous and respected of all American winemakers. When he praised a Gewurztraminer made by Phil Church, another winemaker in the group, as the best American example of this wine he had ever tasted, the group rented a small facility in Kirkland, a suburb of Seattle, and produced their first commercial vintage (1967).

A key element in the winery is David Lake, winemaker since 1979, and now winery vice president. Although Washington is commonly thought of as a white wine region, Lake believes that it is an even better region for red wine, and Columbia Winery's Cabernet Sauvignons are among the best in the state. While very similar in structure and profile to traditional Bordeaux, the scents and flavors bespeak the growing areas of Washington.

Lake works very closely with Columbia's growers, and wines from the different vineyards are often labeled separately. In the Yakima Valley, Otis Vineyards produces an excellent but often atypical Cabernet with a distinctive black cherry flavor and aroma from 20-year-old fan-trained vines. Also in the Yakima Valley, Red Willow Vineyards yields a complex, more textural wine with flavors more closely resembling the style of traditional Bordeaux. Cabernets from the Bacchus and Dionysus Vineyards in the Pasco area of the Columbia Valley are fuller-bodied and display more of the grape's herbaceous elements. The Merlot is more immediately accessible than the Cabernets, but it too benefits from time in the bottle. The best recent vintages for Cabernet and Merlot are 1979, 1981, and 1983.

The best Washington Cabernets require and benefit greatly from lengthy aging. In 1985 Columbia released a special reserve bottling from an exceptional Cabernet vintage, the 1979 Cabernet Sauvignon Millennium, the name coming from the suggestion that the wine should be laid down until the turn of the century.

Of the white wines, Columbia is specializing in another Bordeaux variety, Semillon, and in Chardonnay. Other specialties include Grenache, a sweet Riesling, and a dry Gewurztraminer, a winery trademark.

COMMONWEALTH WINERY
Plymouth, New England

Output: 12,000 cases

Leading Wines: Aurora, Cayuga, Chardonnay, Cranberry Apple, De Chaunac, Gewurztraminer, Red and White, Plymouth Rock Rosé, Seyval, Vidal

More than a dozen small vineyards scattered in southeastern Massachusetts, plus a few in New Hampshire and Long Island, supply Commonwealth with grapes for about the same number of wines.

Most of the grapes used are French-American varieties. Commonwealth's almost-dry, citrusy Cayuga and hearty De Chaunac have become benchmark examples of these varieties. Along with a flinty dry Seyval and German-style Vidal and Aurora, they offer consistently good, affordable drinking. Plymouth Rock, honoring the nearby stepping-stone into the New World, is the name given to the winery's reliable, dry blends; the Harvest blends are sweet and grapey. Winemaker David Tower showed an early interest in the emerging Long Island vineyard district (only 100 miles southeast of Plymouth), the source for some distinguished, sinewy, Commonwealth Chardonnays. Limited edition Riesling has also been successful here in flowery German Kabinett style. This is the largest New England winery, but still small.

CONCANNON VINEYARDS
Livermore, San Francisco Bay South

Output: 100,000 cases

Leading Wines: Burgundy, Chablis, Chardonnay, Chenin Blanc, Livermore Riesling, Petite Sirah,

Concannon Vineyards was founded in 1883 by an Irish immigrant, James Concannon, with the purpose of producing altar wines. This kept the winery operating during Prohibition.

Concannon has been noted for a variety of white wines produced on the gravelly soils (very much like those of Graves in Bordeaux) of the Livermore Valley, and has drawn attention for its experiments with the Russian

Sauvignon Blanc,
Zinfandel Rosé,
Estate-bottled:
Cabernet Sauvignon,
Petite Sirah,
Sauvignon Blanc

white grape known as Rkatsiteli. Concannon was also the first to make Petite Sirah as a varietal wine in 1963. Previously used as a blending wine, Petite Sirah is now accepted as a varietal in its own right.

In recent years the winery has been sold twice — most recently in 1983 to Distillers Company, the producers of Johnnie Walker whisky. James Concannon, Joe's brother and the third generation of Concannons associated with the winery, remains actively involved.

The winery's fortunes have fluctuated with the changes of ownership. One measure of the difficulties has been the vast reduction in acres of vines, owing in part to urban spread in the Livermore area. But a county agricultural preserve ordinance absolutely protects 250 acres of Concannon-owned vineyards, and these form the basis of the estate-bottled program initiated by Concannon with the release of an estate-grown Cabernet Sauvignon. Another cause for optimism at Concannon is the addition of Chilean winemaker Sergio Traverso; as winemaker at Sterling and then at Domaine Chandon, Traverso was responsible for many outstanding California wines in the 1970s. With storage exceeding 500,000 gallons, Concannon maintains a range of 15 different wines.

Concord

The most extensively grown grape in the East by a wide margin (and with the second largest acreage in the United States), Concord is not considered a wine grape, but it is used to make plenty of wine. The rise of Concord wine came after Prohibition, when wine grape vineyards had been pulled out or abandoned, and any grapes available were called into service for winemaking. The pungent flavor of the grape, familiar in grape jelly and juice, requires amelioration with water and sugar to bring wine from this variety into drinkable balance. Few wines labeled Concord are 100 percent varietal, as a little Concord goes a long way in a blend. One of its best uses is in sangrias and other mixes. Certainly the best use Concord has been put to by winemakers is for sherry production, where the processes of heating and oxidation refine the labrusca flavor into mild background fruitiness.

CONN CREEK

Output: 20,000 cases

Leading Wines:
Cabernet Sauvignon,
Chardonnay,
Zinfandel

St. Helena, San Francisco Bay North

Conn Creek began life in 1974 in a ninety-year-old stone building north of St. Helena. After five vintages there, the winery was moved to a new 15,000-square-foot building on Silverado Trail, where storage capacity has been expanded to 135,000 gallons.

Approximately 70 percent of the grapes used by the winery are harvested in the 120 acres of vineyards owned by Bill and Kathy Collins, founding partners of Conn Creek. (Included in this is a 70-year-old Zinfandel vineyard.)

Conn Creek's Cabernet Sauvignon and Zinfandel wines are aged in

60-gallon Nevers oak barrels for 18 for 20 months and released after three years of aging at the winery, including at least one year in the bottle, prior to release. Chardonnay receives wood-aging in Limousin oak and is released after two years (one in bottle) of aging at the winery.

R AND J COOK
Clarksburg, Sacramento Valley

Output: 50,000 cases

Leading Wines:
Cabernet Sauvignon,
Chenin Blanc, Merlot,
Petite Sirah,
Sauvignon Blanc

Roger and Joanne Cook founded this 225,000-gallon winery in 1979, 10 years after Roger's father planted grapes near Clarksburg in the Sacramento River delta. R and J Cook is part of the renaissance of grape-growing in this area. The delta's microclimate, with cool ocean air blowing in off San Pablo Bay, is a radical break in the Region V climate of neighboring areas. In the delta — which is actually as cool as Region III at times — the wind moderates the afternoon heat and enables the grapes to retain their refreshing acidity.

The Cooks own 130 acres of vineyards, and lease another 100. Although five varietals are produced, they specialize in Chenin Blanc made in three distinct styles. One is semidry with 2.3 percent residual sugar; the second is very dry, containing only .28 percent residual sugar; and the third is barrel-fermented, adding an extra dimension of complexity.

Cooperage

A collective term for the containers, large and small, used in making wine. In its more precise definition, cooperage refers to wooden barrels, casks, and tanks. Once the only material used, wood was eclipsed by sanitary, hi-tech stainless steel, but is now enjoying a renaissance in the evolution of American winemaking. White oak is the preferred wood for small cooperage, where the lower surface-to-volume ratio imparts some flavoring to the wine. Varieties of oak native to France add more subtle flavors than American or other oaks, though the choice is a matter of individual taste and wine style.

CORBETT CANYON VINEYARDS
San Luis Obispo, Central Coast

Output: 70,000 cases

Leading Wines:
Chardonnay,
Chenin Blanc,
Pinot Noir,
Pinot Noir Blanc,
Sauvignon Blanc,
Zinfandel

Formerly Lawrence Winery, the name of this winery was changed to Corbett Canyon three years after Glenmore Distillers bought the property from founder Jim Lawrence in 1981. This change illustrates a classic pattern in the California wine industry: a large corporation coming in and putting a small winery on its feet.

Since 1983, Cary Gott, formerly with Montevina in the Sierra Foothills, has been the winemaker at Corbett, which now has 730,000 gallons of storage capacity. Gott, who grew up in a wine-oriented environment, was well-known for his outstanding Zinfandels and Cabernets at Montevina.

C

During his first year at Corbett, he added new equipment and Limousin oak barrels for aging selected wines.

Corbett Canyon Vineyards is the name used on the label for this winery's still wines; Shadow Creek appears on the labels of its sparkling wines. These sparkling wines, made in Sonoma at the Chateau St. Jean facility, are relatively new but have attracted a strong following.

CORDTZ BROTHERS CELLARS
Cloverdale, San Francisco Bay North

Output: 11,000 cases

Leading Wines:
Cabernet Sauvignon,
Chardonnay,
Gewurztraminer,
Mama Tasca's Carignane,
Late-harvest Johannisberg
Riesling, Sauvignon Blanc
Zinfandel

Built on the site of an old winery, this family owned and operated enterprise began winemaking operations in 1979. Storage capacity is now 130,000 gallons.

Cordtz wines have done well in recent competitions; its late-harvest Riesling won a Gold medal in the 1984 Los Angeles County Fair judgings, and Mama Tasca's Carignane, regarded as a specialty of the winery, was awarded a Bronze medal in these judgings. The well-respected Chuck Ortman serves as consulting winemaker.

COTES DES COLOMBES VINEYARD
Banks, Oregon

Output: 2,000 cases

Leading Wines:
Cabernet Sauvignon,
Chenin Blanc,
Gewurztraminer,
Pinot Noir,
Riesling

Founded in 1977 by Joe Coulombe, a former wine retailer in the Portland area, Cote des Colombes's production from its 5-acre vineyard is supplemented by purchased grapes from Oregon and Washington. The winery is focusing on Cabernet Sauvignon, and has experimented with Oregon oak (*Quercus garryana*) chips, and more recently several Oregon oak barrels for aging wine. At this stage, Colombes has not established a track record for these efforts.

H. COTTURRI & SONS
Glen Ellen, San Francisco Bay North

Output: 2,000 cases

Leading Wines:
Cabernet Sauvignon,
Chardonnay, Pinot Noir,
Zinfandel

Founded in 1979, Cotturri is one of Sonoma County's smallest wineries. Cotturri's wines are naturally made without benefit of temperature controls during fermentation, utilizing wild yeasts present on the grapes, and bottled without filtration. Although the winemaker's control is diminished considerably by such practices, Cotturri and the few other winemakers who make natural wines believe that purer wines of greater complexity result.

COWIE WINE CELLARS
Paris, Arkansas

Output: 1,800 cases

Leading Wines:
Cynthiana,

The Cowie family's wine business dates back to the late 1960s but is rooted in local tradition. Arkansas is the western range of the southern

Muscadine grape specie, and Cowie makes half-a-dozen red, white, and rosé wines with assertively regional, muscadine fruit flavors. A delicate, dry Niagara shows considerable skill with that forceful grape. But the real specialty is Cowie's dark red, velvety Cynthiana, the region's best native variety given the body, oak aging, and a measure of dryness (it is still on the soft side) to show character and complexity. Ninety percent of the grapes used are bought from local growers, but the Cowies are building up their own vineyard with Cynthiana and some experimental Chardonnay and Riesling.

Dry Muscadine, Niagara, Villard Noir

CRESTA BLANCA WINERY
Ukiah, San Francisco Bay North

Output: 100,000 cases

Although Cresta Blanca is now part of the huge Guild Wineries and Distillers and has operated out of a Mendocino County location since 1971, the name became famous when it was an independent winery farther north, in the Livermore Valley.

The original Cresta Blanca was founded in 1880 by Charles Wetmore, a San Francisco newspaperman who brought cuttings of Semillon and Sauvignon Blanc from the renowned Chateau d'Yquem to plant in his Livermore vineyards. Under his ownership the winery won an international reputation in the last decades of the 19th century. Cresta Blanca survived Prohibition but was sold in 1941 to Schenley, which continued operations at the Livermore site until it was closed in 1965.

It was in 1956 at Cresta Blanca in Livermore that Myron Nightingale made the wine called Premier Semillon, a lush, dessert-style wine which is still a topic of conversation among wine aficionados today. The Semillon grapes were artificially infected with botrytis mold using a technique devised by Nightingale's wife Alice, to obtain the concentrated flavors, sugars, and aromas that normally develop naturally. After the Livermore winery was closed, Nightingale moved on to Beringer.

Leading Wines: Burgundy, Cabernet Sauvignon, Chablis, Chardonnay, Chenin Blanc, French Colombard, Gamay Beaujolais, Gewurztraminer, Grenache Rosé, Johannisberg Riesling, Grey Riesling, Petite Sirah, Pinot Noir, Zinfandel; sparkling wines, various ports, sherries, and aperitif wines

CRIBARI VINEYARDS
Fresno, Central Valley

Output: 3.5 million cases

Cribari is an old and familiar name in California wine. Now part of the Guild Cooperative, it was founded by Benjamin Cribari in 1906. Prior to the beginning of World War II, Cribari owned thousands of acres of vineyards in the Santa Clara Valley and operated wineries in Madrone, Fresno, and New York City.

The present Cribari winery in Fresno occupies an extensive cellar filled with enormous tanks at the former home of Roma Winery. The sherry cellar, for example, contains twelve 90-year-old redwood tanks, each of which holds 25,000 gallons. A second cellar is filled with six tanks of 60,000 gallons each and eight tanks of 127,000 gallons each.

Albert Cribari, a grandson of the founder, is very much in evidence as winemaker and public relations representative extraordinaire.

Leading Wines: Cabernet Sauvignon, Chardonnay, Chenin Blanc, French Colombard, Spumante (from Muscat grapes), Zinfandel; several generics including sparkling wines; brandies,

C

CRYSTAL VALLEY CELLARS
Modesto, Central Valley

Output: 15,000 cases

Leading Wines:
Cabernet Sauvignon,
Chardonnay,
Johannisberg Riesling,
Merlot, Pinot Noir,
Riesling, Sauvignon Blanc

Although Crystal Valley calls the moderately hot Modesto region home, Mitch Cosentino, winemaker and founder, chooses to make his wines from grapes grown in a variety of cooler areas. Included are several versions of four varietals, each designated by region or origin. Those in the line called Cosentino Select are given imaginative names such as The Novelist (Sauvignon Blanc), and The Sculptor (Chardonnay).

JOHN CULBERTSON WINERY
Fallbrook, South Coast

Output: 4,000 cases

Leading Wines:
Brut, Cuvée Tranquille,
Natural sparkling wines

John Culbertson and his wife Martha have been producing sparkling wines on their Fallbrook ranch near San Diego since 1981. Their specialty has been a *méthode champenoise* sparkling wine in two styles—a natural with no sugar in the dosage, and a brut with less than 1 percent sugar.

CUVAISON
Calistoga, San Francisco Bay North

Output: 20,000 cases

Leading Wines:
Cabernet Sauvignon,
Chardonnay, Pinot Noir

Tracing Cuvaison's history is somewhat difficult, since this Napa Valley winery has been through a number of ownership, wine list, and wine style changes since its inception in 1970. It has achieved stability today under the ownership of Dr. Stefan Scmidheiny and his brother Alexander.

Cuvaison has made a strong commitment to the coolest section of Napa Valley, Los Carneros, and has recently planted 300 acres of grapes there. Los Carneros region was chosen for Cuvaison's new vineyard to take advantage of the cooling effect provided by San Pablo Bay (an arm of San Francisco Bay). This effect allows the grapes to retain high acid levels, and delays bud break in the spring until the danger of frost is past.

Fermentation and vinification techniques for all of Cuvaison's wines are traditional, with such complexity-generating techniques as barrel-fermentation, malolactic fermentation, and aging in barrels employed in various combinations.

Cynthiana

Also called Norton, this was one of the American varieties shipped to Europe late in the 19th century as an antidote to the great phylloxera plague. At that time it made the only wine that met with any favor and today is considered by many to be the only native American grape with potential for high quality red wine.

Today Cynthiana is grown commercially only in Missouri and Arkansas, with very limited but expanding acreage. The vine is a shy bearer of small clusters. This favors the production of intense, dark red wine with full, ungrapey fruit flavors that can develop spicy complexity with age.

D'AGOSTINI WINERY
Plymouth, Sierra Foothills

Output: 50,000 cases

Leading Wines:
Muscat Canelli, Red and White table wines, Sauvignon Blanc, Amador County Estate-Bottled Zinfandel, White Zinfandel

D'Agostini is the oldest winery operating in the Sierra Foothills. With the exception of the Prohibition years, wine has been made there since 1856 when a Swiss emigré constructed the winery from local stone. The D'Agostini family purchased the facility in 1911 and made mainly generic wines after Repeal. But in the late 1960s growing interest in the aggressive, full-flavored Zinfandels of Amador County encouraged D'Agostini to label its own Zinfandel by its varietal name rather than generically (it had been called Burgundy).

With 205,000 gallons of storage capacity, D'Agostini is Amador County's largest winery and in 1984 it was purchased by Armagan Ozdiker. One hundred and eighty-three acres of vineyards are owned, 86 of which are in vineyards in the Shenandoah Valley, the heart of Amador County viticulture.

De Chaunac

Named for Adehemar De Chaunac, the Canadian winemaker, this red French-American hybrid variety was extensively planted in New York in the late 1960s and early 1970s at the urging of the Taylor Wine Company. A high yielder, it was Taylor's choice for a reliable source of robust red table wine. New York acreage in 1980 was 860, largest of the red hybrids. The wine is an all-purpose red with moderate fruitiness and deep color, made light and fresh with cherry-like flavors or more often in a hearty, barrel-aged, pasta-wine style.

DEHLINGER WINERY
Sebastopol, San Francisco Bay North

Output: 7,000 cases

Leading Wines:
Cabernet Sauvignon, Chardonnay, Pinot Noir, Zinfandel

Tom Dehlinger, formerly a winemaker at Hanzell Vineyard, founded his own 35,000-gallon winery in the Russian River Valley in 1975. He owns 31 acres of vineyards. The winery has received critical acclaim for its carefully made, stylish wines that generally exhibit attractive flavors and

D

commendable balance. Furthermore, Dehlinger delivers these well-made wines at very reasonable prices.

Delaware

The quintessential labrusca wine, Delaware has a powerful scent and flavor of the grape, embroidered with floral, citrus, and musky qualities when it has fully ripened. If an eastern winery makes any labrusca wine, it is likely to make this white wine varietal, often the token native in a product line of hybrids and vinifera. Given this role, the prevailing style plays up the variety's lush, fragrant character with at least some, and sometimes much more, residual sugar, which helps mask some bitterness in the finish of Delaware.

Delaware is a low-acid variety, unlike most labruscas. This has kept most of the plantings in northern areas, where cool seasons retain more acidity to balance residual sweetness. In the late 19th century it became a mainstay of sparkling wines made in the Finger Lakes and a 1980 vineyard census listed almost 2,000 acres of Delaware in New York state.

DE LOACH VINEYARDS
Santa Rosa, San Francisco Bay North

Output: 35,000 cases

*Leading Wines:
Chardonnay,
Fumé Blanc,
Gewurztraminer,
Pinot Noir,
White Zinfandel,
Zinfandel*

Christine and Cecil De Loach began their careers in the wine industry by planting vineyards northeast of Santa Rosa in 1972, selling their grapes to other wineries for seven years. Acreage now totals 155, planted to Zinfandel, Pinot Noir, Gewurztraminer, and Chardonnay, all in a cool Region I. De Loach owns 81 of those acres and leases the other 74.

They built a winery in 1979, styled after the barns in the area, with 55,000 gallons of storage capacity. De Loach still sells about half its grapes to the Windsor Co-operative. The winery buys no grapes from other sources, making its line fully estate-bottled, and has recently scored some stunning critical successes. Its powerful Zinfandel has always drawn attention, but its Chardonnay has also emerged with a Gold medal.

Diamond

An old American wine grape producing dry, assertive white wine with flinty undertones and some spiciness. It has minimal labrusca character but tends to be hard and somewhat astringent. Dwindling acreage is about 100, almost all in New York.

DIAMOND CREEK VINEYARDS
Calistoga, San Francisco Bay North

Output: 2,500 cases

*Wine:
Cabernet Sauvignon*

Founded by Al Brounstein, Diamond Creek is known for three distinctly different Cabernet Sauvignons from grapes grown in three equally distinct vineyards, each with its own microclimate and soil. The wines are fermented separately and their labels identify Gravelly Meadow, Red Rock Terrace, and Volcanic Hill as the sources of the grapes.

The Cabernet from Red Rock Terrace is intended for earliest consumption; the Volcanic Hill Cabernet, almost black in color, requires 15-20 years of aging (in good vintages) to reach drinkability. The Gravelly Meadow falls somewhere between the two. A very select fourth wine is sometimes produced from the ¾-acre Lake Vineyard. These wines, which all carry hefty price tags, are much prized by lovers of enormous mountain-grown Napa Cabernet.

DIAMOND OAKS VINEYARD
Cloverdale, San Francisco Bay North

Output: 20,000 cases

Leading Wines:
Cabernet Sauvignon,
Chardonnay, Fumé Blanc,
Sauvignon

This old facility was known as the Rege Winery until it was purchased in 1980 by Denish Maniar. He modernized and enlarged it to 70,000 gallons of storage capacity; 200 acres of vineyards are owned in both Napa and Sonoma counties. Under a second label, Thomas Knight, a Cabernet Sauvignon, Chardonnay, and Sauvignon Blanc are produced.

Disgorging

The classic method for removing the sediment from sparkling wine made by *méthode champenoise,* prior to final corking. The process involves freezing a small plug of wine containing the sediment in the neck of the bottle and expelling this plug before final corking.

DOLAN VINEYARDS
Redwood Valley, San Francisco Bay North

Output: 4,000 cases

Leading Wines:
Cabernet Sauvignon,
Chardonnay

Paul Dolan, a descendant of Italian Swiss Colony pioneer Edmond Rossi, Sr., is a winemaker at Fetzer in addition to running his own winery. The Dolan enterprise is another familiar California pattern: the winemaker at a large winery beginning his own, much smaller operation to make a more personal style of wine. Dolan Vineyards, founded in 1980, has 15,000 gallons of storage capacity and 15 acres of vineyards (Dolan also buys some grapes).

DOMAINE LAURIER
Forestville, San Francisco Bay North

Output: 5,000 cases

Leading Wines:
Cabernet Sauvignon,
Chardonnay,
Pinot Noir,
Sauvignon Blanc

Domaine Laurier, founded by Barbara and Jacob Shilo in 1978, is oriented toward traditional winemaking techniques. A large portion of its white wines are barrel-fermented at 65°F to develop added complexity. Malolactic fermentation is induced in Chardonnay for the sake of roundness and to increase sought-after complexity. Malolactic fermentation also softens a

D

wine's acidity, and for this reason it is not often used in California. But Domaine Laurier is in an area that produces grapes with high acid, by California standards, making malolactic fermentation an attractive option. Domaine Laurier's 30 acres of vineyards are approximately 10 miles from the Pacific Ocean and cooled by the daily incursion of marine air.

Red wines are fermented in open wooden fermenters and the cap is punched down manually several times each day for color and flavor extraction. Some whole clusters of grapes are added to the red must to slow fermentation. Pinot Noir is aged in Burgundy barrels, and Cabernet Sauvignon in Bordeaux barrels (there are 30,000 gallons of storage).

Domaine Laurier's barrel-fermented 1982 Chardonnay won a Gold medal and Best of Class award at the 1984 Los Angeles County Fair competition. Its very delicate Pinot Noirs are often rather Burgundian in flavor.

DONATONI WINERY
Inglewood, South Coast

Output: 1,000 cases

Leading Wines:
Cabernet Sauvignon,
Chardonnay

Repeated successes in competition for homemade wines led Hank Donatoni to enter commercial winemaking in 1980. His 8,000-gallon winery, situated in the shadow of airliners approaching Los Angeles International Airport, uses grapes purchased in other regions of California.

DONNA MARIA VINEYARDS
Healdsburg, San Francisco Bay North

Output: 10,000 cases

Leading Wines:
Cabernet Sauvignon,
Chardonnay,
Gewurztraminer,
Sauvignon Blanc,
Semillon

Frederick Furth, Donna Maria's owner, began his venture into the wine industry in 1974 by planting vineyards in the Chalk Hill Viticultural Area (officially approved in 1983). The area—actually part of Alexander Valley—is noted for its rocky, shallow soil, which affords excellent drainage for the vines.

Storage capacity is 65,000 gallons, and annual production is expected to rise to 30,000 cases as vineyards continue to increase in production as they reach full maturity. Under a second label, the winery offers Chalk Hill Chardonnay and Sauvignon Blanc from purchased grapes.

Dosage

A syrup made of sugar, white wine and (usually) a small amount of brandy, added to sparkling wine to adjust its sweetness before corking. The amount of the dosage determines whether the wine will be brut, dry, extra dry, and so on.

Dry

In its general usage, simply the absence of sweetness; dry wines best complement foods. On the label of a sparkling wine, however, "Dry" indicates a wine with some sweetness, usually about 2.5-4.5 percent residual sugar.

DRY CREEK VINEYARD

Healdsburg, San Francisco Bay North

Output: 50,000 cases

Leading Wines:
Cabernet Sauvignon,
Chardonnay,
Chenin Blanc,
Fumé Blanc,
Gewurztraminer,
Late-Harvest Merlot,
Zinfandel

Dave Stare founded Dry Creek Vineyards in 1972 and began by planting 50 acres of vines on the site of an old prune orchard. The first stage of the winery was completed in time for the 1973 crush. Although he now has 80 acres of vines bearing, Stare still purchases up to 70 percent of his annual grape requirements and has a reputation for seeking out grapes from the finest vineyards. Storage capacity is now 180,000 gallons.

Stare is now the president of Dry Creek and the winemaker is Larry Levin. Grapes come from Dry Creek Valley and Alexander Valley, both officially approved Viticultural Areas. Dry Creek Vineyard is probably best known for its Fumé Blanc, its first wine to win national attention and acclaim. Lovers of Sauvignon Blanc are delighted with its intensely grassy character. Another wine that seems to thrive in this area—and at this winery—is Zinfandel.

GEORGES DUBOEUF AND SONS WINERY

Healdsburg, San Francisco Bay North

Output: 8,000 cases

Leading Wines:
Chardonnay, Gamay

Not only is George Duboeuf a leading *négociant* and a reliable exporter/importer of Beaujolais of the highest quality, but his company is now a producer of fine California wines.

Duboeuf's 12,000-gallon winery was founded in 1981 and specializes in production of the variety that is called Gamay in the United States (thought by some viticulturists to be Gamay Noir à Jus Blanc, the main grape of Beaujolais). Chardonnays are also produced.

All Duboeuf's grapes are purchased in Sonoma and Medocino counties: 60 percent of the Chardonnay grapes come from Knight's Valley and 40 percent from Alexander Valley (both officially recognized Viticultural Areas in Sonoma County). The Gamay grapes purchased by Duboeuf are grown in Mendocino (60 percent) as well as in Sonoma County (40 percent).

DUCKHORN VINEYARD

St. Helena, San Francisco Bay North

Output: 10,000 cases

Leading Wines:
Cabernet Sauvignon,
Merlot,
Sauvignon Blanc

There is no name in California more firmly associated with Merlot than Dan Duckhorn. In the years since Duckhorn Vineyard began in 1978, he has built an enviable reputation for rich, dark, flavorful wine. It is made from grapes grown by a variety of Napa Valley farmers with the most famous grapes provided by the Three Palms Vineyard. Duckhorn Merlot is attractive in its youth, but develops lovely complexity with time.

Duckhorn's success may be traced to his fanatic devotion to the practices of winemakers in the Bordeaux region. The winery itself is functionally and architecturally reminiscent of a Bordeaux winery, down to the low buildings called chais that are used for aging, and Duckhorn brings a number of traditional Bordelaise methods to the treatment of his wines (such as egg white fining, and using a high percentage of new French oak barrels each year). His roster of wines is also reminiscent of Bordeaux; in addition to the Merlot (which is a kind of Napa Valley Pomerol), he makes a Cabernet Sauvignon (that is blended, as in Bordeaux, with Cabernet Franc and Merlot), and a Sauvignon Blanc (that is blended as in Bordeaux, with Semillon).

DUCKHORN VINEYARDS

1982
NAPA VALLEY
MERLOT

*Produced and bottled by Duckhorn Vineyards
3027 Silverado Trail, St. Helena, California. BW CA 4857
Alcohol 13.4% by volume*

DUPLIN WINE CELLARS
Rose Hill, North Carolina

A group of grape growers formed this cooperative winery in 1976, responding to protect the North Carolina grape market from manipulation by out-of-state wine interests. Devoted to the Muscadine grape native to the South, Duplin has developed over a dozen wines from just four grape varieties, and this is the label for exploring the peculiar, striking landscape of Muscadine flavors. Even the dry wines have some sweetness, typical of Muscadines. The product line includes sparkling wines and one of the few brandies made in the East.

Output: 50,000 cases

*Leading Wines:
Carlos, Carolina Red,
Carolina Rosé,
Chablis, Champagne,
Chancellor, Magnolia,
Scuppernong, Sparkling
Scuppernong*

DURNEY VINEYARD
Carmel, Central Coast

Carmel Valley's first winery, Durney Vineyard stands in the midst of a 1,200-acre cattle ranch (Rancho del Sueno or ranch of dreams) owned by Carnation Sea Foods President William Durney and his wife Dorothy. Although four varietals are produced, Cabernet Sauvignon is the hallmark wine of Durney Vineyard. One hundred percent varietal, as are all of the Durney wines, it is dark, intense, and intended for long aging.

Output: 12,000 cases

*Leading Wines:
Cabernet Sauvignon,
Chenin Blanc,
Gamay Beaujolais,
Johannisberg Riesling*

Dutchess

Of all the native American varieties, Dutchess has the most delicate, vinous character, without grapiness but still showing some labrusca flavor. The vine was introduced by a grape breeder in the Hudson Valley, working on the site occupied by Benmarl Vineyards today. Unlike other labruscas, this white native can be successful as a dry wine. About 400 acres are planted in the eastern United States.

Early Burgundy

Not widely known or heavily planted red vinifera, this variety is generally used for blending but is made by Frank Cadenasso as a varietal at his winery in Fairfield in northern California and labelled simply as Burgundy.

EBERLE WINERY
Paso Robles, Central Coast

Output: 8,000 cases

Leading Wines:
Cabernet Blanc,
Cabernet Sauvignon,
Chardonnay,
Muscat Canelli

Gary Eberle left Estrella in 1980 to launch his own small winery near Paso Robles and Estrella River. Eberle was completed in June of 1984, but an Eberle Wineries 1979 Cabernet Sauvignon was made in leased space at Estrella River Winery.

Eberle Winery has seven stainless steel tanks with a total capacity of 34,500 gallons and 202 Nevers oak barrels of 60 gallons each for storage and aging. Although it owns no vineyards at present, there are plans to plant vines on part of the 60 acres owned by the winery. In the meantime, grapes are purchased from nearby vineyards, mainly Estrella River.

EDMEADES VINEYARDS
Philo, San Francisco Bay North

Output: 24,000 cases

Leading Wines:
Cabernet Sauvignon,
Chardonnay,
Gewurztraminer,
Opal (Pinot Noir Blanc),
Pinot Noir,
Rain Wine (White Riesling),
Whale Wine (Colombard
and Riesling blend),
Zinfandel

One of the first new wineries in Mendocino County, Edmeades was founded in 1972. The winery currently has 70,000 gallons of storage capacity and 108 acres of vineyards in the cool and remote Anderson Valley. It has attracted interest in its spicy Zinfandel, made in part from old Zinfandel vines on the property. Edmeades is also noted for its line of proprietary wines, the labels of which stress ecological themes.

E

EDNA VALLEY VINEYARD
San Luis Obispo, Central Coast

Output: 30,000 cases

Leading Wines:
Chardonnay,
Pinot Noir,
Vin Gris of Pinot Noir

Edna Valley Vineyard is jointly owned by the Chalone Winery in Monterey and by Paragon, a 600-acre vineyard in Edna Valley. Dick Graff is the consulting winemaker, and grapes come from the prestigious Paragon vineyard. Graff and his colleagues at Chalone were among the first to see the potential of the Edna Valley (just south of San Luis Obispo) for Pinot Noir and Chardonnay; the air corridor through the valley acts like a funnel to the sea, producing extremely low temperatures and the chance to properly mature the finicky Burgundian grapes.

When it was built in 1977, Edna Valley Vineyard became the second jewel in Chalone's crown (soon to be followed by a third, Carmenet). It has 75,000 gallons of storage capacity and an enviable reputation for Chardonnay.

EHLERS LANE
St. Helena, San Francisco Bay North

Output: 12,000 cases

Leading Wines:
Cabernet Sauvignon,
Chardonnay,
Sauvignon Blanc

Using the old Conn Creek stone winery building dating from 1886, John Jensen and Michael Casey installed a thoroughly modern winery in 1983. Their intention is to produce only three varietals in limited quantities. Storage capacity is 87,000 gallons and annual sales are projected at 15,000 cases.

Their first release, a 1983 Sauvignon Blanc, was made in fall of 1984. Blended with 23 percent Semillon, the wine was aged for three to four months in Nevers and Limousin oak puncheons.

ELK COVE VINEYARDS
Gaston, Oregon

Output: 12,000 cases

Leading Wines:
Cabernet Sauvignon,
Chardonnay,
Gewurztraminer,
Pinot Noir, Riesling

Pat and Joe Campbell, owners and operators of Elk Cove Vineyards, had their first commercial crush in 1977. Twenty-four acres of their 136-acre northern Willamette Valley hilltop estate are now in vine, and expansion is planned.

Elk Cove is among those Oregon wineries most oriented to European viticultural and winemaking practices. As in Europe, its vines are spaced very tightly in narrow rows. Chardonnay is fermented in French oak barrels with the Montrachet yeast strain. Pinot Noir is left to macerate in the must for five days, and the wine is then racked into Allier oak barrels. These Burgundian practices enhance the wine's structure and transform some of the immediate fruity flavors into more complex nuances.

Because of the frequently rainy fall season, most Oregon winegrowers avoid any kind of mold, including botrytis. But the Campbells often encourage botrytis in their Riesling, and in the best years release a heavily botrytised dessert wine from individually selected clusters in the traditional German style.

ELLENDALE VINEYARDS
Dallas, Oregon

The first Ellendale vineyard, planted in 1975, was destroyed by deer, and the current 13-acre vineyard dates from 1980 and 1981. Owners Robert and Ella May Hudson will continue to make fruit and berry wines, but emphasis will shift to premium grape wines as the vineyard matures. The meads, offered in three finishes from dry to sweet, are a specialty.

Output: 1,500 cases

Leading Wines: Gewurztraminer, Riesling, fruit and berry wines, mead

Emerald Riesling

This cross by Harold Olmo is one of his most successful. Created at U.C. Davis from a cross of Johannisberg Riesling and Muscadelle, it is used to make a light, fresh, fruity, and frequently sweet, table wine. Over 3,000 acres are planted in California, mostly in the Central Valley.

ENZ VINEYARDS
Hollister, Central Coast

Enz is one of three small wineries operating in Lime Kiln Valley, a Viticultural Area approved in 1983. Its vineyards include acreage of three varieties planted in 1895 — Orange Muscat, Zinfandel, and Pinot St. George. The Pinot St. George is thought to be the oldest planting of that variety in the state, and Enz is one of the very few wineries producing either Pinot St. George or Orange Muscat.

The Enz winery was established in 1973. It now includes 50,000 gallons of storage capacity and owns 800 acres of vineyards.

Output: 10,000 cases

Leading Wines: Fumé Blanc, Limestone Wine Cocktail, Pinot St. George, Orange Muscat, Zinfandel, White Zinfandel,

Estate-Bottled

No guarantee of superiority, "Estate-Bottled" on a label simply means the entire production from grapegrowing to bottling has taken place on the producer's property. In many cases this does indeed benefit the all-important connection between winery and vineyard and give the producer an extra measure of quality control.

ESTRELLA RIVER WINERY
Paso Robles, Central Coast

This large winery began in 1972 with Cliff Giacobine's purchase of 1,000 acres of fallow land east of Paso Robles. Cliff's half-brother, Gary Eberle, developed a vineyard on a portion of the property, and their first small crop of less than 300 tons was harvested in 1976.

There are now 875 acres of producing vineyards in Estrella River's holdings. All grapes are grown on the property. Among the many varieties, the

Output: 320,000 cases

Leading Wines: Barbera, Chardonnay, Chenin Blanc, Johannisberg Riesling, Muscat Canelli (both regular and late-harvest),

Sauvignon Blanc,
Syrah, Zinfandel,
White Zinfandel,
méthode champenoise
sparkling wine

Syrah is perhaps the most unusual. Estrella River is one of only three wineries in California to make wine from the true Syrah grape of the Rhône Valley in France: there are only 95 acres planted to it in California.

Extra Dry

Paradoxically, this designation is for sparkling wine that is finished semi-sweet to sweet. "Extra Dry" indicates a sweeter wine than "Dry."

THE EYRIE VINEYARDS
Dundee, Oregon

Output: 7,000 cases

Leading Wines:
Chardonnay,
Muscat Ottonel,
Pinot Gris,
Pinot Noir

One of the true pioneers of Oregon's modern wine industry, David Lett came to Oregon in 1965 and became the first modern winemaker to grow grapes in the Willamette Valley. Lett was also the first to focus his efforts on Pinot Noir, now Oregon's most renowned grape.

With a degree in viticulture from U.C. Davis and some practical California winemaking exprience, Lett had left California in search of a cool growing site for Burgundian grape varieties. Few then agreed with his assessment of the Willamette Valley as a good location.

But Lett's choice of the Willamette Valley and Pinot Noir was vindicated in a dramatic way by the now-famous tastings published in *Gault/Millau*, the French food and wine magazine. Eyrie's 1975 Pinot Noir Reserve came in a close second against top Burgundies, bringing instant recognition to the winery and to the Oregon wine industry.

Lett's Pinot Noirs are noted for their perfumed delicacy, moderate tannin, silkiness, and moderately high acidity. The wines age very well, often far better than other Pinot Noirs that may have seemed sturdier and more robust in their youth. But in recent years Lett has routinely released a reserve Pinot Noir as well as a regular bottling. The reserve Pinots are darker and more tannic, but more important they have good acid and concentrated varietal fruit.

Lett's principal white wine is Chardonnay, the Burgundian white varietal, which like the Pinot Noir is aged in French oak barrels. Unusual for an Oregon winery, Eyrie produces no Riesling. Lett prefers dry wines to go with food and believes other varietals make a better dry wine than Oregon Riesling.

More recently, Lett has begun to emphasize Pinot Gris, an authentic white wine relative of Pinot Noir, and will eventually devote half of Eyrie's production to this varietal. If the growing climate is too warm, Pinot Gris can be heavy and flat with some bitterness in the finish, but in Oregon Pinot Gris produces a crisp, full-flavored, distinctive wine.

Lett also makes very limited quantities of dry Muscat Ottonel, a refined but shy-bearing and unusual member of the Muscat family.

LOUIS FACELLI WINERY
Wilder, Idaho

In 1980 Louis Facelli planted 5½ acres of vines in the Snake River Valley, intending to operate a small premium winery on a parttime basis. In 1981, his first commercial vintage, Facelli made a mere 700 cases, but of these the Riesling was highly successful in regional judgings. In 1982 Facelli joined with Fred and Norm Batt in managing the finances and operation of the winery. The Batts had already planted 37 acres of grapes east of Wilder the year before, and 120 more acres were planted in 1983 in the Arena Valley area west of Wilder, a more gravelly growing site than most in the greater Snake River Valley area.

Like many new Northwest wineries, Facelli relies heavily on Washington grapes while waiting for its own vineyards to mature fully. Washington grapes will gradually be phased out and Facelli will make its targeted 50,000-case production entirely from grapes grown in the winery's own vineyards. Facelli continues to make fruit and berry wines in very small quantities, but the major focus is toward premium vinifera wines from Idaho grapes.

Facelli is a dedicated wine craftsman, and his Riesling is consistently successful: delicate, flavorful, and finished with residual sweetness. The Facelli Chardonnay is barrel-fermented but the oak flavors are not emphasized in aging. Although Facelli is the first Idaho winery to make a major commitment to red wine from Pinot Noir grapes, 37 acres are planted to the Pommard and Wadenswil clones of Pinot Noir.

Output: 10,000 cases

Leading Wines:
Chardonnay,
Gewurztraminer,
Pinot Noir, Riesling, fruit
and berry wines

1983
IDAHO
Johannisberg Riesling
A semi-dry wine with
fine varietal flavors.

PRODUCED AND BOTTLED BY LOUIS FACELLI WINERY
WILDER, IDAHO BWID-9
ALCOHOL 10.8% BY VOLUME

FAMILI PUCCI VINEYARDS
Sandpoint, Idaho

With a family tradition of home winemaking, Skip Pucci founded a small commercial winery in 1982, specializing in red, white, and rosé Zinfandel from California grapes and other varietals from Washington grapes. All are unblended, fermented and aged in oak, and bottled dry.

Output: 2,000 cases

Leading Wines:
Cabernet Sauvignon,
Chardonnay, Riesling,
Zinfandel

F

FAR NIENTE WINERY
Oakville, San Francisco Bay North

Output: 11,500 cases

Leading Wines:
Cabernet Sauvignon,
Chardonnay

Far Niente has been revived from a long-dormant state by Gil Nickel, who in 1979 purchased the old stone chateau nestled against the western foothills of the Napa Valley. Built in 1885, the three-story building had stood empty and neglected for more than 50 years.

A modern, 125,000-gallon winery was completed on the ground floor in time for the 1982 vintage (the 1982 Cabernet Sauvignon will be released in 1985). Far Niente's full-blown Napa Valley style Chardonnay received almost instant recognition and acceptance by an already Chardonnay-deluged public in the early 1980s.

FELTON-EMPIRE VINEYARDS
Felton, Central Coast

Output: 20,000 cases

Leading Wines:
Chardonnay,
Gewurztraminer,
Pinot Noir, Petite Sirah,
White Riesling

When Felton-Empire Vineyards was founded in 1976 on the site of the former Hallcrest winery, the founders' goal was to develop a reputation as a producer of a single varietal, Johannisberg Riesling. Their line has subsequently been extended to encompass a total of five varietals.

Two lines of wine are produced, the Maritime Series and the Tonneaux Series. The former is made from grapes grown in the cool regions of the Central Coast. The Tonneaux Series includes only barrel-fermented Chardonnays and Pinot Noirs, designated as either Tonneaux Français or Tonneaux Américain according to the source of the barrels.

Felton-Empire owns 8 acres of Region I vineyards that border a majestic, virgin redwood forest. Grapes are also purchased from various areas in California. One unusual feature of this winery is that varietal grape juice is also produced and sold under the Empire Vineyards label.

The winery now has 72,000 gallons of storage capacity and supplements its annual output with 20,000 cases of grape juice that are sold to other wineries. The winery's original success with Riesling has, in recent years, been matched by its success with Gewurztraminer.

FENESTRA WINERY
Livermore, San Francisco Bay South

Output: 2,700 cases

Leading Wines:
Cabernet Sauvignon,
Chardonnay,
Sauvignon Blanc,
White Riesling,
Zinfandel

Chemistry professor Lanny Replogle began making wine commercially in 1976, but did not establish his winery in its present Livermore Valley location until 1980. Fenestra is built on the site of a winery that dates from 1880, and unlike many other Livermore wineries it is set in pastureland, not vineyards. All grapes are purchased from Viticultural Areas along the California coast in Monterey and San Luis Obispo counties, and the vineyards are given credit on Fenestra's labels when appropriate.

All of Fenestra's white wines are aged in French (mostly Limousin) oak, and the Chardonnay is barrel-fermented in French oak. When conditions are suitable, Fenestra makes a late-harvest Chenin Blanc. Each of the reds receives a period of time in American oak.

F

FENN VALLEY VINEYARDS
Fennville, Michigan

The Welsch family bought their 230-acre farm after searching Michigan and other states for a location suited to cool-climate wine. As a site for their vineyards they chose several broad, sandy hilltops close enough to benefit from Lake Michigan. In the lee of the lake, the growing seasons are cooled and extended, and winters are tempered; heavy snows act to insulate the vines.

The slow, extended ripening of the grapes gives the intense fruitiness that is most important in Fenn Valley's winemaking style. It is best-known for late-harvest Vignoles, often botrytised, ranging in some years to Auslese and Beerenauslese levels of concentration and sweetness. Riesling is lighter, flowery, and Germanic. Acid levels tend to run high in the whites, balanced with some residual sweetness, and alcohol tends to be low. Vidal is also made in a German style — light, fruity, off-dry — a quaffing wine. Seyval is dry, with firmer structure, and given more than the usual time in steel cooperage to fill out.

Output: 29,000 cases

Leading Wines:
Chancellor,
Johannisberg Riesling,
Regal Red, Regal White,
Seyval Blanc, Vidal Blanc,
Vignoles

Fermentation

In winemaking, the process in which yeast cells convert the sugar in grape juice into ethanol (alcohol), carbon dioxide, and small amounts of other compounds contributing to the smell, flavor, and color of wine. Red wines are typically fermented on the skins (with grape skins and juice mixed together), adding color and more intense flavors, while white wines are made by fermenting the separated juice.

Winemakers are learning how to manipulate the fermentation process more precisely — mainly through yeast strain selection and temperature control — to affect the compounds produced. Slow, cool fermentations tend to preserve delicate flavors and aromas of fruit; warm fermentations yield flavors less associated with fruit. Fermentation was one of the first areas of study of the modern sciences of microbiology and biochemistry, and yet it is still not fully understood.

FETZER VINEYARDS
Redwood Valley, San Francisco Bay North

A family-run winery that has grown to prominence at a phenomenal pace, Fetzer was one of Mendocino County's early successes. In 1958 Barney and Kathleen Fetzer bought a ranch in Redwood Valley that included a small 80-year-old vineyard. The Fetzers replanted and restored the vines to production, and grapes were sold to commercial wineries and home winemakers. Fetzer's winery was not started until 1968, but today it owns 800 acres of Mendocino vineyards and controls an additional 2,000 acres through contracts with several growers in Mendocino, Lake, Sonoma, and Monterey counties.

Output: 450,000 cases

Leading Wines:
Blanc de Blancs,
Cabernet Sauvignon,
Chardonnay, Chenin
Blanc, French Colombard,
Gamay Beaujolais,
Gewurztraminer,

Johannisberg Riesling,
Muscat Canelli, Petite
Sirah, Pinot Blanc,
Pinot Noir, Sauvignon
Blanc, Zinfandel; White,
Red, and Rosé table wines

fetzer

1984
mendocino county
sundial chardonnay

produced and bottled by fetzer vineyards
redwood valley, california, u.s.a. alcohol 12.4% by volume

Output: 6,000 cases

Wine: Tinto Port

Two completely separate wineries—one for white wines and the other for reds—have been built on the home vineyard in Redwood Valley, and each is stocked with the latest winemaking equipment. The 2.5 million gallons of storage capacity is divided between stainless steel (which accounts for 80 percent of the total) and small oak barrels. Fetzer uses a lot of oak-aging in its wines. All red wines, including a generic called Mendocino Premium Red, receive a minimum of 8 months of aging in American oak; dry white wines spend up to 6 months in French oak.

Fetzer's meteoric growth began with their first releases of excellent Cabernet Sauvignon and Zinfandel and its reputation for reds has continued. But the secret of its success has been its ability to produce both white and red wines that are good-value and high quality.

Fetzer also produces a White Cabernet and a White Zinfandel under another label, Bel Arbres.

FICKLIN VINEYARDS
Madera, Central Valley

The Ficklins were the first California winery to plant Portuguese grape varieties used in the production of Porto wines in the Douro River Valley in 1944. Today they have approximately 200 acres of Tinta Madeira, Tinta Cao, Souzao, and Ouriga planted near the Central Valley town of Madera.

When the late Walter Ficklin, Sr., founded his winery in 1946, to produce red dessert wines from these grapes, it was not only the first in California to produce wines entirely from Portuguese grape varieties but also the first to specialize in this style. Ficklin's first Port was made in 1948.

As in Portugal, most Ficklin ports are blends of wines from different vintages. Some, again following Portuguese practice, are bottled as vintage ports. This means that wine from only one vintage is used—it must be an exceptional vintage—and that the wine is held for a shorter time in wood.

Field-Crushing

A California innovation during the early 1970s to reduce the vulnerability of harvested grapes to spoilage. Mobile crusher-stemmer machines are taken from the winery into the vineyard so that machine-harvested grapes can be immediately destemmed, crushed, and stored in sealed tanks until they reach the winery for fermentation or pressing, particularly in large operations, providing wineries with cleaner, fresher raw materials.

FIELD STONE WINERY
Healdsburg, San Francisco Bay North

This is the first underground winery to be built in California in the 20th century. Excavations were made in 1966 into a wooded knoll in the midst

Output: 14,000 cases

Leading Wines:
Cabernet Sauvignon,

F

of founder Wallace Johnson's 850-acre estate at the southern end of the Alexander Valley, and 30,000 gallons of wine storage capacity were erected there. The only visible evidence of the winery from the outside is the stone wall across the front.

Field Stone owns 140 acres of vineyards, and the first wines were released in 1977. It is known for its consistent ability to produce reasonably big wines—mostly red. An outstanding example of Field Stone's style is the enormous Petite Sirah, made from 80-year-old vines on the property. These vines produce only 1½ tons of grapes per acre at the present time, accounting for the intensity of the wine. Field Stone plans to produce Petite Sirah from these vines for 20 years more—until the yield slips considerably under 1 ton per acre (a startlingly low yield).

Spring Cabernet (a rosé of Cabernet Sauvignon), Chenin Blanc, Gewurztraminer, Johannisberg Riesling, Petite Sirah, Rosé of Petite Sirah

J. FILIPPI VINTAGE COMPANY
Mira Loma, South Coast

When Giovanni Filippi and his son Joe migrated from northern Italy to the Cucamonga Valley in 1922, the region was already famous as a grape-growing area. At their peak, vineyards in Cucamonga exceeded 20,000 acres, and there were in excess of 30 wineries in the area. But vineyard acreage and wineries have been declining since the 1960s: acreage is now barely a third of its peak level, while only two producing wineries still operate in Cucamonga—Filippi and Galleano.

Storage capacity at Filippi amounts to more than 1 million gallons. Nearly 40 wines are bottled under four labels and are nearly all sold through the chain of Filippi outlets. Chateau Filippi and Joseph Filippi are considered by the winery to be its best wines, and are sold at the winery and through five off-premise tasting rooms located throughout southern California, from San Diego to the San Fernando Valley. Pride of Cucamonga and Pride of California identify generics that are also sold through wholesale outlets.

Output: 125,000 cases

Leading Wines: Chateau Filippi: Chianti Rosé, Chianti Supreme, Emerald Riesling, French Colombard, Gamay Beaujolais, Gewurztraminer, Green Hungarian, Grenache Rosé, Zinfandel, Sparkling wines, various fruit wines; Joseph Filippi: Johannisberg Riesling, Pinot St. George, St. Emilion

Filtration

Wine is pumped through a filter up to three times between fermentation and bottling to remove suspended material that doesn't settle out and can leave the wine unstable. The procedure may also strip out some small measure of the wine's desirable characteristics. This double-edged sword has become sharper with the development of filter media so fine that they can trap individual yeast cells. Such a "sterile filtration" can protect a sweet wine from refermentation in the bottle without the use of a preservative chemical, but more desirable elements may also be removed. Occasional labels proclaim a wine to be unfiltered, a winemaker's gamble with instability in exchange for minimal interference with flavor and aroma.

F

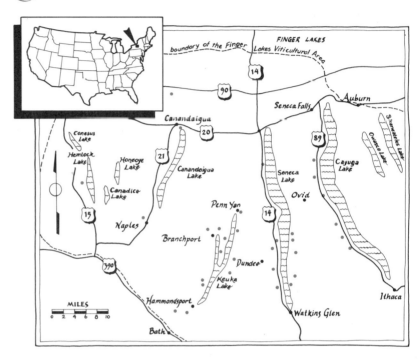

FINGER LAKES

The Finger Lakes district of New York accounts for close to half of all United States wine production outside California. About 15,000 acres of vineyards hug the shores of four of a dozen long, narrow lakes carved by glaciers 10,000 years ago. As a region it represents a textbook example of the importance of viticultural microclimate and the affinity of grapevines for bodies of water. Vineyards are planted only in narrow bands where land slopes evenly down to the lakes. Continuous air circulation by convection in these basins moderates temperatures in summer and winter and keeps vine foliage dry.

The dynamics of microclimate and well-drained shale soils made the Finger Lakes a natural haven for winegrowing in years following the Civil War. A reputation for sparkling wines from Catawba, Delaware, and Isabella grapes was well-established by the turn of the century. At this time there were more than 40 wineries clustered around the village of Hammondsport, at the head of Keuka Lake.

In the second flowering of Finger Lakes wineries, since the 1960s, the focus of winegrowing has shifted from Keuka and Canandaigua lakes east to the biggest lakes: Seneca and Cayuga. Lower in altitude and so deep that they almost never freeze, these bodies of water have supported the shift in Finger Lakes wine from the old American grapes to more delicate French-American hybrid and vinifera varieties. The geography can be tasted by comparing a glass of crisp, appley, Keuka Lake Chardonnay with a big, melony Chardonnay from Seneca Lake's east shore. Chardonnay is a variety just taking its place among those making the best Finger Lakes wines: Riesling, Seyval Blanc, Ravat, Cayuga — all whites. This is a

F

cold-climate district where white grapes ripen best, with intense fruitiness, firm acid, and clean flavors. With some exceptions they make light wines to be drunk young, within two or three years. Even the red wines, while they benefit from that much time, are not keepers. Wood-aged Chancellor and youthful Maréchal Foch have been most successful.

Sparkling wines are enjoying a renaissance in the Finger Lakes. The best are now made from Chardonnay, Seyval, Aurora, and Riesling, instead of Catawba. Late-harvest wines from Riesling, Ravat, and Vidal are produced in dry falls and have the acid backbone to carry honeyed, concentrated fruit. (The botrytis mold is very prevalent.)

Native labrusca wines still account for most Finger Lakes production. Perfumed Delaware and vividly flavored Niagara are the best. Labruscas remain the base of sherries that spend considerable time mellowing in barrel, losing native grape flavor in the benign neglect of a weak market.

FINGER LAKES WINE CELLARS
Branchport, Finger Lakes

Output: 4,500 cases

Leading Wines: Cayuga, Classic Red, Delaware, Johannisberg Riesling, Marechal Foch, Seyval

At the tip of Keuka Lake's west branch, this small farm winery has quickly established a reputation for exceptional Delaware and Cayuga white. A relatively cool site captures the lush fruit character of these varieties and retains grape acids to balance their semisweet finish. Since the first vintage in 1981, Finger Lakes Cellars wines have dried out somewhat and developed more refined style as the product line added more French-American hybrid varieties and viniferas (from purchased grapes).

Fining

Like filtration, fining is a procedure for clarifying and stabilizing the wine. While filtration removes suspended particles, fining takes out compounds dispersed or dissolved in the wine through a "fining agent" that draws them out of solution. Gelatin and a clay-like mineral called betonite are commonly used fining agents in American wine cellars, but more complex, synthetic materials are being introduced. Unfined wines are unusual attempts to minimize the processing of wine and any attendant stripping of character.

THE FIRESTONE VINEYARDS
Los Olivos, Central Coast

Output: 75,000 cases

Leading Wines: Cabernet Sauvignon, Rosé of Cabernet Savignon, Chardonnay, Gewurztraminer, Johannisberg Riesling, Merlot, Pinot Noir

Firestone is the largest winery in the still-developing Santa Ynez Valley in northern Santa Barbara County. It was founded in 1973 by Brooks Firestone, heir to the Firestone Tire Company of Akron, Ohio.

The first 250 acres of vineyards were planted in 1973, and the winery was built in stages. Now completed, it houses 300,000 gallons of storage capacity and is a joint venture of the Firestone family and the Suntory Company of Japan.

1984

THE
FIRESTONE
VINEYARD

Santa Ynez Valley
Rosé of Cabernet Sauvignon

100% Cabernet Sauvignon
Grown, Produced, and Bottled by The Firestone Vineyard
Los Olivos, California, U.S.A. - Bonded Winery No. 4720
Alcohol 11.5% By Volume

Output: 7,000 cases

Leading Wines:
Cabernet Sauvignon,
Chardonnay

The Santa Ynez Valley is an elevated region that is cooled by its proximity to the ocean, benefiting cooler-ripening varieties. Firestone's well-balanced Riesling and its Chardonnay have shown best among its generally superior whites. Among the reds, the Pinot Noir has traditionally been most interesting for its strong varietal definition.

Winemaker Alison Green replaced Tony Austin, who built a reputation for intensely varietal wines created by extreme stressing of the vines. Austin has gone on to found his own winery and Green promises more readily accessible wines from Firestone.

FISHER VINEYARDS
Santa Rosa, San Francisco Bay North

Julie and Fred Fisher cleared 70 acres of hillside on the Sonoma side of the Mayacamas Mountains — which separate the Napa and Sonoma valleys — and planted vineyards in 1973.

A winery was completed in 1979 and there are now 75 acres of vineyards. Production is limited but Fisher has developed a reputation particularly for its stylish, elegant Chardonnay.

FITZPATRICK WINERY
Somerset, Sierra Foothills

Output: 4,000 cases

Leading Wines:
Cabernet Sauvignon,
Chardonnay,
Chenin Blanc, Sauvignon
Blanc, Zinfandel

Founded in 1980, Fitzpatrick Winery owns 80 acres of vines in El Dorado County but buys grapes from other vineyards and credits them on the label. Winery storage capacity is 17,000 gallons. It offers estate-bottled Cabernet Sauvignons and a Chardonnay, produced from its own El Dorado grapes — a relatively new practice that is becoming a trend in an area that had always been Zinfandel country. More conventionally, Fitzpatrick also produces vineyard-designated Zinfandels (there were three from the 1981 vintage) from grapes grown in nearby Shenandoah Valley.

The Fitzpatricks are known for their innovative practices in the winery as well as in the marketplace, and their stylishly balanced wines have won many medals in judgings since their debut.

Flora

A U.C. Davis cross of Gewurztraminer with Sauvignon Blanc. The best-known use of Flora is by Schramsberg in its Cremant, a lightly sweet, sparkling dessert wine. There are over 350 acres planted in California.

FLORA SPRINGS
St. Helena, San Francisco Bay North

Output: 10,000 cases

Leading Wines:
Cabernet Sauvignon,

Flora and Jerry Kome purchased the old Louis M. Martini winery and vineyards in 1977. Since then the winery has been renovated, enlarged, and stocked with modern winemaking equipment, including small oak barrels for fermentation and aging.

The Chardonnay is produced in two styles. One is completely barrel-fermented in limited quantities (only 800 cases in the 1982 vintage) and the second is partially barrel-fermented. Both styles have won a following, as has their Bordeaux-style blend of Cabernet Sauvignon, Merlot, and Cabernet Franc.

Chardonnay, Sauvignon Blanc

THOMAS FOGARTY WINERY AND VINEYARDS
Portola Valley, San Francisco Bay South

Situated in the Santa Cruz Mountains Viticultural Area, Fogarty began operations in 1981. Thirteen acres of Chardonnay and Pinot Noir grapes had been planted in 1984 in its own vineyards, and storage capacity is 30,000 gallons. The winery has a reputation for seeking out grapes from leading vineyards such as Winery Lake and Ventana.

Output: 4,500 cases

Leading Wines: Cabernet Sauvignon, Chardonnay, Gewurztraminer, Pinot Noir

FOLIE à DEUX WINERY
St. Helena, San Francisco Bay North

This small 10,000-gallon winery is appropriately named. Freely translated from the French, Folie à Deux means "shared fantasy," and it is in this spirit that it was founded in 1981.

The 13 acres of vineyards are young, so grapes were purchased for the first vintages, but as the vines mature, the wines will be estate-bottled. In some vintages Chardonnay is partially barrel-fermented and aged in oak; the 1983 vintage was aged solely in Limousin barrels. Chenin Blanc receives no wood development, but Cabernet Sauvignon spends up to 18 months in oak.

Output: 2,500 cases

Leading Wines: Cabernet Sauvignon, Chardonnay, Dry Chenin Blanc

Folle Blanche

With under 300 acres of this white vinifera planted in California, its best-known use is by Louis Martini, the only winery in the state to make a varietal from this grape. As produced by Martini, it is light, dry, and relatively high in acidity, but without pronounced aroma or flavor. The home of Folle Blanche is the Charantes region of France, where it was used to make cognac until it was supplanted by Colombard.

E.B. FOOTE WINERY
Seattle, Washington

A senior engineer at Boeing, Gene Foote began his second occupation as winemaker in 1978 with his first commercial crush of 500 cases. Instead of making Chenin Blanc, Riesling, and Gewurztraminer in the more typical fresh, fruity, semidry style, he produces wines that are completely dry, in

Output: 4,000 cases

Leading Wines: Cabernet Sauvignon, Chardonnay, Chenin Blanc,

F

Gewurztraminer,
Pinot Noir, Riesling

a less fruity but more substantive style, intended to complement food. None of Foote's wines are fined or filtered, in the interest of preserving flavor elements that might be stripped away.

LOUIS J. FOPPIANO WINERY
Healdsburg, San Francisco Bay North

Output: 100,000 cases

Leading Wines:
Cabernet Sauvignon,
Chardonnay,
Chenin Blanc,
Petite Sirah,
Sauvignon Blanc,
Zinfandel

This winery was founded in 1896 and is now in the hands of the fourth generation of Foppianos to make wine in the Russian River Valley in Sonoma County. Recent modernization and replanting have resulted in a remarkable improvement in Foppiano wines. Generics and varietals labeled Riverside Farm have been especially good value from this one million gallon-winery.

FORGERON VINEYARD
Eugene, Oregon

Output: 5,500 cases

Leading Wines:
Cabernet Sauvignon,
Chardonnay,
Chenin Blanc,
Pinot Noir, Riesling

Lee and Linda Smith began planting their 20-acre vineyard in 1972 in a warm and sunny microclimate. Riesling is Forgeron's leading white wine, occasionally made in a botrytised dessert style. Forgeron is also one of the few Willamette Valley wineries producing Cabernet Sauvignon. In the vineyard's warmer microclimate, the grapes ripen reliably in most years, and in the best years produce wines of depth and complexity.

Fortified

Sherry and port are the primary examples of wine fortified with a small amount of brandy (distilled wine), elevating the level of alcohol in the wine to 18-21 percent. This has several effects. The alcohol acts as a natural preservative and stabilizer, so that fortified wines can be left open or stored half-empty without significantly affecting the wine. The addition of brandy also arrests biological activity in the wine, stops fermentation, and naturally preserves sweet sherries, ports, muscatels, etc. The type of brandy used and its interaction with the properties of the base wine create particular characteristics of taste and smell.

FORTINO WINERY
Gilroy, San Francisco Bay South

Output: 15,000 cases

Leading Wines:
Barbera,
Cabernet Sauvignon,
Charbono, Johannisberg
Riesling, Petite Syrah,
Sauvignon Vert,
Zinfandel,
several generics

The Italian-born Fortinos began making wine in Gilroy in 1970, having taken over the operation of an old winery. Fermentation of their red wines in open-top redwood fermenters permits the Fortinos to claim that their wines are made in the traditional manner. This may be the secret of their great success with consumers and wine judges alike.

Perhaps the Fortinos' most remarkable wine is Charbono, which regularly brings home awards. (There are only 95 acres of Charbono grapes planted in California.)

F

FOUR CHIMNEYS FARM WINERY
Himrod, Finger Lakes

In the temperate microclimate of Seneca Lake, this small Finger Lakes farm has undertaken to make the first organic wines in the East, and perhaps in America. The 15-acre estate vineyard relies on herbal sprays, seaweed, mulch, and insect predators to produce grapes without chemicals. But reduced yields are part of the bargain, along with a restricted selection of only hardy labrusca varieties.

The wine cellar also limits chemical applications. Most of these wines are finished semidry to sweet, with simple fruitiness. Four Chimneys also purchases (nonorganic) grapes from other Finger Lakes vineyards for an intriguing selection of vinifera and French-American hybrid varietals. All wines are vintage-dated, limited bottlings.

Output: 2,500 cases

Leading Wines:
Cabernet Sauvignon,
Catawba, Chardonnay,
Eye of the Dove,
Johannisberg Riesling,
Kingdom Red and White,
Late-Harvest Delaware,
Pinot Noir

Foxy

The distinctive taste of labrusca wine has been described as foxy for centuries. The term first appeared in 17th-century accounts of Europeans encountering wild American grapes and their wines. Their musky scent recalled the smell of the fox. Over the centuries it has been generalized to refer to the pungent, grapey character of labrusca wines, although muskiness is only one component of that character that comes through in some varieties and not in others. In fact, the musky smell associated with foxes is more characteristic of southern Muscadine wines than northern labruscas. It is not surprising, then, that the term "foxy" is tossed around wine circles without a clear sense of its meaning.

FRANCISCAN VINEYARDS
St. Helena, San Francisco Bay North

Franciscan Vineyards has been through several changes of ownership in the years after its founding in 1971. Since 1979 it has been owned by the West German Peter Eckes Company.

Under winemaker Tom Ferrell, Franciscan produced several notable Chardonnays (the 1982 exhibited a genuine Meursault character) and Cabernet Sauvignons, and was beginning to establish a style for these two leading Franciscan varietals when he left in 1984.

Franciscan owns 250 acres of vineyards in the Napa Valley and an additional 225 acres in Sonoma's Alexander Valley. Chardonnay and Cabernet are produced with both appellations, the Cabernet also being offered in a Reserve.

Output: 150,000 cases

Leading Wines:
Cabernet Sauvignon,
Charbono, Chardonnay,
Fumé Blanc,
Johannisberg Riesling,
Merlot, Zinfandel,
sparkling wine

F

FREEMARK ABBEY WINERY
St. Helena, San Francisco Bay North

Output: 26,000 cases

Leading Wines:
Cabernet Bosche,
Cabernet Sauvignon,
Chardonnay, Edelwein,
Johannisberg Riesling,
Petite Sirah

1982
NAPA VALLEY
CHARDONNAY

PRODUCED AND BOTTLED BY
FREEMARK ABBEY WINERY, ST. HELENA, CALIFORNIA, U.S.A.
Alcohol 12.5% by volume

In 1977, on the site of the old winery built around 1885, the Freemark Abbey name was reactivated in this winery. Storage capacity is now 200,000 gallons, and Freemark Abbey's 130 acres of vineyards are supplemented by the vineyards owned by each of the partners. (Still, most of the output of the 720 acres owned jointly by several of the partners goes to Rutherford Hill Winery.)

Freemark Abbey's early fame is partly due to former winemaker Jerry Luper, now at Chateau Bouchaine. In 1973 he made a wine called Edelwein from botrytised Johannisberg Riesling grapes. It was a big, liqueur-like wine, full of varietal flavors and the honeyed nuances of the botrytis mold, which won widespread critical acclaim. Subsequent versions of Edelwein have been made when growing conditions encouraged the development of botrytis, but they have lacked the intensity and complexity of the 1973 vintage.

But another wine that achieved early success—and has maintained its stature—is Freemark Abbey's Chardonnay. This wine lighted the path for a whole generation of California winemakers toward oakier, more varietally intense Chardonnay. Many of the latter-day Chardonnay monsters produced by other wineries are clumsy imitations of a style originally produced with taste and restraint at Freemark Abbey.

Free-run

The juice (or wine from the juice) that flows from crushed grapes before pressing. Containing a minimum of components from the grape skins and pulp, it yields lighter wine with more delicate fruit flavors than when the grapes are pressed. Sometimes free-run and press-run batches of a wine are made separately; sometimes they are blended, giving the winemaker another way to manipulate style.

French-American Hybrid

When the phylloxera epidemic swept across Europe in the late 19th century, one strategy for saving the vineyards was hybridization of American and European vinifera grapevines to create new varieties with New World pest resistance and Old World wine quality. Breeders in France—François Baco, Eugene Kuhlmann, Pierre Landot, J.F. Ravat, J.L. Vidal, Albert Seibel, Bertille Seyval, and others—worked for decades to create and market new varieties with the best combinations of vineyard and wine qualities. Nearly a million acres of these French-American hybrids were eventually planted in France, although the best wine vineyards maintained their classic, vinifera varieties by grafting them onto hardy American rootstocks.

American winegrowers began to realize the potential of the hybrids in this country in the 1930s. At a time when European varieties in the East were still succumbing to American diseases and winters, the French-American hybrids were found to be hardy survivors and to produce wines similar to European wines. Philip Wagner at Maryland's Boordy Vineyards and Charles Fournier at New York's Gold Seal Vineyards were among the first to grow the new varieties commercially. They were not extensively planted until the 1960s, when a new generation of eastern American wines began to emerge.

French Colombard

The most heavily planted white wine grapes in California. Favored in the Central Valley for its high acidity despite the heat of that growing region, its chief use is as a significant component of jug white wines and of inexpensive sparkling wines. A few producers do make a light, fruity varietal from French Colombard, however. Of over 73,000 acres planted in California, 54,000 are in the Central Valley.

FRENCH CREEK CELLARS
Seattle, Washington

French Creek Cellars was founded by two University of Washington professors and their families. The principal winemaker is Hans Doerr, a psychology professor and long-time home winemaker. The winery is in the Seattle suburbs and purchases grapes from Columbia Valley growers. The first crush was in 1983. French Creek's first releases included a well-regarded dry Riesling. In the coming years Cabernet Sauvignon will receive special emphasis.

Output: 1,500 cases

Leading Wines:
Cabernet Sauvignon,
Chardonnay,
Gewurztraminer,
Muscat of Alexandria,
Riesling

FREY VINEYARDS
Redwood Valley, San Francisco Bay North

This 30-acre winery was founded in 1980 with the aim of using only grapes that met the standards of natural farming set by California Certified Organic Farmers. Both vineyards and wines are free from chemical additives. Even the addition of sulfur dioxide to prevent oxidation and browning, one of the most common of winery practices, is said by Frey to be unnecessary, because of its natural farming and because its grapes are harvested at high acid levels which act as a preservative. Storage capacity is now 15,000 gallons.

Output: 6,000 cases

Leading Wines:
Cabernet Sauvignon,
Chardonnay,
French Colombard,
Gewurztraminer,
Pinot Noir, Grey Riesling,
White Riesling,
Sauvignon Blanc,
Zinfandel

F

FRICK WINERY
Santa Cruz, San Francisco Bay South

Output: 3,500 cases

*Leading Wines:
Chardonnay, Petite Sirah,
Pinot Noir, Zinfandel*

Hidden on a back street in Santa Cruz, Frick produces wines essentially made by hand from start to finish in a small, 10,000-gallon winery founded in 1976. Frick owns no vineyards and buys grapes from growers in Monterey, Santa Clara, and San Luis Obispo counties. The idiosyncratic, whimsical labels that Frick affixes to its wines point up the off-beat nature of this excellent winery, which specializes in Pinot Noir.

FROG'S LEAP WINERY
St. Helena, San Francisco Bay North

Output: 7,000 cases

*Leading Wines:
Cabernet Sauvignon,
Chardonnay,
Sauvignon Blanc*

This winery takes its name from the frog farm that once occupied the site that has been its home since 1981. Planting of 5 acres of Sauvignon Blanc preceded the conversion of the old livery stable on the property to a 20,000-gallon winery. The first wine produced was a very successful Loire-style Sauvignon Blanc, and Chardonnay and Cabernet Sauvignon have been added to the list of releases.

E & J GALLO WINERY
Modesto, Central Valley

The story of the Gallo brothers, Ernest and Julio, is perhaps the great American success story in wine. Today, they own the largest winery in the United States, and one of the largest in the world. Yet it is little more than fifty years since they began producing wine in a rented railroad shed, with a $2,000 grape crusher, a few redwood tanks bought on credit and some pre-Prohibition how-to-make-wine pamphlets which they found in Modesto Public Library. By anticipating the end of Prohibition the Gallos were ready at repeal with wines which they could sell in bulk to eastern bottlers, a practice they followed for the next several years. (The Gallo label did not appear on a bottle of wine until the 1940s.)

It is as difficult to convey the size of Gallo today as it is to measure its influence. Perhaps more than anyone else it has taught Americans to drink wine with everyday meals, simply by producing and selling reliable wine at attractively low prices. Its Hearty Burgundy and Chablis Blanc, introduced 20 years ago, epitomize this policy and are considered by both consumers and knowledgeable critics to be good value and soundly made wines.

At the same time, the Gallos were also the first to apply modern marketing techniques to the sale of wine. Their efforts were instrumental in convincing retailers to display wines prominently in the front of their stores, while they convinced wholesale distributors of the wisdom of training specialists to sell wine.

Gallo was among the first California wineries to establish a research department. The facility at Modesto has the appearance of a university campus and employs a team of enologists and researchers which is the largest in the world.

Gallo was also among the first to replace wooden fermentation and storage tanks with the now generally adopted stainless steel fermentation and storage tanks. This was one of the most important innovations in modern winemaking, paving the way for the immensely popular current style of fresh, clean, fruity wine, and winemakers around the world have followed Gallo's lead in this area.

Output: 40-50 million cases

Leading Wines: Varietals: The Wine Cellars of Ernest and Julio Gallo: Cabernet Sauvignon, Chardonnay, Chenin Blanc, French Colombard, Gewurztraminer, Johannisberg Riesling, Sauvignon Blanc, Zinfandel; Generics: Hearty Burgundy, Reserve Burgundy, Chablis Blanc, Reserve Chablis; Sparkling wines; Fruit and fruit flavored wines; Dessert and aperitif wines

G

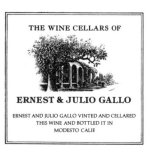

Still, it is the sheer size of the Gallo operation that is often the most lasting impression. The warehouse at the Modesto headquarters, from which Gallo wines are shipped to all 50 states and to foreign countries as well, covers 25 acres, is served by five separate railroad spurs and at any time contains about 2.5 million gallons of wine awaiting shipment. Gallo's bottling operation is so large that they have built their own glass factory to assure a supply of bottles (uniquely amber-green in color) that is uninterrupted by strikes or delays in shipping.

Altogether, the Gallos operate four wineries at Modesto, Fresno, Livingston, and Healdsburg. No grapes are crushed or vinified at Modesto, but it is here that blending, oak-aging, bottling, binning, and shipment, as well as research take place. Through these wineries pass the grapes from thousands of acres of California vineyards: both Gallo's own and those independents under long-term contracts. Total storage capacity of all of these wineries is more than 300 million gallons according to the company (the Livingston facility alone has more than 100 million gallons of capacity).

Altogether, Gallo requires approximately 700,000 tons of grapes from an annual California harvest of approximately 2 million tons. Approximately 30 percent of Sonoma County's harvest, 20 percent of Napa County's harvest, and over 30 percent of the Monterey/Central Coast harvest go to Gallo wines. Annual sales of Gallo wines can only be estimated as they are never revealed to the public.

Gallo may not only have taught many Americans to drink wine with their meals, but it has also schooled some of today's wine industry leaders in the making and merchandising of wine. Among these are: Leigh Knowles, Chairman of Beaulieu; Dick Maher, head of Seagram's Wine Company; Terence Clancy, President of Callaway Vineyards and Winery; and Art Ciocca, President of Wine Group (which includes Franzia). Winemakers who at one time were at Gallo include Dick Peterson, Monterey Vineyard; Bill Bonetti, Sonoma-Cutrer; Doug Davis at Sebastiani; Walter Schug, Storybook Mountain Vineyards; Jerry Luper, Chateau Bouchaine; and Brad Webb at Freemark Abbey.

Gallo wines go to market under a long list of brand names. In addition to the Gallo label and that of the Wine Cellars of Ernest and Julio Gallo; there are Boone's Farm for fruit wines; André for sparkling wines; Carlo Rossi for their budget priced table wines; Livingston Cellars for ports and sherries; Polo Brindisi for Gallo's lightly effervescent, low-alcohol answer to Italy's lambruscos; Ballatore for spumante, Spanada (a sangria), and Tyrolia. There is also a Gallo brandy, under the E & J label.

In addition to both varietal and generic table wines the Gallos also make appetizer and dessert wines, such as ports and sherries. Nine cork-finished varietals and two generics are now marketed under a Gallo label. New introductions in late 1984, the cork-finished generics are a Reserve Burgundy and a Reserve Chablis.

Varietals were first introduced by Gallo in 1974, but have evolved continuously as their vineyards have come into production. The first release included no oak-aged wines, and neither of the "big two" for California,

Chardonnay and Cabernet Sauvignon. In 1979 the Gallos introduced a new label for their varietals, "The Wine Cellars of Ernest and Julio Gallo." Subsequently, after aging in the oak cellar in Modesto, a Chardonnay was released in 1981, followed by a Cabernet Sauvignon in 1982. The Chardonnay is aged entirely in French oak. The Cabernet is aged in Yugoslavian oak.

The first release of the Cabernet Sauvignon was not vintage-dated despite the fact that it was produced entirely of the 1978 vintage (and entirely of Sonoma grapes). A second release did carry a 1978 vintage date, the first Gallo wine to do so in fifty years of commercial winemaking. Both wines are 100 percent Cabernet Sauvignon and are entirely from the 1978 vintage.

Gamay

Commonly thought to be the same as the predominant variety of Beaujolais, France. But in recent years controversy has arisen over its identification and it may, in fact, be Verdigue. Nevertheless, under the identity of Napa Gamay or simply Gamay it is used to make a fruity, fresh red wine in the style of the Beaujolais wines. There are over 3,400 acres of this variety planted in California.

Gamay Beaujolais

Although this red vinifera has been identified as a clone of Pinot Noir, many wineries make varietals from it and label it as Gamay Beaujolais. Most often they are light and fruity in the style of Beaujolais.

GEMELLO WINERY
Mountain View, San Francisco Bay South

Gemello has been tucked away behind a retail establishment on El Camino Real in Mountain View since 1934, somehow managing to survive the urbanization of the Santa Clara Valley. New ownership has brought a new vision to this winery. Gemello once specialized in simple, powerful reds, but now it is moving toward the production of higher quality wines. Storage capacity is 5,000 gallons.

Output: 2,500 cases

Wine:
Cabernet Sauvignon

Generic

American wine (or any other non-European wine) labeled with a classic European appellation such as Burgundy, Chablis, Rhine, or Sauterne, or wine style such as Claret or Rosé. Such wines usually show little resemblance to (or attempt at copying) the European originals and are usually a producer's basic everyday blend, and rather undistinguished. But generic wine from better wineries can be quite good, when

G

winemakers feel released from the American cult of varietals and do some creative blending. More and more frequently in these cases, generic labels are being replaced by proprietary names.

Gewurztraminer

Alsatian in origin, there are over 4,400 acres of this variety planted in California, nearly half in San Francisco Bay North. Particularly aromatic and spicy when allowed to ripen fully, California Gewurztraminers are sometimes harvested slightly under-ripe in order to reduce these varietal characteristics. The wines are frequently finished with a touch of sweetness, in order to soften the bitter aftertaste which can develop as the grapes approach maturity. In the Northwestern and eastern vineyard districts, Gewurztraminer has begun to produce delicately balanced wine.

GEYSER PEAK WINERY
Geyserville, San Francisco Bay North

Output: 1.1 million cases

Leading Wines: Burgundy, Cabernet Sauvignon, Rosé of Cabernet, Chablis, Chardonnay, Chenin Blanc, Soft Chenin Blanc (low alcohol), Fumé Blanc, Gewurztraminer, Soft Johannisberg Riesling, Pinot Noir, Pinot Noir Blanc, Sauvignon Blanc, Zinfandel; Brut and Blanc de Noir sparkling wines;

Geyser Peak was founded in 1880 by one of Sonoma County's pioneers, Augustin Quitzow, and is now owned by the Trione family. At one time vinegar, under the Four Monks label, was the only product offered for sale by the winery. During the 1970s, under Schlitz (Stroh) Brewing Company ownership, the winery was completely rehabilitated and Geyser Peak pioneered bag-in-box packaging of its Summit generic wines. Packaging in aluminum cans and plastic bottles has since been added.

A long list of vintage-dated varietals and two sparkling wines are produced under the Geyser Peak label. The wide selection is popularly priced, offering many things to many consumers.

Geyser owns 1,050 acres of vineyards in the Alexander Valley, Russian River Valley, and in the Los Carneros region. Storage capacity is 2.6 million gallons.

GIBSON WINERY COMPANY
Sanger, Central Valley

Output: 1.4 million cases

Leading Wines: Table, dessert, and fruit wines; hard cider

Gibson is a cooperative winery (one of the few still operating in California) with approximately 150 grower members. Its enormous storage capacity, of over 11 million gallons, and annual sales make Gibson one of the largest wineries in California, eleventh by sales volume. Still, it is not a name that is generally known to the wine-drinking public.

Grapes grown in Fresno, Madera, Tulare, and Kings counties in the Central Valley are supplied to two wineries owned and operated by Gibson—at Elk Grove, south of Sacramento, and at Sanger, near Fresno. Gibson distributes under its own labels—Gibson, California Villages, Silverstone Cellars, Romano and Farley's (hard cider) and the company is also one of the largest suppliers of private-label wines in California, selling to large beverage stores and to supermarket chains.

GIRARDET WINE CELLARS
Roseburg, Oregon

A native of Switzerland, Philippe Girardet established an 18-acre vineyard in the Umpqua Valley in 1971. After initially selling his grapes to other wineries, Girardet started a winery of his own and is virtually the only Oregon winegrower devoting a significant portion of his production to French-American hybrids. Girardet's releases emphasize his interest in blending different varietals for good, easily accessible wines at a moderate price.

Output: 2,500 cases

Leading Wines: Gewurztraminer, Riesling, blends of vinifera and French-American hybrids

GIRARD WINERY
Oakville, San Francisco Bay North

Fifty acres of Chardonnay and Cabernet Sauvignon vines provided the basis for Girard when the property was purchased in 1974. A winery was built in 1980 and acreage has been increased significantly. Some wines are made from purchased grapes, and these are bottled under the "Stephens" label. Their wines have generally shown good fruit and better-than-average complexity.

Output: 12,500 cases

Leading Wines: Cabernet Sauvignon, Chardonnay, Chenin Blanc, Sauvignon Blanc

GLEN CREEK WINERY
Salem, Oregon

The few experimental vines Thomas and Sylvia Dumm planted in 1976 were planned to supply their home winemaking. But in 1982, using Washington grapes, Glen Creek crushed its first commercial vintage. Sauvignon Blanc in particular was an immediate success. Glen Creek continues to use Washington grapes, although the Dumms will shift more to Oregon fruit as their own vineyard matures.

Output: 3,000 cases

Leading Wines: Chardonnay, Gewurztraminer, Sauvignon Blanc

GLEN ELLEN WINERY
Glen Ellen, San Francisco Bay North

The site of Glen Ellen Winery saw vines as early as 1868 and it is not hard to understand why the property was seen as a prime spot for grape-growing. It sits in a glen, nestled in the side of Mount Sonoma, that features two markedly different soils: one red (rich in iron), and one white. (Mount Sonoma is an inactive volcano, and its past created this unusual topographical situation.) Additionally, the steep terraced slopes insure good drainage for the vines, and the hot-at-noon, cool-at-night microclimate ripens the grapes to an unusual intensity.

Glen Ellen produces five varietals with the emphasis on estate-bottled Chardonnay, Sauvignon Blanc, and Cabernet Sauvignon. In all, Glen Ellen owns 85 acres of vineyards (including five acres each of Merlot and Cabernet Franc used for blending with Cabernet Sauvignon) and leases 200 additional acres. Its wines have drawn critical acclaim at every level;

Output: 40,000 cases

Leading Wines: Cabernet Sauvignon, Chardonnay, Fumé Blanc,

G

Muscat Canelli,
Sauvignon Blanc

of especially good value are the Proprietor's Reserve Red (made from Cabernet) and Proprietor's Reserve White (made from Chardonnay and French Colombard).

GLENORA WINE CELLARS
Dundee, Finger Lakes

Output: 15,000 cases

Leading Wines:
Cayuga, Chardonnay,
Johann Blanc,
Johannisberg Riesling,
Seyval Blanc, Sparkling
Ravat, Blanc de Blancs

Glenora has played a prominent role in refining the crisp, citrusy style characteristic of premium northeastern white wines. Dry or sweet, Glenora wines generally build on a structure of acid that gives them an austerity and an affinity for food. After early experiments with labrusca, French-American hybrids, and vinifera varieties, its line of wines was narrowed to five grapes Glenora believes are most consistent in the Finger Lakes. (Small releases of Gewurztraminer have been added in occasional years, and the winery bottles a wine cooler.)

Four grape grower-entrepreneurs built the winery in 1977. With large vineyards directly opposite one another on both sides of Seneca Lake, they could fill the cellar many times over and most of the wines are estate-grown, particularly as new vinifera vineyards come into bearing. But Glenora also buys grapes from other vineyards on the three lakes, adding 'colors' to their winemaking palette.

Notwithstanding a high turnover of winemakers (five in the first eight vintages), Glenora is known for consistency of quality and style. Riesling, however, has stood out from year to year. Made in dry (labeled Johann Blanc), semidry (Johannisberg Riesling), and occasionally in late-harvest versions, its floral finesse presents strong evidence for the Finger Lakes as Riesling's home away from home. Glenora's Seyval Blanc is also exceptional, in a bright crisp style. Cayuga is made dry for this variety, more reserved and food-oriented than the norm. But Ravat comes through mezzo-forte with pineapple-grapefruit flavors and residual sugar to match acidity. Chardonnay has been Glenora's problem child, stylistically unresolved as a varietal.

GOLD SEAL VINEYARDS
Hammondsport, Finger Lakes

Output:
about 1 million cases

Leading Wines:
Blanc de Blanc, Blanc de
Noir, Brut Champagne,
Catawba, Chablis,
Chardonnay,
Gewurztraminer,
Johannisberg Riesling, Dry
Riesling, Rhine

The second winery established in the Finger Lakes, as the Urbana Wine Co. in 1865, Gold Seal has remained a pioneer. The first large eastern winery to experiment with French-American hybrid grape varieties in the 1930s and 1940s, it resurrected Catawba, once the sparkling star of American wine, as one of the hot pink pop wines of the 1960s, and introduced the classic, European vinifera varieties to eastern American vineyards. After 25 years of uneven progress with these vinifera grapes, Gold Seal's Riesling and Chardonnay have reached a quality level that is consistent and frequently excellent.

Much of this innovation can be credited to Old World winemakers. Before and after Prohibition, Gold Seal made a practice of hiring French winemakers from the venerable cellars of Champagne who helped to build the Finger Lake's early reputation for sparkling wine. Gold Seal champagne still stands among the best of eastern American sparkling wines. But most of their sparkling wines rely on labrusca grapes and remain somewhat provincial, eclipsed by the finest California sparklers and by the winery's own vinifera varietals. Blanc de Blanc and Blanc de Noir are exceptions and Gold Seal's best sparkling wines.

The late Charles Fournier, an emigré from Veuve Cliquot in Champagne, guided Gold Seal through many of the last 50 years. He hired Russian expatriate Konstantin Frank in 1952 on the chance that Frank's speculations about growing European grapes in New York might prove correct. They did, although subsequent experience has narrowed the winery's offerings to Riesling and Chardonnay, with Gewurztraminer added in occasional years. Dry (not completely), semi-dry (labeled "Johannisberg Riesling"), and Late-Harvest Riesling are all reliable examples of the Finger Lake's capacity to grow fragrant, lively, German-style wines with finesse and depth of fruit. Gold Seal's Chardonnay is also impressive, balancing rich fruit with prominent acidity and moderate oak, mistakable for a lean north coast California Chardonnay. These estate-bottled wines are from Gold Seal's own large vineyard on Seneca Lake's east shore, an area gaining a reputation for producing the region's 'biggest' wines.

Semisweet, grapey Pink Catawba is Gold Seal's biggest seller and a good example of the old line of labrusca wines. But although it was one of the pioneers with French hybrids, the winery has done nothing remarkable with these varieties for many years.

Gold Seal is a subsidiary of the Seagram conglomerate which also owns Paul Masson Vineyards and Taylor Wine. In 1984 Seagram consolidated its Finger Lakes operations at the Taylor winery and closed the century-old Gold Seal facility on Keuka Lake. Gold Seal vinifera wines continue to be made separately from the same vineyards.

ESTATE BOTTLED

GOLD SEAL VINEYARDS
Johannisberg Riesling
NEW YORK STATE WHITE WINE

Made and bottled at the Winery
by Gold Seal Vineyards
Hammondsport, New York
Alcohol 12% by Volume *Charles Fournier*

GOOD HARBOR VINEYARDS
Lake Leelanau, Michigan

Good Harbor added vineyards to a large, successful orchard in Michigan's northern fruit belt, on the Leelanau Peninsula, and entered the wine business in 1980. The surrounding waters of Lake Michigan extend the growing season enough to bring the peninsula into low Region I on the U.C. Davis climate scale. Good Harbor concentrates on white wine varieties that consistently ripen well, and gives its dry wines (Seyval Lot 2 and Vignoles) a touch of oak.

Output: 5,000 cases

Leading Wines:
Baco Noir, De Chaunac
Rosé, Marechal Foch,
Riesling, Seyval Blanc,
Vignoles, three fruit wines

GORDON BROTHERS CELLARS
Pasco, Washington

Jeff and Bill Gordon, grape growers in the Columbia Valley near Pasco, founded Gordon Brothers Cellars in 1983 to control better the pricing of

Output: 1,000 cases

Leading Wines:
Chardonnay, Chenin

Blanc, Riesling,
Sauvignon Blanc

their grape crop. The Gordons are leaders in an increasing trend of Washington grape growers seeking to assume more complete control over their crop. Most of the grapes from the Gordons' 80-acre vineyard, however, is still sold to other wineries.

GRAND CRU VINEYARDS
Glen Ellen, San Francisco Bay North

Output: 40,000 cases

Leading Wines:
Cabernet Sauvignon,
Chenin Blanc,
Gewurztraminer,
Sauvignon Blanc, Vin
Maison: White, Rosé, Red

Founded in 1970, Grand Cru first attracted attention with its Gewurztraminers, which are from botrytised grapes. Since 1975, Grand Cru Chenin Blancs, made from grapes grown in the Clarksburg Viticultural Area in the Sacramento River Delta, have also been winning a following of consumers and medals from wine judges. The wines are made in a Vouvray style but exhibit greater fruitiness and intensity of varietal character.

Grand Cru's Collector Series of Cabernet Sauvignons is also attracting a following for its intensity and complexity. The Cabernet is produced from grapes grown in Garden Creek Vineyard in the Alexander Valley, in northern Sonoma County. The small, 20-acre vineyard yields only 2½ tons per acre (3-4 tons is not unusual for quality Cabernet) and the grapes possess great richness and flavor.

GRAND RIVER WINE
Madison, Lake Erie

Output: 4,000 cases

Leading Wines:
Old Mill Claret,
Rick's Blend

Originally a vinifera winery but it has shifted to hardier French hybrids in the face of damaging winters. Although whites predominate in the 20-acre vineyard, Grand River is best known for red blends with firm, spare structure and dry fruit resembling wines of northern Italy. Chambourcin, Leon Millot, and Chancellor are variously fermented on and off the skins and in the carbonic maceration technique famous in Beaujolais Nouveau.

GRANITE SPRINGS WINERY
Somerset, Sierra Foothills

Output: 7,000 cases

Leading Wines:
Cabernet Sauvignon,
Chenin Blanc, Petite
Sirah, Sauvignon Blanc,
Sierra Gold, Sierra Red,
White Zinfandel, Zinfandel

Granite Springs is another of the new, small wineries that have begun appearing in the El Dorado Viticultural Area, renewing the 19th-century viticultural traditions of this region.

It is family owned and operated, and began in 1981 with the planting of vineyards at the 2,400-foot level in the Sierra Foothills. Construction of a 25,000-gallon winery was begun in 1981 and was completed in time for the crush of that year.

Winemaking practices combine traditional techniques with modern. Red wines are fermented in open-top redwood tanks and the cap is punched down by hand several times each day to assure maximum color and flavor extraction. White wines, however, are fermented in the modern style: in temperature-controlled, stainless steel tanks. Granite Springs has garnered a reputation for consistent, straightforward wines.

Grey Riesling

Not actually a member of the Riesling family, this variety is properly identified as the French Chauché Gris. Several wineries produce it as a varietal. As such, it can be rather thin and acidic. There are over 2,600 acres of this grape planted in California.

Green Hungarian

Without a great deal of varietal character, Green Hungarian is nevertheless a white vinifera favored by a few wineries and consumers as a varietal table wine. As such, it is light in body and usually fairly neutral in flavor. There are 470 acres planted in California.

Grenache

A widely favored variety California for rosés — it is the grape used in Tavel in the Rhône. There are nearly 18,000 acres planted in California, of which over 12,000 are in the Central Valley.

GRGICH HILLS CELLARS
Rutherford, San Francisco Bay North

Output: 17,000 cases

Leading Wines:
Cabernet Sauvignon,
Chardonnay, Fumé Blanc,
Johannisberg Riesling,
Late-Harvest Johannisberg
Riesling, Zinfandel

Miljenko (Mike) Grgich had already established a reputation as a world-class winemaker when he and Austin Hills founded Grgich Hills Cellars in 1977. Grgich had worked at Beaulieu with the famed André Tchelistcheff, and had achieved international acclaim at Chateau Montelena for his Chardonnay.

At Grgich Hills, Mike makes wine from five grape varieties. His rich Chardonnay still is popular, but his Zinfandel is made in an uncommonly firm, complex, tannic style. The Cabernet Sauvignons benefit from aging, but the softness of their tannins makes them drinkable at an early age. Grgich's rich Sauvignon Blanc has recently been attracting a lot of attention. It is usually full, aromatic, and flavorful, with an apple-like crispness that makes it attractive with many foods.

Grgich Hills Cellars owns 100 acres of vineyards and has storage capacity for approximately 60,000 gallons.

Grown, Produced, and Bottled by

These words before the winery name on a label are the best assurance that the entire process from vine to bottle was carried out by a single operator. It has replaced "estate-bottled" on many labels because of abuse of the term "estate" in recent years (vineyards managed, but not owned, by wineries were considered part of the estate). But whether labeled "estate-bottled" or "grown, produced and bottled by," ultimately the quality of the wine depends on the reputation and performance of the winery.

G

GUNDLACH-BUNDSCHU WINERY
Vineburg, San Francisco Bay North

Output: 30,000 cases

Leading Wines:
Cabernet Sauvignon,
Chardonnay,
Gewurztraminer,
Kleinberger, Merlot, Pinot
Noir, Sonoma Red,
Sonoma Riesling, Sonoma
White, Zinfandel

Gundlach-Bundschu traces its origins to 1858, when Jacob Gundlach, a Bavarian emigré who owned a vineyard near the town of Sonoma, released his first wines. This vineyard, called Rhinefarm, was later expanded to 400 acres, the current size, and produced wines that won worldwide acclaim. A series of late 19th-century and early 20th-century disasters — phylloxera, earthquake, fire, Prohibition — eventually brought winery production to a halt. It was not until 1970 that the winery was revived. In that year Jim Bundschu, the great-great grandson of one of the original partners, and his brother-in-law John Merritt began to rebuild the winery on the site of the original building. Their first crush, of Zinfandel only, in the rebuilt winery was in 1973.

The winery has now grown to 120,000-gallons of storage capacity. Gundlach-Bundschu produces 10 wines, including the only Kleinberger made in the United States (a German variety grown in California only by this winery).

Gundlach-Bundschu's reds are known for their attractive firmness and for their aging ability. This is not uncommon for a wine like Cabernet Sauvignon, but even the Merlots from this winery show a stiff tannic backbone. A partly barrel-fermented Pinot Noir took its place beside these two varietal reds in 1982.

GUENOC RANCH
Middletown, San Francisco Bay North

Output: 40,000 cases

Leading Wines:
Cabernet Sauvignon,
Chardonnay, Chenin
Blanc, Petite Sirah, Red
table wine, Sauvignon
Blanc, White table wine,
Zinfandel

The proprietors of Guenoc — the only winery in Guenoc Valley (a BATF-approved Viticultural Area) — are also the owners of the only vineyards planted in this valley. There are 4,398 acres in the two-mile-long, crescent-shaped Viticultural Area, but only 270 acres are planted to vineyards. These vineyards include the less-common red Bordeaux grapes, Cabernet Franc and Malbec, as well as the more common red Bordeaux grapes, Cabernet Sauvignon and Merlot. There are plans to add Petite Verdot, another red Bordeaux variety.

The 200,000-gallon winery, the largest in Lake County, was completed in 1981 in time for the early crush of that year. Winemaker Walter Raymond and viticulturist Roy Raymond also share ownership of the winery bearing their name in the Napa Valley. They have developed a reputation at Guenoc for very reasonably-priced wines that feature outstanding varietal definition.

HACIENDA WINE CELLARS
Sonoma, San Francisco Bay North

The name of Agoston Haraszthy figures heavily in the history of Hacienda Wine Cellars; roughly half its vineyards are on 50 acres that Haraszthy first planted to vines in 1862. (Another 60 acres of vineyards do not boast such a pedigree.) But Hacienda is a modern winery, established in 1973.

The winery, housed in a former hospital, has 86,000 gallons of storage capacity. Wines are fermented in stainless steel with the exception of 25 percent of its Chardonnay, which is barrel-fermented. Most wines are aged in small oak cooperage. Zinfandel goes into American oak. Cabernet Sauvignon, Chardonnay, and Pinot Noir receive their barrel development in a variety of French oak barrels. Hacienda's wines are assertive indeed, often featuring significant levels of oakiness and alcohol.

Output: 20,000 cases

Leading Wines:
Cabernet Sauvignon,
Chardonnay,
Dry Chenin Blanc,
Gewurztraminer,
Pinot Noir,
Sauvignon Blanc,
Zinfandel

HAFNER
Healdsburg, San Francisco Bay North

Founded in 1982, Hafner produces only two varietals in its 50,000-gallon winery. Vineyards totaling 95 acres in the Alexander Valley are owned. The winery itself is a reconstruction of an 1893 building.

Output: 8,000 cases

Leading Wines:
Cabernet Sauvignon,
Chardonnay

HAGAFEN CELLARS
Napa, San Francisco Bay North

"Hagafen" is Hebrew for "the vine," and since 1980 this winery has been the only one in the United States making dry kosher varietal table wines.

Hagafen Cellar's wines are perhaps the most interesting of kosher wines. Two of their varietals, Johannisberg Riesling and Chardonnay, are made from grapes grown in the famous Winery Lake Vineyards of Rene Di Rosa, who is a partner in the enterprise.

Output: 5,000 cases

Leading Wines:
Cabernet Sauvignon,
Chardonnay, Johannisberg
Riesling, Pinot Noir Blanc

H

HAIGHT VINEYARD
Litchfield, New England

Output: 6,000 cases

Leading Wines: Chardonnay, Covertside Red, Covertside White, Marechal Foch, Riesling

Haight was the first winery established in Connecticut after the state's farm winery law opened the door for small vineyards in 1978. The rocky hillsides and cold winters of northwestern Connecticut have forced the vineyard to concentrate on a few varieties that produce small crops with some reliability of quality.

Not surprisingly, white wines show best. A blend labeled Covertside White balances the acid structure of Seyval with a semidry finish and the richer dimensions of Chardonnay. Even in warm years that generate high sugar levels, the grapes tend to retain their acid. Haight's Riesling puts this to good use with consistently elegant, semidry, Mosel-style wine with crisp edges and a long finish. Chardonnay is more sporadic in quantity and quality—hence its use with Seyval in the Covertside blend and in a *méthode champenoise* sparkling wine. In exceptional years like 1983, the elements of classic Chardonnay can come together for a wine with intense varietal fruit and acid rounded by light aging in Limousin oak. Covertside Red is a light, fruity blend based on Marechal Foch, which in favorable years is also made as a full-bodied, barrel-fermented varietal.

HAMLET HILL VINEYARDS
Pomfret, New England

Output: 9,000 cases

Leading Wines: Charter Oak Red, méthode champenoise sparkling wine, Seyval Blanc

In rolling New England countryside new to grapes, Hamlet Hill has planted one of the region's most diverse vineyards. One variety showing an immediate affinity to this northeastern corner of Connecticut was Seyval, here finished dry but full of tart fruit—a New England shellfish wine. The experimental nature of the vineyard led to the East's only planting of Muscadet and Pinot Meunier. The latter is destined for a sparkling wine cuvée with Chardonnay and Pinot Noir. Another sparkling wine made in the *méthode champenoise* from Seyval and Chardonnay is aged for a period of years on the yeast. A red blend, Charter Oak Red, is also barrel-aged over a year.

HANZELL VINEYARDS
Sonoma, San Francisco Bay North

Output: 2,500 cases

Leading Wines: Cabernet Sauvignon, Chardonnay, Pinot Noir

Hanzell Vineyards owes its existence to the late James D. Zellerbach's love for fine Burgundies. Pinot Noir and Chardonnay grapes were planted on his Sonoma property in 1952 while he was living in Italy as U.S. ambassador. The winery's exterior facade is patterned after that of Clos de Vougeot in Burgundy. In 1957 with the first Hanzell Chardonnay he firmly established a reputation for quality which continues to this day.

Not so incidentally, Zellerbach is credited with introducing California wine producers to the beneficial effects of aging wines in French oak and with arousing interest in the idea of making a fine California Pinot Noir.

He was thoroughly dedicated to the dream of Burgundian-style wine in California and, to this end, brought in Burgundian machinery and Burgundian techniques that had never been seen before in California.

After Zellerbach's death in 1963, the winery and 32-acre vineyard has changed hands a couple of times but the standard of wines has not declined. A Cabernet Sauvignon is expected shortly.

HARGRAVE VINEYARD
Cutchoque, Long Island

Output: 8,000 cases

Leading Wines:
Cabernet Sauvignon,
Chardonnay, Fumé Blanc,
Merlot, Sauvignon Blanc

It seems extraordinary that a region so well-suited to winegrowing as Long Island should wait for a scholar of Chinese literature and an educator to plant the first wine vineyard in 1973. Alex and Louisa Hargrave chose the Island's North Fork after a search on both coasts for a site to ripen classic European varieties with European acid levels reliably, in the service of food.

From the first crush in 1975, the early vintages resisted clear varietal definition. But by 1980, vineyard and cellar began to come into their own with Chardonnay and Sauvignon Blanc. Their balance, depth of fruit, and silky finish pegged the winery's style. The herbal fruit of the Sauvignon Blanc shows through in a separate batch of Sauvignon aged in French oak for Fumé Blanc. New French oak barrels are added to the cellar yearly for whites and reds (except Riesling and Sauvignon Blanc). Woody tones and the complexity and buttery lactic flavors of malolactic fermentation are important elements of style here. Cabernet stays in barrel 2-2½ years for release in its third year, and is a wine built to last. Hargrave's Riesling stands apart in style — crisp and floral, off-dry. Pinot Noir has been uncooperative. The Collector's Series of Chardonnay may or may not surpass the regular bottling depending on vintage, but does carry evocative original art labels from Long Island painters. All wines are estate-bottled from 55 acres.

1982

Hargrave Vineyard
North Fork
Long Island   New York

Fumé Blanc

Grown, Produced & Bottled By Hargrave Vineyard
Cutchogue, N.Y.   12% Alcohol By Volume

HAVILAND VINTNERS
Lynwood, Washington

Output: 12,500 cases

Leading Wines:
Cabernet Sauvignon,
Chardonnay, Merlot,
Riesling, Sauvignon Blanc

Founded in 1981 in the suburbs of Seattle by winemaker George Dejarnatt, Haviland has a reputation for fine dry wines. It owns one of the oldest producing Cabernet vineyards in Washington; half the 11-acre vineyard was planted in 1961, the other half in 1965. (The vineyard was the source of Chateau Ste. Michelle's first Cabernet Sauvignons.) Recently acquired, and under development, are an additional 60 vineyard acres contiguous with the Cabernet vineyard. The new acreage, on the former Corral Creek Ranch property, is devoted principally to Merlot and Chardonnay. All other Haviland grapes are purchased from Columbia Valley growers.

Chardonnay is the most important white wine. Haviland partly ferments its Chardonnay in French oak to give the wine a more rounded, textural quality. DeJarnatt avoids malolactic fermentation, believing that it sacrifices too much of the fruit of the grape.

Although the red wine focus is on the Bordeaux grape varieties, Haviland is one of the few wineries achieving some measure of success with Pinot Noir from Columbia Valley grapes.

HAYWOOD WINERY
Sonoma, San Francisco Bay North

Output: 10,000 cases

Leading Wines: Cabernet Sauvignon, Chardonnay, Estate White, White Riesling, Spaghetti Red, Zinfandel

Haywood's careful matching of grape variety to vineyard site — Cabernet nearer to the valley floor, for example, and Riesling higher up — at its steeply terraced Chamisal Valley location helped initiate a trend that has vastly improved the quality of California wine. The generic red, Spaghetti Red, Haywood whimsically calls it, frequently wins medals and the hearts of budget-conscious consumers.

HEITZ WINE CELLARS
St. Helena, San Francisco Bay North

Output: 35,000 cases

Leading Wines: Burgundy, Cabernet Sauvignon, Chablis, Chardonnay, Grignolino, Pinot Noir, Treasure Port, Zinfandel

Heitz Wine Cellars is another California wine success story. When its founders Joe and Alice Heitz purchased a small vineyard and winery south of St. Helena, they were among the first "outsiders" to enter the California wine industry after Repeal; they had no long family history in winemaking.

Their early years were difficult, but the wines of Heitz Wine Cellars, particularly the Cabernet Sauvignon made from the grapes of Martha's Vineyard, are now world famous.

In the beginning, Heitz purchased most of the grapes used to make its wines. In addition to 8 acres of vines around the tasting room, there were 20 acres of Zinfandel and Grignolino (a variety for which Heitz also has a high reputation), surrounding the Taplin Road winery. Since the mid-1960s the Heitzes have added 30 acres of Chardonnay to their vineyards, and in 1984 purchased another 77-acre vineyard in the Napa Valley, planted mainly to Cabernet Sauvignon and some Zinfandel. All of this amounts to a move toward estate-grown grapes.

Heitz Cellars is noted for Cabernet Sauvignons, particularly those of Martha's Vineyard, Bella Oaks, and Fay Vineyard. Martha's Vineyard is a special plot that produces uniquely flavorful Cabernet grapes. Time after time in tastings this wine is identified for its richness, intensity, and characteristic bouquet of eucalyptus. Martha's Vineyard is virtually synonymous with Heitz and with a definitive style of Napa Cabernet Sauvignon. But Heitz produces several vineyard-designated Cabernet and a cheaper and often good-value version with a Napa Valley apellation. Heitz Chardonnays have also been sought after by consumers.

VINTAGE 1975   BOTTLED JULY, 1979
Magnum   of a total of 2,400 Magnum

NAPA VALLEY
CABERNET SAUVIGNON
ALCOHOL 13½% BY VOLUME
PRODUCED AND BOTTLED IN OUR CELLAR BY
HEITZ WINE CELLARS
ST. HELENA, CALIFORNIA

H

HENRY WINERY
Roseburg, Oregon

Output: 6,300 cases

Leading Wines:
Chardonnay,
Gewurztraminer,
Pinot Noir

Henry's winegrowing practices differ considerably from the Oregon norm. Pinot Noir and Chardonnay are planted on the valley floor, not a southerly hillside where air movement and sunshine would dispel frosts. But neither frost nor ripening have been problems and yields are six to eight tons an acre, two to three times Oregon's usual yield. Both wines are aged in American oak before release, producing riper and fuller-bodied wines in a markedly different style to most Oregon wine.

HERON HILL VINEYARDS
Hammondsport, Finger Lakes

Output: 10,000 cases

Leading Wines:
Aurora, Cayuga,
Chardonnay, Johannisberg
Riesling, Ravat, Seyval
Blanc

Unlike many of its Finger Lakes neighbors, Heron Hill began as a vinifera-only enterprise, inspired by the success of Dr. Konstantin Frank's Vinifera Wine Cellars a few miles away on Keuka Lake. White Riesling and Chardonnay were planted beginning in 1968, making this one of the oldest vinifera vineyards in the Finger Lakes. The winery's first vintage in 1977 included an exceptional, Mosel-style Riesling that began a remarkably consistent reputation for quality with this variety. German cellaring techniques keep the wine in a cold, reduced state to produce an American Riesling close to wines of the German Saar Valley.

As in the Saar, the finesse of Heron Hill Riesling is bred in a difficult microclimate. Upland air drainage through the vineyard makes it one of the coldest in the Finger Lakes, frequently damaging the vines and reducing the crop. (A second estate property on Canandaigua Lake, Ingle Vineyard is not much warmer.) As a result, hardier French hybrid varietals have become an important part of the product line. Grapes for these wines are generally grown on the cool, western Finger Lakes (Keuka and Canandaigua), holding to a light, German-style with residual sugar balancing crisp, appley acidity. Ravat is a specialty and the wine with biggest proportions, emphasizing the variety's pineapple-grapefruit character. Seyval Blanc picks up some richness and complexity of fruit from blending with Ravat.

Chardonnay has struggled to find its place in Heron Hill's wine style. Recent vintages tend to show more wood from Nevers cooperage and somewhat more body, but are still lithe, Chablis-structured wines with firm acidity.

Otter Spring is a second Heron Hill label added in 1980 to accommodate a broader range of wine styles. Used for the same line of hybrid varieties as the Heron Hill label, it identifies wine lots made somewhat drier, with warmer fermentation temperatures and some wood-aging producing rounder body and more muted fruitiness. Otter Spring Riesling and Chardonnay are made from free-run juice, showing more delicacy than their Heron Hill counterparts.

H

HIDDEN SPRINGS WINERY
Amity, Oregon

Output: 4,000 cases

Leading Wines:
Chardonnay,
Pinot Noir,
Riesling

A northern Willamette Valley winery founded in 1980, Hidden Springs is owned jointly by two families, Don and Carolyn Byard and Al and Jo Alexanderson. In all, 28 acres are in vine and each family owns its own section and sells the grapes to the winery. The Byards are participating in an Oregon State University test program, using a thermograph to automatically record data on temperature, humidity, and sunlight intensity. Hidden Springs is also conducting experiments with three different Riesling clones and small test plots of other grapes.

HILLCREST VINEYARD
Roseburg, Oregon

Output: 10,000 cases

Leading Wines:
Cabernet Sauvignon,
Chardonnay,
Pinot Noir, Riesling,
Sauvignon Blanc,
Zinfandel

1979

**Hillcrest
Vineyard**

OREGON
PINOT NOIR

alcohol 10.7% by volume

PRODUCED AND BOTTLED BY HILLCREST VINEYARD
ROSEBURG, OREGON   BONDED WINERY OR-44

A pioneer of modern winemaking in Oregon, Hillcrest began in 1961 when Richard Sommer came to the Umpqua Valley in search of a cooler winegrowing climate. At that time nothing was left of the winegrowing industry except the decayed remnants of earlier efforts. Despite the recommendations of Oregon State University, Sommer planted vinifera grapes in the valley and bonded a winery two years later. His solitary faith in vinifera over labrusca as a viable commercial species in Oregon was borne out, and for many years Sommer's Hillcrest Vineyard and premium Oregon wine were synonymous.

At 850 feet above sea level, the Hillcrest Vineyard is higher and slightly cooler than most Umpqua Valley growing sites. From the beginning Sommer focused his efforts on the cool-ripening Riesling, and fully two-thirds of his 30-acre vineyard are planted to the grape.

Hillcrest's Rieslings are fermented in stainless steel tanks at a temperature of about 50°F. At about 2 percent sugar, fermentation is stopped. In the best years, Sommer releases late-harvest Riesling from exceptionally ripe grapes and occasionally an ice wine. Sommer also makes small quantities of Oregon Mist, a bottle-fermented sparkling Riesling.

Most Oregon wineries use Riesling as a cash flow wine: one to bottle and sell as soon as possible after the vintage. Rieslings, however, do need some bottle age to show their best. Sommer does not release his Rieslings until about two years after the vintage, ready to drink but still capable of developing further with cellar age.

Sommer also produces red wines in small quantities. Pinot Noir is routinely successful, and in the best years Sommer's Cabernet Sauvignon ripens well.

HINMAN VINEYARDS
Eugene, Oregon

Output: 13,000 cases

Leading Wines:
Chardonnay,

A partnership of Doyle Hinman and David Smith, Hinman Vineyards has 19 acres of vines in the southern Willamette Valley. While neighboring Oregon winegrowers look primarily to France's Burgundy district for perspectives on their own winemaking methods and styles, Hinman has shown a marked German influence in its wines since its first commercial crush in 1979. All the white wines including the Chardonnay are low alcohol, relatively high in acid, and finished with slight residual sugar.

Gewurztraminer,
Pinot Noir, Riesling, Tior

HINZERLING VINEYARDS
Prosser, Washington

Output: 5,000 cases

One of the pioneers in the Washington wine industry, Mike Wallace planted a 23-acre vineyard in the Yakima Valley in 1972.

Leading Wines:
Cabernet Sauvignon,
Chardonnay,
Gewurztraminer,
Riesling

Cabernet Sauvignon is Hinzerling's best wine. At a time when many dismissed Washington as a red wine growing region, Hinzerling provided a strong contrary argument in estate Cabernets made with little compromise. Made from 100 percent Cabernet Sauvignon, full-bodied, rough, and tannic in their youth, Hinzerling's Cabernets need and reward time in the cellar. (The 1978 vintage is often regarded as the best to date.) Hinzerling has also begun releasing a second Cabernet for more immediate consumption, produced from non-estate grapes.

Hinzerling has also been something of a pioneer in botrytised wines, making sweet dessert wines from both Riesling and Gewurztraminer. Not a usual grape for botrytised wines, Gewurztraminer is slightly more resistant to the noble mold than Riesling and is easier to manage in the vineyard. The results have been highly successful.

HMR ESTATE WINERY
Paso Robles, Central Coast

Output: 35,000 cases

HMR's original vineyards were planted near Paso Robles, beginning in 1964, and eight years later a winery was completed in the midst of the maturing vines. After 10 years as Hoffman Mountain Ranch, during which a reputation was achieved for quality Pinot Noir, the winery and vineyards were sold to a group of investors (HMR Limited) who changed the name of the winery to HMR Estate Winery (or Hidden Mountain Ranch). Pinot Noir continues to be a specialty. But the winery also produces very exciting Cabernet Sauvignon from its estate vines. The rare but delicious Doctor's Reserve Cabernet Sauvignon is one of the outstanding examples of this variety from this region of California.

Leading Wines:
Cabernet Sauvignon,
Chardonnay,
Chenin Blanc,
Pinot Noir,
Franken Riesling
(Sylvaner),
Sauvignon Blanc

THE HOGUE CELLARS
Prosser, Washington

Output: 34,000 cases

Long-time residents of the Yakima Valley, the Hogue Family manage a diversified agricultural operation raising cattle, hops, asparagus, mint, and Concord grapes as well as wine grapes. Grapes from other growers in the Yakima Valley supplement the Hogues' 200-acre estate vineyards.

From the first crush of Chenin Blanc in 1982, winemaker Mike Conway created something of a sensation, setting a style for the wine now emulat-

Leading Wines:
Cabernet Sauvignon,
Chardonnay,
Chenin Blanc, Riesling,
Sauvignon Blanc

ed by other Washington winemakers. Intensely fruity, with crisp acidity and some residual sugar, the wine resembles Yakima Valley Rieslings but has its own distinctive scent and taste, sometimes described as honeysuckle in character. Sauvignon Blanc and Chardonnay, are also harvested and fermented to emphasize crisp acidity and fruit of the grape. (The Chardonnay is aged in French oak, the Sauvignon Blanc in a combination of French and American oak.)

The Hogue family also partly financed Conway's own winery, Latah Creek, and after assuming dual winemaking roles in 1982 and 1983, Conway left Hogue for full-time duties at his own expanded winery. Conway remains available for consultation and Rob Griffin, formerly winemaker at Preston Wine Cellars, assumed winemaking duties.

HOOD RIVER VINEYARDS
Hood River, Oregon

Output: 2,500 cases

Leading Wines:
Gewurztraminer,
Pinot Noir,
Riesling,
fruit and berry wines

Situated on Oregon's northern boundary, Hood River has a unique microclimate in the Columbia River Gorge, where the opposing climates of east and west Oregon meet. Compared with the winegrowing regions in the Willamette Valley, the summers are warmer, the winters colder, and there is less rainfall. Sensing the potential for grapes, owners Clifford and Eileen Blanchette planted an experimental acre of Riesling in 1974 on their fruit farm. The vineyard now totals 12 acres, and recent results with Gewurztraminers have been especially promising.

HOODSPORT WINERY
Hoodsport, Washington

Output: 4,000 cases

Leading Wines:
Chenin Blanc,
Gewurztraminer,
Island Belle, Merlot,
Riesling;
various fruit and
berry wines

Founded in 1979, Hoodsport is situated on Hood Canal in western Washington and is known primarily as a fruit and berry winery. However, the winery is increasing its emphasis on vinifera wines from Columbia Valley grapes and also makes a wine associated with the earliest years of the state's wine industry, a native variety known locally as Island Belle.

HOP KILN WINERY
Healdsburg, San Francisco Bay North

Output: 8,000 cases

Leading Wines:
Cabernet Sauvignon,
Chardonnay, Napa
Gamay, Gewurztraminer,
Johannisberg Riesling,
Pinot Noir, Petite Sirah,
Marty Griffin's Big Red,
A Thousand Flowers (A
French Colombard-White
Riesling blend), Zinfandel

Founded in 1975, Hop Kiln is situated on a 240-acre Russian River ranch with 70 acres planted to vineyards. The cool benchland along the Russian River provides growing conditions that are beneficial to the Johannisberg Riesling, Gewurztraminer, and Chardonnay planted there.

The red wines at Hop Kiln are vinified in open fermenters. This method, which was in common use in California until the mid-1960s, is no longer a widespread practice, although it may be coming back into vogue. Hop Kiln's reds tend to be fuller bodied, deeper colored, and have more intense varietal flavors as a result.

HOPKINS VINEYARD
New Preston, New England

Hopkins Vineyard was started in 1979 with a selection of French-American hybrid varieties hardy enough for winters in the Berkshire foothills. The goal is country wines closely identified with this corner of Connecticut, where the Hopkins family has farmed for eight generations, over 200 years — no allusions here to European or California wine styles.

Ravat Blanc (Vignoles) shows well in a slightly sweet, signature varietal and adds freshness and spice to the Waramaug white blend (mostly Aurora). Like other New England wineries, Hopkins makes a range of white varietals and blends and one red blend, here a Barn Red emphasizing the bright fruit flavors of Marechal Foch.

Output: 6,000 cases

Leading Wines:
Barn Red,
Lakeside White,
Ravat Blanc,
Seyval Blanc,
Waramaug White

HUDSON RIVER VALLEY

Vineyards first appeared along the Hudson River Valley with French Huguenot settlements in the 17th century, making this one of the nation's original winegrowing districts. By the early 19th century, thousands of acres of grapevines draped the hills abruptly rolling out from the river. The Brotherhood Winery in Washingtonville remains from that era and is the oldest continuously existing winery in the United States.

The Hudson River forms a corridor which carries the temperate effects of the Atlantic about 100 miles inland, extending the growing season and cushioning winter cold snaps. Stony, well-drained soils and undulating terrain favor small-scale viticulture; and the irregularity of the land accentuates microclimatic (and soil) variations, resulting in a good deal of variation in growing conditions, wine styles, and vintage responses. This is compounded by the scattering of wineries from Catskill foothills to the river's edge and back up onto the shoulder of Connecticut's Berkshire Mountains. Total vineyard area in the region is about 1,000 acres.

With the exception of Brotherhood, little of the valley's vinous history is evident today. Most of the two dozen wineries are relatively new, small farm operations growing French-American hybrids. Unlike other northern wine districts, the Hudson region puts considerable energy into the production of red wines, taking advantage of the maritime influence and extra degree days to put more body and depth in red varieties. At their best the wines resemble the village wines of Beaujolais and Burgundy. Even so, white wines are the region's best overall, with Seyval a specialty and Chardonnay a promising varietal.

H

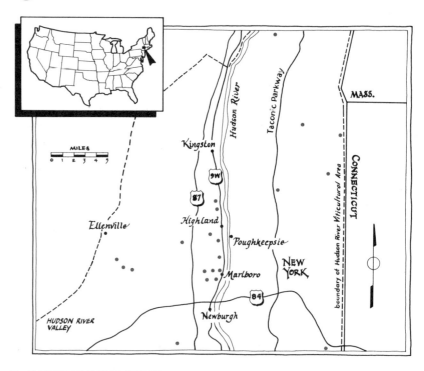

ROBERT HUNTER
St. Helena, San Francisco Bay North

Output: 8,000 cases

Wine:
Brut de Noirs
sparkling wine

In cooperation with St. Helena Wine Company and Chateau St. Jean, Robert and Sylvia Hunter began in 1980 to produce *méthode champenoise* wine from a blend of Pinot Noir, with Chardonnay and Pinot Blanc.

Grapes grown in Hunter Farm Vineyards, situated in the Valley of the Moon in Sonoma County, are picked by hand at low 18° to 10° Brix in the cool morning hours. The wines remain in contact with the yeasts of the second fermentation for at least 30 months, and a portion is held for 36 months for late-disgorged lots. The result is a complex, yeasty character with only a hint of varietal flavors and aromas. Dosage sugar levels are kept low to maintain a crisp character in the wine.

HUSCH VINEYARD
Philo, San Francisco Bay North

Output: 12,000 cases

Leading Wines:
Cabernet Sauvignon,
Chardonnay,
Chenin Blanc,
Gewurztraminer,
Pinot Noir,
La Ribera Blanc,
Sauvignon Blanc

Husch Vineyards is the oldest winery in the Anderson Valley, one of the most recently approved Viticultural Areas of California. All Husch wines are made from grapes grown in their own vineyards and are estate-bottled. The cool vineyards near the winery are planted to Pinot Noir, Gewurztraminer, and Chardonnay. The warmer La Ribera vineyard is planted to Sauvignon Blanc, Chardonnay, Cabernet Sauvignon, and Chenin Blanc.

I

IDAHO

The Idaho wine industry is the Northwest's newest and smallest. Although some wines were made in Idaho as early as the 19th century, the state lapsed into a long viticultural dormancy. The new Idaho wine industry was born in 1976 when Ste. Chapelle Vineyards had its first commercial crush from vines planted in the early 1970s. Ste. Chapelle remained the state's only winery until the early 1980s, when several smaller wineries came into being.

The Clearwater Valley in the northern part of Idaho was the site of some of the winegrowing efforts in the last century, and although several other areas in the state appear suitable for grape growing in the modern era, the Snake River Valley in the southwest is the only area that has been developed in any significant way.

In the Northwest, the Snake River Valley's climate is closest to Washington's Columbia Valley. The summer days are warm, dry, and sunny, and the temperatures are cool at night; the winters are cold and the growing season is generally shorter and cooler than Washington's. The Snake River Valley is also much higher than the Columbia Valley. Most northwest grape growing regions are at an elevation of less than 1,000 feet, but growing sites along the Snake River Valley are as much as 3,000 feet above sea level. In other circumstances, the higher elevation might mean greater temperature extremes and severe frost problems. But the valley's low elevation, relative to the surrounding terrain, and the marine airflow through the Columbia and Snake River gorges from the Pacific Ocean, hundreds of miles away, moderate the climate throughout the year.

Winter cold can be a problem. Frosts threaten the vines in spring, and winter brings the threat of cold temperatures and sun scalding. Bright sunlight reflecting off the snow can warm parts of the vine well above freezing, but this is often followed by a dramatic drop in temperature at nightfall. In spite of the dangers, vine damage and crop loss have been minimal so far and Idaho has experienced fewer problems with winter cold than Washington.

With the exception of a few fruit and berry wines, Idaho's premium wine industry is based virtually entirely on vinifera grape varieties, with Riesling at the forefront. A very cold-hardy grape that develops varietal character at low sugar levels, Riesling was a logical choice for Idaho's first winegrowing efforts, and the grape is made in styles ranging from semisweet to late-harvest, as well as sparkling versions via the charmat process in the manner of German sekt.

Chardonnay has followed Riesling, and changed the perception of Idaho as a marginal region. The state's first Chardonnay from the 1978 vintage was not steely and austere as many expected, but just the opposite: ripe, full-bodied, moderately high in alcohol, with modest acidity. Although acclaimed nationally, the wine was almost too different from what was expected, and subsequent Idaho Chardonnays have tended more toward balance and elegance, with crisper, balancing acidity. But this first Chardonnay clearly demonstrated that the state was not a region constrained by its climate, but capable of producing a spectrum of wines.

Idaho is adding more grape varieties as experimental plantings prove successful. Idaho Chenin Blancs, for example, are made in a semidry style, and have a flavorful raciness that raises them above most American examples of this varietal. Very little Gewurztraminer is yet produced, but those that have been are distinctive, with a spicy varietal character, adequate acidity, clean fruit, and an absence of the flaws that sometimes befall the grape. Pinot Noir may be the only suitable red wine grape. The first experimental wines were lacking in color and varietal definition, but serious efforts in selected growing sites are not yet fully bearing, and the grape may also find a role in Idaho's premium sparkling wine industry. Other experimental plantings in the state include Muscat Canelli and Sauvignon Blanc.

INGLENOOK VINEYARDS
Rutherford, San Francisco Bay North

Output: 1.25 million cases

Leading Wines:
Inglenook-Napa Valley:
Beaujolais, Cabernet
Sauvignon, Charbono,
Chardonnay, Chenin
Blanc, Gamay,
Gewurztraminer,
Johannisberg Riesling,
Merlot, Muscat Blanc,
Petite Sirah, Pinot Noir,
Rosé of Cabernet
Sauvignon, Sauvignon
Blanc, Zinfandel;
Inglenook-Navalle: Blanc
de Blanc, Burgundy,
Chablis, Chenin Blanc,
French Colombard, Rhine,

Inglenook, one of the oldest names in the Napa Valley, was founded by a retired Finnish sea captain, Gustave Niebaum, in 1879. Niebaum retained the Scottish name of Inglenook for his property and built the three-story stone winery building in 1887, which still stands in the Rutherford vineyards and serves as an aging cellar and visitors' center.

Prohibition closed the winery from 1920 through 1933. When Inglenook was reopened at Repeal, Niebaum's widow asked Carl Bundschu (of Gundlach-Bundschu) to take charge of the winery's rehabilitation. She worked to restore Inglenook's wines to the quality level and reputation they had obtained when they received awards at the Paris International Exposition in 1889. It seems that this goal was achieved, but at a cost. During the following decades Inglenook's wines were considered to be among the best in the world, but they were rarely if ever profitable to their producers. Aside from quality, the winery had a reputation for being traditional. This did not preclude innovation, however. Inglenook was one of the first wineries to label their wines as estate-bottled and to label their wines by their varietal name rather than generically.

In 1964 the winery was abruptly sold to United Vintners, which included, among others, Italian Swiss Colony and Petri, and who thoroughly modernized the winery. When control in United Vintners was acquired, in turn, a few years later by Heublein, Inglenook became embroiled in the ensuing legal battles. At their conclusion Inglenook was established as an independent Heublein subsidiary and divided into Inglenook-Napa Valley and Inglenook-Navalle.

Inglenook-Napa Valley functions as a "boutique" winery, producing 250,000 cases of higher-quality wine per year. It is separated from Inglenook's Navalle wines, which are produced at Heublein's large winery in Madera, and are jug wines produced in large quantities.

Inglenook-Napa Valley emphasizes Cabernet Sauvignon, Merlot, and Sauvignon Blanc—the Bordeaux varieties—made from grapes grown in Inglenook's vineyards at Rutherford, and Chardonnay and Pinot Noir—Burgundy varietals—from vineyards being developed at Oak Knoll and Carneros. Zinfandel and Charbono complete the list of varietals. Charbono, produced by fewer than 10 wineries in California (there are only 90 acres of this robust grape planted in the state) has been an Inglenook specialty for over 40 years.

Ruby Cabernet, Vin Rosé, Zinfandel

INGLESIDE PLANTATION VINEYARDS
Oak Grove, Virginia

In the capable hands of winemaker Jacques Recht, a retired professor of enology from Belgium, Ingleside quickly established a reputation for consistent quality with its first few vintages in the early 1980s. The 30-acre estate vineyard grows mostly French-American varieties for blends designed to provide clean, fruity, dry table wines accessible in character and price. Seyval Blanc is singled out for a lean, tart-fruit varietal in the style of Muscadet. Ingleside's location on the estuary of the Potomac River cools the vineyard in summer and helps keep the wines more supple than the Virginia norm. The winery's first *méthode champenoise* sparkling wines made an auspicious debut in 1984. Some hybrids and most of the vinifera grapes used are purchased from other Virginia vineyards. Cabernet Sauvignon and Chardonnay from Ingleside—medium-bodied wines with balance and breed that indicate careful crafting—have both ranked among the East's best.

Output: 10,000 cases

Leading Wines:
Cabernet Sauvignon,
Champagne, Champagne Rosé, Chardonnay,
Roxbury Red, Seyval Blanc

IRON HORSE VINEYARDS
Sebastopol, San Francisco Bay North

Iron Horse owns 140 acres of vineyards in two Viticultural Areas. Chardonnay and Pinot Noir are planted in Green Valley/Sonoma Viticultural Area. Proximity to the ocean is one factor behind the crisp leanness of Green Valley grapes—a perfect area for the Burgundian varieties.

Generic wines are sold under a second label, Tin Pony. Sparkling wines have recently been introduced and initial releases have drawn unqualified

Output: 25,000 cases

Leading Wines:
Cabernet Sauvignon,
Chardonnay, Fumé Blanc,
Pinot Noir, Zinfandel;

Blanc de Noir, Blanc de Blanc, Brut, sparkling wines

praise, leading many to believe that Green Valley is also an ideal spot for sparkling wine grapes.

Isabella

This blue American grape is the most widely grown variety in the world, according to Pierre Galet, the French viticultural authority, having been generally planted after the phylloxera plague. With Catawba, it was one of the building blocks of the 19th century American wine industry. But in this century, Isabella has dwindled in its home territory of the eastern states. Fewer than 100 acres are planted to Isabella.

ISC WINES OF CALIFORNIA
Asti, San Francisco Bay North

Output: 5 million cases

Leading Wines:
Colony varietals:
Cabernet Sauvignon,
French Colombard,
Chenin Blanc, Zinfandel;
Colony generics: Chablis,
Burgundy, Rosé;
Colony proprietaries:
Emerald Chablis, Pink
Chablis, Gold Chablis,
Ruby Chablis, Moselle,
Vin Rosé;
Petri table wines:
Burgundy, Chablis Blanc,
Chianti, Pink Chablis,
Grenache Vin Rosé, Rhine;
Sparkling wines: Jacques
Bonet and Lejon pink and
white, Cold Duck

ISC, formerly known as Italian Swiss Colony, was founded in 1881 by Andrea Sbarboro, who had seen it originally as a cooperative venture in which Italian and Swiss immigrants would participate. The cooperative idea remained a dream, but a winery was built in 1887. Colony became famous in its early years for two wines sold in raffia-covered bottles: Tipo Red and Tipo White, which were withdrawn only in the 1970s.

During the 1950s, Italian Swiss Colony became part of the United Vintners grower cooperative. But when Heublein took a majority interest in the cooperative, the winery became entangled in protracted legal battles that were not resolved until the early 1980s. In 1983, the labels were acquired from Heublein by the newly formed ISC Wines of California. (Allied Grape Growers is a major shareholder in this new enterprise.)

In addition to the acreage owned by the 1,300 members of Allied Grape Growers, ISC Wines owns 500 acres. A portion of the acreage is in Sonoma County and some of the Colony varietals are so designated. Storage capacity of the several wineries owned by ISC totals 55 million gallons, making the company one of the ten largest in the United States.

Ives

Inky color, intense, grapey flavor and full body characterize this labrusca variety. Acreage is about 600 and declining, and Isabella is still produced as a varietal by only a few wineries in Arkansas and New York.

J

JAEGER INGLEWOOD WINERY
St. Helena, San Francisco Bay North

The Jaeger family has long been identified as producers of high quality grapes which have gone into the wines of Freemark Abbey and Rutherford Hill (the Jaegers are partners in both wineries). In 1983 the family completed a small 10,000 gallon winery that will produce only Merlot, blended with small amounts of Cabernet Sauvignon and Cabernet Franc.

Output: 4,000 cases

Wine: Merlot

JEKEL VINEYARD
Greenfield, Central Coast

Television producers Bill and Gus Jekel began planting vineyards in Monterey County in 1972. By the time these vines — 140 acres of them — matured in 1978, a winery had been built in the Salinas Valley.

Their first release of a Johannisberg Riesling was an instant success and established a firm niche for Jekel wines in markets throughout the United States. Jekel has remained remarkably consistent with this variety; in each vintage, the full Riesling flavors, aromas, and fruitiness are balanced by crisp acidity. In some vintages — the 1983 is an example — the development of botrytis adds nuances of honey.

Another white variety that is recognized as a Jekel specialty — the not-too-common Pinot Blanc, a white-fruited member of the Pinot Noir family — is vinified and aged in a Chardonnay style. The result is a wine that is a virtual Chardonnay substitute, at a lower price. Of course the Jekel Chardonnay itself is not to be overlooked; Bill Jekel recently took home a best-of-show award for his 1982 Chardonnay in a London tasting that included the greatest Chardonnays from around the world.

Though Jekel's reputation has always been strongest for white wines, the winery is also capable of producing magnificent reds. In the same year that Jekel won the top Chardonnay award in London, its 1979 Private Reserve Cabernet Sauvignon also defeated first-growth Bordeaux, and far more expensive California Cabernets. The wine is rare, but Jekel also

Output: 30,000 cases

Leading Wines:
Johannisberg Riesling,
Pinot Blanc, Pinot Noir;
Special releases:
Private Reserve Cabernet
Sauvignon,
Private Reserve
Chardonnay,
Late-Harvest
Johannisberg Riesling,
Muscat Cannelli

bottles a more widely available Cabernet — also first-rate — that is labeled Home Vineyard.

Proficiency with reds is further demonstrated in Jekel's treatment of Pinot Noir; the fickle grape responds to the Monterey environment with a wine of delicacy, charm, and a set of flavors reminiscent of wines from Burgundy, the home of Pinot Noir.

Jekel Vineyard is near Greenfield in the Arroyo Seco Viticultural Area (officially approved in 1983) in the heart of the Salinas Valley, one of the coolest winegrowing regions in the United States. This allows long, slow ripening of the grapes grown there, which maintains high acidity but delays completion of the harvest until mid-November or, sometimes, early December. Grapes such as these often feature greater flavor intensity.

Expansion is currently underway to increase vineyards to 320 acres.

JIMARK WINERY
Healdsburg, San Francisco Bay North

Output: 8,000 cases

Leading Wines:
Cabernet Sauvignon,
Chardonnay

A recent addition to the growing number of wineries that call Healdsburg home, Jimark was founded in 1982. It leases 140 acres of vineyards, and has storage capacity of 65,000 gallons. Jimark specializes in only two varietals: Cabernet Sauvignon, and a ripe, oaky Chardonnay. They are bottled under the Michtom label.

Johannisberg Reisling, See White Riesling

JOHNSON ESTATE WINE
Westfield, Lake Erie

Output: 10,000 cases

Leading Wines:
Aurora, Cascade,
Chancellor, Delaware,
Liebestropfchen,
Seyval Blanc

In the heart of western New York's Chautauqua grape district, Johnson Estate has been vineyard land for well over a century. The Johnson family started producing wine in 1861, making this the oldest farm winery in New York State.

The estate concept is an important part of Johnson's identity; all grapes come from 125 acres of vineyards immediately surrounding the winery. Johnson's varieties reflect a strong sense of regionalism, bordering on Chautauqua chauvinism. The native-American Delaware grape is prominent in four of the eleven wines made, including Johnson's hallmark dessert wine, Liebestropfchen, with its florid nose and lush, musky fruit flavor. Ives Noir and Cascade are two less familiar varieties from New York's vinous past that have faded away elsewhere but keep plugging along at Johnson Estate. The intent here is to make unpretentious, affordable wine for the average consumer who knows what he likes. Seyval and Chancellor are the dry dinner wines.

J

JOHNSON TURNBULL VINEYARD
Oakville, San Francisco Bay North

Output: 1,500 cases

Wine:
Cabernet Sauvignon

Only one varietal, estate-bottled Cabernet Sauvignon, is produced by this 20,000-gallon winery, which was opened in 1977. The grapes are field crushed, then fermented in stainless steel. The wine is aged in upright oak tanks and small Limousin barrels for nearly two years. Given egg white fining prior to bottling, the Johnson Turnbull Cabernet receives additional aging in bottle before release.

Johnson Turnbull is small but its wine has already received very favorable critical attention.

JORDAN VINEYARD AND WINERY
Healdsburg, San Francisco Bay North

Output: 60,000 cases

Leading Wines:
Cabernet Sauvignon,
Chardonnay

Tom Jordan's original impulse for his winery came from his love of Bordeaux wines. French laws prevented him from buying a Medoc chateau and Jordan was forced to look elsewhere.

After an encounter with Beaulieu Vineyards Private Reserve Cabernet Jordan became convinced that fine Cabernet Sauvignon could be made in California, and many years of planning went into the creation of a winery in Sonoma's Alexander Valley in 1976. The winery clearly shows the influence of Jordan's first love; it is inspired both functionally and aesthetically by the chateaux of the Bordeaux region. More important, the wine that is produced there is also decidedly French in style.

To achieve this, Jordan hired the ubiquitous California wine consultant André Tchelistcheff. Cabernets are made from grapes in the Alexander Valley (Cabernet Sauvignon and Merlot), see aging for approximately two years in a combination of French and American oak, and are not released until approximately four years after the vintage date. The Jordan style is easily recognizable: the wines are rich and luscious, with an impression of sweetness on the tongue (despite the fact that they're fermented completely dry). They are accessible in youth, though they also age marvelously. A canny marketing campaign has helped to establish Jordan Cabernet Sauvignon as the first choice of many Cabernet drinkers seeking a high-quality wine at a price to match.

Jordan has 280 acres of vineyards and 250,000 gallons of storage capacity. The current winemaker is Mike Rowan.

J

CHATEAU JULIEN
Carmel, Central Coast

Output: 20,000 cases

Leading Wines:
Cabernet Sauvignon,
Chardonnay,
Private Reserve
Chardonnay,
Chateau Blanc,
Chateau Rouge,
Johannisberg Riesling,
Merlot,
Sauvignon Blanc

Located in Carmel Valley, Chateau Julien owns 8 acres of vineyards and leases an additional 45. The winery, housed in a building styled after a French country chateau, contains 64,000 gallons of fermentation capacity and produces five varietals. Its Private Reserve Chardonnay is probably the most interesting of its line. In addition to the five varietals, Chateau Julien is cellaring a sparkling wine and releases two Sherries from a solera dating to 1955.

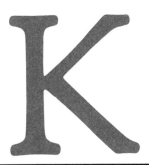

KALIN CELLARS
Novato, San Francisco Bay North

A small urban winery that draws upon some of the best north coast vineyards to make vineyard-designated wines, using "traditional" European techniques.

Output: 5,000 cases

Leading Wines:
Chardonnay, Pinot Noir

KARLY WINES
Plymouth, Sierra Foothills

A small, Shenandoah Valley winery, built in 1979, Karly's wines are produced from its own vineyards and purchased grapes. Chardonnay grapes are bought entirely from Central Coast vineyards and output of Zinfandel is supplemented with grapes from older Amador County vines.

Output: 5,000 cases

Leading Wines:
Chardonnay, Estate Red
(Barbera, Zinfandel and
Petite Sirah blend),
Petite Sirah, Zinfandel

KATHRYN KENNEDY WINERY
Saratoga, San Francisco Bay South

This Santa Cruz Mountain winery, founded in 1979, produces one intense varietal, Cabernet Sauvignon, by "natural" winemaking techniques.

Output: 400 cases

Wine: Cabernet
Sauvignon

KENWOOD VINEYARDS
Kenwood, San Francisco Bay North

Kenwood Vineyards dates from 1970, when six wine enthusiasts purchased the old Pagani Brothers Winery (built in 1906) in the Valley of the Moon. Modern winemaking equipment was installed, designed to vinify each lot of grapes separately: Kenwood produces anywhere up to 40 different wines in a vintage.

In addition to grapes grown in its own vineyards, Kenwood purchases grapes from well-known vineyards, such as Beltane Ranch. All wines are made from grapes grown in the Sonoma Valley Viticultural Area and carry this appellation on their labels. Many of the wineries in this area produce big-style wines — as opposed to the more northerly and westerly

Output: 75,000 cases

Leading Wines:
Cabernet Sauvignon,
Chardonnay, Chenin
Blanc, Gewurztraminer,
Johannisberg Riesling,
Pinot Noir, Sauvignon
Blanc, Zinfandel

Sonoma wineries — and Kenwood is no exception to this rule.

Kenwood is especially known to wine lovers for its Sauvignon Blanc, whose distinctive varietal character is enhanced by aging in small oak cooperage, and their rich Artist Series Cabernet Sauvignon.

KIONA VINEYARDS
Benton City, Washington

Output: 7,000 cases

Leading Wines: Cabernet Sauvignon, Chardonnay, Chenin Blanc, Lemberger, Riesling

A partnership of two families, Jim and Pat Holmes and John and Ann Williams, Kiona planted its first vines in 1975 on Red Mountain at the far eastern end of the Yakima Valley. Thirty acres are now in vine, and 20 more are planned.

Kiona was the first to plant Lemberger commercially, a little-known vinifera red wine grape principally from Wurttemberg, Germany, and release it as a varietal wine. But, whereas German Lemberger is a light fruity wine of modest distinction, Kiona's Lemberger is deeply colored, oak-aged, full-bodied, and somewhat tannic. Their version has recently garnered much interest.

KISTLER VINEYARDS
Glen Ellen, San Francisco Bay North

Output: 6,000 cases

Leading Wines: Cabernet Sauvignon, Chardonnay, Pinot Noir

Chardonnay is considered the specialty of this 19,000 gallon winery: three vineyard-designated Chardonnays are in current release: Dutton Ranch, Winery Lake, and Sonoma Valley. Founded in 1978, Kistler has a good reputation for its rich, complex versions of this varietal and its similarly full-bodied vineyard-designated reds.

KNUDSEN ERATH WINERY
Dundee, Oregon

Output: 20,000 cases

Leading Wines: Chardonnay, Gewurztraminer, Pinot Noir, Riesling, Sauvignon Blanc, sparkling wine

One of the founding fathers of the modern Oregon wine industry, Dick Erath first became interested in starting a commercial winery on a 1967 trip to the state. In 1972 Erath developed a vineyard for Cal Knudsen in the Red Hills near Dundee, in the northern Willamette Valley, and a partnership was formed in 1975, with Erath functioning as the winemaker and vineyard manager.

In the late 1960s and early 1970s Riesling was considered the safe grape for the fledgling Oregon wine industry, but Dick Erath was one of the first to give significant emphasis to Pinot Noir. Oregon Pinot Noirs were not always consistently good in the early days, but Erath developed a reputation for producing some of the best. Pinot Noir is still the lead wine, full-bodied and full-flavored, sometimes fairly tannic, often moderate in acidity, and immediately engaging in youth with an almost sweet character. The Pinots with higher acidity from good years age well.

Chardonnay and Riesling are Knudsen Erath's other principal wines.

The winery produces several other varietals, including small quantities of a fine Sauvignon Blanc from Oregon grapes. The best wines from the best years are given the designation Vintage Select.

Knudsen Erath is also moving into the production of bottle-fermented sparkling wine from a blend of Pinot Noir and Chardonnay. New vineyards have been planted on cooler slopes for a steady supply of suitable grapes, and in cooler vintages, less-ripe grapes are set aside for the sparkling wine.

KONOCTI WINERY
Kelseyville, San Francisco Bay North

Konocti has been in the forefront of the renaissance of grape growing and winemaking in Lake County, north of the Napa Valley. A cooperative of 25 Lake County growers who formerly sold their grapes to wineries in Napa, Sonoma, and Mendocino counties, Konocti produces two blanc de noirs wines and a crisp Fumé Blanc, considered the specialty.

Output: 40,000 cases

Leading Wines:
Cabernet Sauvignon,
Fumé Blanc, Sauvignon
Blanc, White Riesling,
White Zinfandel

KORBEL
Guerneville, San Francisco Bay North

Korbel is the oldest and, by a wide margin, the largest producer of *méthode champenoise* sparkling wines in the United States. The founding Korbel brothers, Francis, Anton, and Joseph, immigrants from Bohemia, produced their first crush of 25,000 gallons in 1882, three years after they had begun planting vines on the banks of the Russian River.

The Korbel cellars are now owned by the Heck family, who purchased the winery and vineyards from the Korbels in 1954. Adolf Heck, who guided the company until his death in 1984, is credited with a number of innovations in the production of bottle-fermented sparkling wines. Best known is his technique for automatic riddling; riddling is the process of twisting sparkling wine bottles to accumulate the sediment in the neck, and the riddling machine saves many hours of hand labor. At a time when most California sparkling wines were sweet, he began producing drier cuvées, introducing Brut in 1956, with only 1 percent dosage sugar. He followed Brut with Natural, with 0.5 percent dosage sugar, in 1959. Both were instantly successful. A Blanc de Blancs — made completely from Chardonnay grapes — was introduced in 1982.

Korbel owns 650 acres of vineyards, but fills 70 percent of its needs for grapes by purchases. Storage capacity is 2,800,000 gallons.

Output: 600,000 cases

Leading Wines:
Blanc de Blancs, Blanc de
Noirs, Brut, Extra Dry,
Natural, Rosé, Rouge, Sec

HANNS KORNELL CHAMPAGNE CELLARS
St. Helena, San Francisco Bay North

Since 1952 Kornell has made sparkling wines by *méthode champenoise*. All Kornell's base wines are purchased from selected wineries in Napa,

Output: 85,000 cases

Leading Wines:
Blanc de Blancs, Brut,

K

Sonoma, and Alexander valleys. These base wines are not the traditional Pinot Noir and Chardonnay of Champagne, but primarily Johannisberg Riesling and Chenin Blanc. This tends to come through in Kornell's wines as a fruity quality which appeals to some, but others find excessive.

Sehr Trocken (German for very dry) is Kornell's equivalent to a *Tête de Cuvée*, and is completely dry. Blanc de Blancs is the latest Kornell wine, made entirely of Chenin Blanc, and like most of Kornell's other wines is drier than its equivalents and shows good effervescence.

CHARLES KRUG WINERY
St. Helena, San Francisco Bay North

Output: 1.5 million cases

Charles Krug is credited for making the first wine in the Napa Valley by European techniques — in a proper press, not in stretched cowhide. In 1861 he founded the winery bearing his name — the oldest in the Napa Valley. Krug operated the winery until his death in 1892, although phylloxera devasted his vineyards in the 1880s.

Since 1940 the winery has been run by the Mondavi family who began to bottle some of their wines under the Charles Krug label and slowly and persistently built up a reputation for the wines.

Peter Mondavi now runs the 6-million gallon winery. Fourteen varietals and three generics are sold under the Charles Krug label; under the second label of C.K. Mondavi it produces four generics and three varietals.

L

LA CREMA VINERA
Petaluma, San Francisco Bay North

Founded in 1979, La Crema Vinera specializes in the two Burgundian varieties, Pinot Noir and Chardonnay, made from grapes grown in the cool Carneros Viticultural Area and in Sonoma County. In any given vintage they produce a non-vineyard designated "California" Chardonnay and a "California" Pinot Noir. But their leading wines are vineyard-designated; notably a Winery Lake Pinot Noir, Winery Lake Chardonnay, and Dutton Ranch Chardonnay (other vintage vineyards).

This vineyard-designated program promises some outstanding wines. The Carneros district Winery Lake Vineyard, owned by Rene di Rosa, is well-known for the quality of both its Chardonnay and Pinot Noir grapes. Dutton Ranch's reputation for Chardonnay is also well-established; in 1982 it produced the grapes from which half a dozen wineries produced outstanding Chardonnays.

Output: 10,000 cases

Leading Wines:
Chardonnay, Pinot Noir

LAKE ERIE

Lake Erie exerts a complex influence over the climate of its shoreline, particularly to the south and east where it borders western New York, the northwest corner of Pennsylvania, and northern Ohio. Its most beneficial effect is to extend the growing season here by warming arctic air masses as they pass over its open water. Vineyards close to the lake have frost-free seasons of 175 to 200 days, longer than any other part of the northeast except Long Island, and grapes often ripen well into November.

But Erie is a shallow lake and loses its stored heat early in winter. (It is the only Great Lake that usually freezes.) In the spring, this ice mass delays bud break in nearby vineyards until after the danger of spring frosts. But in the middle of winter, the lake's frozen surface gives no protection against Canadian cold fronts. Cold-sensitive grape varieties that otherwise flourish here are occasionally ravaged by temperatures down to –20°F, and winds that help flush out fungus diseases in summer can desiccate exposed vines in February.

L

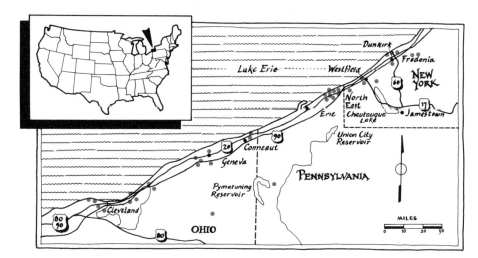

While climate binds the vineyards of Lake Erie, soil and history give the wines variety. On the New York-Pennsylvania end of the grape belt, deep, well-drained glacial till predominates. In northern Ohio topsoil gets shallower over limestone.

Vineyards were planted rapidly along the lake in the mid-19th century, and Ohio's Erie Islands became one of the East's early wine centers. Some of the oldest wineries have survived and continue making Catawbas and other old varieties that, perhaps more than anywhere else, sustain the legacy of Eastern wine. At the other end of the lake, the temperance movement organized at the Chautauqua Institution in the 1870s persuaded farmers to plant the Concord grape for fresh fruit and juice. As a result, winemaking did not become significant here until after Prohibition, when the first kosher wineries began making sweet Concord for specialized markets. This remains the major wine market for Lake Erie grapes. But since the 1960s, small farm wineries ringing the lake from Cleveland to Buffalo have discovered the potential for French-American hybrid and vinifera varieties.

LANDMARK VINEYARDS
Windsor, San Francisco Bay North

Output: 22,000 cases

Leading Wines:
Cabernet Sauvignon,
Chardonnay, Petit Blanc

Landmark Vineyards has been a family operation since its founding in 1974 by retired Air Force officer William Mabry, Jr. and his wife and son.

Landmark owns 90 acres of vineyards in three Viticultural Areas: Alexander Valley, Sonoma Valley, and Chalk Hill. Approximately two-thirds of Landmark's production is Chardonnay. Fermented at 48°F to 57°F, the young wine is aged in small oak cooperage for 4 to 8 months, depending on the age of the barrel.

The balance of Landmark's production is mostly Cabernet Sauvignon. It is aged for 12 to 18 months in wood, a fairly lengthy stay, followed by an additional 2 years in the bottle before release. A third wine called Petit Blanc is a proprietary blend of Chenin Blanc and Sauvignon Blanc.

F.W. LANGGUTH WINERY
Mattawa, Washington

Output: 600,000 cases

Leading Wines:
Chardonnay,
Gewurztraminer, Riesling

F.W. Langguth Winery was the first in the Northwest to be principally financed by a foreign corporation, in this instance F.W. Langguth Erben GmBh, a giant German winemaking operation. In the late 1970s, the corporation began exploring winemaking regions as widespread as Australia, Italy, Spain, and California. On the advice of Dr. Helmut Becker, director of the famous viticultural school at Geisenheim in Germany, Langguth came to Washington.

Langguth chose the Wahluke Slope in Washington's Columbia Valley, a new and highly promising Viticultural Area. The first vines of the 221-acre vineyard were planted in 1981, but grapes for Langguth wines are also purchased from other Columbia Valley growing areas.

Since the first crush in 1982, the parent company in Germany has exercised close supervision of winemaking operations. But winemaker Max Zellweger, a Swiss-trained enologist, is being granted increasing authority, and recent wines have shown very well.

Not unexpectedly for a winery with German parentage, Riesling is the flagship wine, and Langguth takes advantage of the exceptionally favorable Washington growing conditions. Washington Riesling can easily be cropped to six or more tons an acre with intense fruit and excellent sugar and acid balance. Thus there is little need for a high cropping, low-acid grape like Muller-Thurgau, the principal grapes of Liebfraumilch, even for Langguth's inexpensive generic blends. Recent Langguth Riesling special selections and individual vineyard bottlings are among the state's best.

Saddle Mountain is a new label for a line of moderately priced varietals, which includes Cabernet Sauvignon, Gewurztraminer, and Chardonnay, all made in a fruity style for early drinking. None of Langguth's wines see oak.

Late Harvest

Wines made from grapes picked significantly later than the normal harvest time are often labeled "Late Harvest." Residual sugar and concentrated flavor are typical of these wines, as the grapes begin to lose some of their water content in advanced stages of ripeness. Residual sugar in a late-harvest wine may range from 4-16 percent. The effects of *Botrytis cinerea* ("the noble mold") on the grapes are often evident in honey and apricot flavors in the wine. But acetic acid is the nemesis of these wines, and its vinegary taste indicates that the grapes have begun to break down.

Because of reduced yields, risks in delaying the harvest, and selective hand-picking, late-harvest wines are almost always limited in production and high priced.

L

LATAH CREEK WINE CELLARS
Spokane, Washington

Output: 12,000 cases

*Leading Wines:
Chardonnay, Chenin
Blanc, Fumé Blanc, May
Wine, Merlot, Muscat
Canelli, Riesling*

Latah Creek is one of three wineries in the Spokane metropolitan area of eastern Washington. Grapes are purchased from Columbia Valley growers, principally the Hogue Ranches in the Yakima Valley.

Light and fruity wines have been winemaker Mike Conway's specialty since Latah Creek began in 1982, and his Riesling and Chenin Blanc have set a style now emulated by other Washington winemakers. The wines are characterized by low alcohol, crisp acidity, some residual sugar, and intense fruity flavors.

The Chenin Blanc is particularly notable. Normally a wine of modest interest, Conway's rendition displays a distinct varietal profile and a balanced interplay between its residual sugar and acidity. A specialty of Latah Creek is the Hungarian May Wine, which Conway learned to make when he was assistant winemaker at Parducci from cellarmaster Joe Monostori. Latah Creek's May Wine, made from Chenin Blanc flavored with woodruff and strawberry concentrate, is a luscious wine with a harmonious intermingling of flavors.

LAUREL GLEN VINEYARD
Santa Rosa, San Francisco Bay North

Output: 4,500 cases

*Wine:
Cabernet Sauvignon*

Founded in 1980, Laurel Glen produces Cabernet Sauvignon exclusively. Its 35 acres of vineyards were first planted to vines in the 1880s, and have been active continuously since then. In 1968 they were replanted to Cabernet Sauvignon, with a small amount of the other Bordeaux grapes (Cabernet Franc, Malbec, and Petit Verdot) which are used for blending. At 1,000 feet above sea level, the vines are above the fog line and as a result of their northeast exposure, receive the benefit of mild morning sunshine and oblique afternoon sun. As a consequence, the growing season is long and cool, and the grapes ripen with high acidity and intense fruitiness. These qualities in the grapes make for long life and varietal intensity in the wines.

LEELANAU WINE CELLARS
Omena, Michigan

Output: 10,000 cases

*Leading Wines:
Aurora, Baco Noir,
Cabernet Sauvignon,
Chardonnay,
Chelois Rosé, De Chaunac
Rosé, Merlot,
Leelanau White,
Rosé, and Red,
Vignoles*

The warmth of the surrounding waters of Lake Michigan spawned a community of fruit farms on the Leelanau peninsula that inevitably led to wine, pioneered by Leelanau Wine Cellars in 1975. Its line of 14 wines consists mainly of semidry varietals and blends from French-American hybrid varieties.

At least a touch of residual sweetness is used to balance relatively high acid levels from Leelanau's cool climate. In the better varietals, this is accomplished with a "sweet reserve" of grape juice added back to the wine. The Leelanau White blend is the flagship wine: light, crisp, and fruity.

Lees

Sediment collected at the bottom of tanks or other containers after fermentation or clarification. Lees are composed of dead yeast cells and other precipitated solids.

LEEWARD WINERY
Oxnard, Central Coast

This 40,000-gallon winery, founded in 1978, has captured a deserved reputation for full-bodied vineyard-designated Chardonnays. Beginning with its first vintage in 1979, Leeward purchased grapes in four highly-touted and widely separated vineyard areas: Santa Maria Valley, Edna Valley, Monterey, and Amador counties.

Output: 8,500 cases

Leading Wines:
Chardonnay, Coral (Pinot Noir Blanc), Sauvignon Blanc, Zinfandel

LENZ VINEYARDS
Peconic, Long Island

Lenz was established in 1978 on Long Island's North Fork by the former owners of a restaurant well-known for classic interpretations of local produce. As might be expected, the 30-acre estate is devoted to wine varieties and styles that complement local foods, especially shellfish. The best example is Gewurztraminer, dry with delicate, clovelike spice and good acid. The densely planted vinifera vineyard is reined-in for yields of 2 to 3 tons per acre to intensify varietal character. Lenz Reserve blends Cabernet Sauvignon, Merlot, and Cabernet Franc for a classically structured claret.

Output: 6,000 cases

Leading Wines:
Chardonnay, Gewurztraminer, Merlot, Pinot Noir, Reserve

LIVERMORE VALLEY CELLARS
Livermore, San Francisco Bay South

Formerly a grower only, Livermore Valley Cellars now specializes in production of estate-bottled white wines. All the grapes are grown in 34 acres of Livermore Valley vineyards, which are carefully pruned to yield less than 2 tons per acre (a phenomenally low amount). Founded in 1978, the winery has 15,000 gallons of storage capacity. All wines are aged in small oak barrels.

Output: 2,000 cases

Leading Wines:
Blanc de Blancs, Chardonnay, Fumé Blanc, Grey Riesling, Pinot Blanc, Servant Blanc

LLANO ESTACADO WINERY
Lubbock, Texas

The winery name means "staked plains," referring to wooden markers set out by Francisco Coronado on his 16th century search for gold in this part of north-central Texas. But today, the vineyard trellis posts stencilling new vineyards around Lubbock give the name fresh meaning. Llaño Estacado buys grapes from several of these independent vineyards.

Output: 25,000 cases

Leading Wines:
Cabernet Sauvignon, Rosé of Cabernet, Chardonnay, Chenin Blanc, French

L

Colombard,
Gewurztraminer,
Johannisberg Riesling,
Zinfandel

The winery began in 1976—the first new Texas winery in this century—and has become the acknowledged quality leader among the state's dozen and a half wineries, repeatedly earning top honors at the state fair wine judgings. A rich, lemony Gewurztraminer, flinty Colombard, and ripe, fleshy Cabernet Sauvignon suggest a big future for high plains Texas wine. Cool nights preserve high fruit acids despite relatively hot summers, and the wines inherit firmness and keeping power without hot-climate muscle. Nonvintage red and white blends are marketed under a "Staked Plains" label.

LLORDS AND ELWOOD WINERY
San Jose, San Francisco Bay South

Output: 25,000 cases

Leading Wines:
Cabernet Sauvignon,
Chardonnay, Pinot Noir,
Port, Rosé of Cabernet,
Sherry (dry, medium,
sweet), sparkling wine

Founded in 1955, Llords and Elwood was one of the first California wineries to produce premium quality ports and sherries. The first releases of dessert and aperitif wines were made in 1961, and the list has been extended to include several table wines and a sparkling wine.

In early 1985, the sale of Llords and Elwood to Jay Corley, owner of Monticello Cellars in the Napa Valley, was announced. At that time also plans were announced to move the 150,000-gallon Llords and Elwood operation to the Napa Valley, where it would continue to operate as a separate entity under its own name.

J. LOHR WINERY
San Jose, San Francisco Bay South

Output: 240,000 cases

Leading Wines:
Cabernet Sauvignon,
Chardonnay, Chenin
Blanc, Fumé Blanc,
Gamay, Johannisberg
Riesling, Pinot Blanc,
Pinot Noir, Petite Sirah

On a site formerly occupied by a brewery in downtown San Jose, Lohr Winery was established in 1974. Although an unlikely location, it has produced some fine Pinot Blancs, made in a full-bodied style, and Gamays that have been flavorful and dark, one of the closest American equivalents to Beaujolais.

Grapes are brought to the winery from various areas: the Napa Valley, Arroyo Seco in Monterey County, and Clarksburg in Sacramento County. Five hundred acres of vineyards are owned in Monterey. Storage capacity is 980,000 gallons.

LONG ISLAND

The twin forks of Long Island jutting into the Atlantic have seen the most explosive growth of any new wine district in the eastern United States. In 1972 there was only one commercial vineyard on New York's Long Island, with a few acres of table grapes supplying a roadside stand. Its success with cold-sensitive vinifera varieties inspired the island's first wine grape vineyard near Cutchogue. Barely a decade later, there were more than 1,000 acres of grapevines spreading over the island's East End. Failing potato and vegetable truck farms have been reborn in vines, followed by wineries that found the old potato storage barns well suited to barrels and tanks.

Long Island is the only eastern viticultural district planted exclusively in European vinifera grapes. Growers have put their faith in the warming waters of the Atlantic that moderate winter temperatures and extend the growing season (the first killing frost of fall rarely comes before November). Cabernet Sauvignon, Pinot Noir, and Sauvignon Blanc flourish on all sites and ripen regularly on most, in stark contrast to the state's other grape regions. Chardonnay, White Riesling, and Gewurztraminer are the other principal varieties, producing wines with more body and color than their upstate counterparts.

Each fork has secured its own official label "appellation" (North Fork of Long Island and The Hamptons), reflecting some distinction between their growing conditions. More protected from off-shore weather patterns (and from urban development), the North Fork has attracted most of the activity. But Long Island wine styles have barely begun to take shape. Among the challenges are buffeting winds, extremely fertile soils, vigorous growth, and high pH values that jeopardize wine stability.

LONG VINEYARDS
St. Helena, San Francisco Bay North

Output: 1,500 cases

Leading Wines: Chardonnay, Johannisberg Riesling

Vineyards for this small winery were first planted in 1966, but it wasn't until 1978 that Zelma and Bob Long opened their winery. In the meantime Zelma Long had studied at U.C. Davis and established her place as one of the premier winemakers in California, usually a male preserve.

Now at Simi, Long also shares winemaking responsibilities with her husband at their own winery, producing estate-bottled wines that are generally of a very high standard.

LOS VINEROS WINERY
Santa Maria, Central Coast

Output: 15,000 cases

Leading Wines: Cabernet Sauvignon Blanc, Cabernet Sauvignon, Chardonnay

With 80,000 gallons of storage capacity, Los Vineros purchases grapes from Santa Maria and Santa Ynez vineyards owned by the winery partners.

LOWDEN SCHOOLHOUSE WINERY
Walla Walla, Washington

Output: 1,500 cases

Leading Wines: Gewurztraminer, Merlot, Semillon

First crushing grapes in 1983, Lowden Schoolhouse Winery is one of several new small wineries in the Walla Walla Valley. Owned and operated by Baker and Jean Ferguson, the winery is in a converted rural schoolhouse and all grapes are purchased. The winery's focus is on Semillon and Merlot.

L

LOWER LAKE WINERY
Lower Lake, San Francisco Bay North

Output: 7,500 cases

Leading Wines:
Cabernet Sauvignon,
Fumé Blanc, "White"
Cabernet Sauvignon

Lower Lake Winery was founded in 1977 and was the first commercial winery to operate in Lake County (north of Napa Valley) after Prohibition. Although Lower Lake owns 53 acres of vineyards, it also purchases grapes from other Lake County vineyards. Recent approval of Clear Lake as a Viticultural Area permits Lower Lake to identify it as the appellation of its wines.

LYETH
Geyserville, San Francisco Bay North

Leading Wines:
Lyeth Red, Lyeth White

Founded in 1981, Lyeth (pronounced leeth), owns 300 acres of vineyards in the Alexander Valley from which it produces two wines. Most significant is that Lyeth has chosen to label its wines simply as red or white, after the Bordeaux style, and not as varietals. The red is a blend of Bordeaux varieties — Cabernet Sauvignon, Cabernet Franc, Merlot, and Malbec — as is the white — Sauvignon Blanc, Semillon, and Muscadelle de Bordelaise. Exact percentages of each are not given, and the winery hopes to encourage and add further to the trend away from the American pattern of varietal labeling. First released in 1985, early response to the red wine has been extremely favorable. Sales of 10,000 cases annually of both wines are anticipated.

LYNFRED WINERY
Roselle, Illinois

Output: 4,000 cases

Leading Wines:
American (CA) Cabernet
Sauvignon, Chardonnay,
Illinois Apple,
Johannisberg Riesling,
Michigan Seyval Blanc,
Michigan Vidal Blanc

In an elegant house on the suburban fringe of Chicago, this unlikely little winery shops for grapes and fruit in Michigan, Washington, California, and Illinois. Batches are made and labeled separately, although everything ages for at least a few months and up to two years in oak. Geographically and viniculturally, Lynfred's 16 varietal and 13 fruit wines are all over the map.

LYTTON SPRINGS WINERY
Healdsburg, San Francisco Bay North

Output: 10,000 cases

Leading Wines:
Valley Vista Private
Reserve Zinfandel,
Sonoma County Zinfandel

The source of Lytton Springs widely-known Zinfandel is Valley Vista Vineyard which owns 50 acres of 80 year-old Zinfandel vines. Wines made from these grapes are dark, heavy, and intensely varietal.

Since 1979, Lytton Springs has also purchased grapes from other nearby vineyards, blending them with Valley Vista grapes to produce a Sonoma County Zinfandel.

Lytton Springs Zinfandels are among the most sought-after of California Zinfandels by lovers of old-fashioned, powerhouse Zins.

Made and Bottled by

This phrase on the label indicates that at least 10 percent of the wine was fermented at the winery named, according to federal regulations, and most of the wine was purchased from other sources. This low percentage requirement enables a winery to pass off purchased wine as its own. (If the wineries truly made (fermented) all the wine, the label would read "produced and bottled by.") Generally this phrase does not indicate a top-quality wine.

MADRONA VINEYARDS
Camino, Sierra Foothills

Output: 4,000 cases

Leading Wines:
Cabernet Franc, Cabernet Sauvignon, Chardonnay, Gewurztraminer, Johannisberg Riesling, Merlot, White Zinfandel, Zinfandel

Dick and Leslie Bush were aware of the history of winegrowing in El Dorado County, which had more vineyards growing there than did either Napa or Sonoma counties in the 19th century, when they bought 50 acres of land five miles north of Placerville in 1972. During the following two years they planted 35 acres to vines on a ridge 3,000 feet above sea level, the highest vineyard in California.

By 1980, when their vines were mature, they had completed a small, modern winery, housed in an equally modern building, surrounded by conifers and oaks, and containing 63,000 gallons of storage capacity.

Malolactic Fermentation

The same type of bacteria that sours milk, and produces cheese and sauerkraut can also affect wine. Called malolactic fermentation, the action of the bacteria converts malic acid (associated with apples) in the wine to lactic acid (associated with milk). It is a conversion encouraged in many red wines to transform simple, fruity qualities of the grape into more complex scents and flavors, among them a buttery quality. Malolactic fermentation is usually avoided in the production of white wines to preserve their fruitiness; but it is sometimes used with Chardonnay and a few other varieties when fruitiness is not a primary element of the style.

M

Another aspect of malolactic fermentation — the reduction of acidity — recommends it to cool-climate districts producing high acid wines. When it occurs inadvertently after a wine is bottled, malolactic fermentation spoils wine flavors and leaves it murky and gassy.

Malbec

A red vinifera, Malbec is used in California primarily for blending with other Bordeaux varieties, as it is in France. About 60 acres are planted in California.

Marechal Foch

Often simply called Foch, this is the most widely grown red French-American hybrid variety (De Chaunac probably has more total acreage but all concentrated in the Finger Lakes area). With acreage of about 500, it has become a fixture in vineyards from New England to New Mexico and Virginia to Minnesota, even popping up in Oregon. The vines are vigorous, adaptable, and relatively disease resistant.

White Riesling was one of the grandparents in the cross-breeding of Foch and a bright, berrylike fruitiness is prominent in the nose and taste of the wine. This, along with a high malic component in the acidity and a tendency to mature quickly, has led vintners to pattern their winemaking style after Beaujolais. Foch is typically light-to-medium bodied, ready to drink within a year of the vintage, with little or no flavor of wood cooperage to interfere with fresh berry aromas and flavors. The challenge to winemakers is a degree of bitter weediness picked up in fermentation on the skins. Skin contact is usually limited, sometimes totally eliminated for a claret-style or rosé. The technique of carbonic maceration used to make Beaujolais Nouveau works well with Foch, for holiday wines also labeled "nouveau."

MARKKO VINEYARD
Conneaut, Lake Erie

Output: 1,500 cases

Leading Wines:
Cabernet Sauvignon,
Chardonnay, Covered
Bridge White and Red,
Pinot Noir, Riesling,
Underridge

Markko's diminutive scale belies its accomplishments and stature among the quality leaders of eastern American wine. The vineyard has slowly grown to just 14 acres since 1968, when Arnulf Esterer, an industrial engineer, founded Markko.

One of the early disciples of Konstantin Frank, the pioneer of vinifera viticulture in New York State, Esterer concentrated on Riesling and Chardonnay. Smaller plantings of Cabernet Sauvignon and Pinot Noir (first vintage 1985) were added as the variables of Markko's site revealed themselves. Situated in the extreme northeastern corner of Ohio, the vineyard benefits from nearby Lake Erie for a long ripening season but is periodically hard hit by winter freezes. This translates into relatively full-bodied white wines and marginally varietal, spicy Cabernets in variable quantities from year to year. Rain during harvest is sometimes a problem, adding to significant difference between vintages. Nevertheless Markko has established a distinctive style of earthy, mature wines, often with mellow wood tones.

MARK WEST VINEYARDS
Forestville, San Francisco Bay North

Output: 18,000 cases

Leading Wines: Chardonnay, Gewurztraminer, Johannisberg Riesling, Pinot Noir, Pinot Noir Blanc, méthode champenoise sparkling wine

A 68,000-gallon winery founded in 1976, Mark West's 62 acres of vineyards are evenly divided between Chardonnay, Johannisberg Riesling, Gewurztraminer, and Pinot Noir.

Each of the three white varieties receives some skin contact before fermentation to increase varietal complexity. The Chardonnay get special treatment; half the must is barrel-fermented, and half is cold-fermented in stainless steel. The two lots are later blended and aged in small oak.

The winery had been best known for its crisp varietal Gewurztraminer, but the recent critical success of its 1981 Chardonnay has broadened its reputation.

LOUIS M. MARTINI WINERY
St. Helena, San Francisco Bay North

Output: 300,000 cases

Leading Wines: Barbera, Cabernet Sauvignon, Chardonnay, Chenin Blanc, Folle Blanche, Gamay Beaujolais, Gewurztraminer, Johannisberg Riesling, Merlot, Moscato Amabile, Petite Sirah, Pinot Noir, Sauvignon Blanc, Semillon, White Zinfandel, Zinfandel

In 1983, the Louis Martini Winery celebrated 50 years of winemaking in the Napa Valley. The winery is still a family enterprise operated by the second and third generations, and is one of three (of 54) wineries established in the Napa Valley at Repeal still owned and operated by its founding family.

Louis M. Martini had produced wines, grape juice, and concentrates before Prohibition. But the history of the winery dates from 1940 when Martini released the entire range of vintage-dated, aged varietals he had been storing at the St. Helena winery he built after Repeal. It was a bold pioneering move, but one which immediately established a reputation for the quality of Louis Martini wines.

Martini remained a pioneer in many other ways. Long before refrigerated fermentation tanks became common in the industry, he built a large, insulated cold room to cold-ferment his white wines. In order to control grape quality and variety, Martini was one of the first major wineries to buy and develop its own vineyards. (One of the legacies of Prohibition which is still evident today is the separation of vineyard and winery ownership.)

Despite its size (3.6 million gallons), Martini retains something of the atmosphere of a much smaller winery. Both Martini's son and grandson (who is now winemaker) have preserved the spirit of experimentation, whether it be with yeast strains or fermentation temperatures, or with the line of wines they release.

Louis Martini is probably best known for its red wines, which comprise nearly two-thirds of its output, particularly Cabernet Sauvignon, Zin-

fandel, and Barbera. However, its Gewurztraminer, in the dry, full-bodied Alsatian style, has long been valued by wine lovers. Folle Blanche, produced as a varietal only by the Martini Winery, has its followers, while the fruity, slightly effervescent Moscato Amabile, also uniquely Martini, has a host of admirers. Said by Louis M. Martini to be the result of a happy accident, this wine is available almost exclusively at the winery.

Martini has always been a reliable source of attractive, well-priced wines that have rarely reached great heights but have always avoided the lows. The current generation appears to be pushing the winery towards the production of complex and exciting varietal wines through the addition of Vineyard Selection to the Private Reserve and Special Selection lines begun in earlier years. Private Reserve and Special Selection are offered only in certain years. Of the two, the Special Selection generally represents more interesting wines and is given extra barrel-aging prior to release. This is put to good use in better vintages by Martini's Cabernet Sauvignon and Pinot Noir.

Chardonnay, Merlot, Pinot Noir, Cabernet Sauvignon, and Zinfandel are currently offered with vineyard designations.

PAUL MASSON VINEYARDS
Saratoga, San Francisco Bay North

Paul Masson and Almadén both trace their origins to Etienne Thée, the Bordeaux winemaker who planted vineyards near Los Gatos in 1852. Control of these vineyards eventually passed to Paul Masson, a phylloxera-refugee from a Burgundian winemaking family. Masson planted his own mountainside vineyards which he called La Cresta, overlooking the Santa Clara Valley in 1896. In 1905, he built a winery on the vineyards and continued to operate his mountainside winery until he sold it to Martin Ray in 1936. In 1942, Ray sold the business to the House of Seagram, the Canadian-based distillers and wine distributors who are the present owners.

At the end of World War II, when urban development in Santa Clara County replaced thousands of acres of vineyards with housing tracts, the Paul Masson winery began looking southward to Monterey County, eventually planting 3,400 acres of grapes there. In 1966, a new winery was built in nearby Soledad to produce table wines.

The flagship wines of Paul Masson are those carrying the Pinnacles Estates designation. Many of Masson's grapes are planted on slopes on the eastern side of the Salinas Valley in two vineyards designated as Pinnacles I and Pinnacles II. When these grapes were fully mature, Paul Masson released its first vintage-dated wines, beginning with a 1977 Pinnacles Estate Chardonnay in 1979. This program has expanded to include several white varietals, but has so far met with mixed success. About 50,000 cases of the Estates program are released each year.

Output: 8 million cases

Leading Wines:
Varietals:
Cabernet Sauvignon,
French Colombard,
Gamay Beaujolais,
Grenache Rosé,
Johannisberg Riesling,
Petite Sirah, Pinot Blanc,
Sauvignon Blanc;
Pinnacles Estates
Selections:
Chardonnay, Fumé Blanc,
Gewurztraminer;
Dessert and Aperitif
wines, Sparkling wines,
brandy

With over 37 million gallons of storage capacity in four locations, Paul Masson is today on the edge of becoming one of the ten largest wineries in the United States. For years Masson has provided dependable wines at reasonable prices. The wines rarely exhibit uncommon complexity, but the selections from the Pinnacles Vineyards clearly stand out as excellent values in mid-range premium wines. Masson produces a list of more than 40 wines, including a dozen generics, nearly 20 varietals, 4 sparkling wines, and 10 aperitif and dessert wines.

MASTANTUONO WINERY
Paso Robles, Central Coast

Pasquale Mastantuono founded his 25,000-gallon winery in 1977. It is best-known for its rich flavored, full-bodied Zinfandels, and for several years this was the only wine Mastantuono made. Fifteen acres of Zinfandel vines in the vineyards are supplemented by purchases from Dusi Vineyard in which 75-year-old vines yield grapes of marked varietal intensity. All grapes are purchased for the other varietals.

MATANZAS CREEK WINERY
Santa Rosa, San Francisco Bay North

Matanzas Creek Winery, established in 1977, is situated in the Bennet Valley, a microclimate just west of the more famous Sonoma Valley. First harvest was in 1978, and the winery has quickly established a wide and enthusiastic following. Both the 1982 Chardonnay and Sauvignon Blanc have topped lists of the best California wines made from those varietals in that year.

Nearly half the output of the winery is its full, oaky Chardonnay. Seventy percent of the wine is barrel-fermented from initiation of fermentation to its completion. The Sauvignon Blanc contains a small percentage of Semillon and is aged in small French oak barrels.

MAYACAMAS VINEYARDS
Napa, San Francisco Bay North

At the end of a narrow, winding road, Mayacamas is perched on a ridge separating the Napa and Sonoma Valleys. The 45 acres of hillside vineyards are on steep, terraced slopes. Mayacamas is the prototypical Napa mountain winery: the grapes and wines produced here demonstrate the full intensity of mountain-grown grapes.

Mayacama's rich and powerful Cabernets and Zinfandels have a legion of admirers who wait for the completion of aging in the bottle that is required to bring them to their most enjoyable drinking. Mayacamas produced one of California's first late-harvest Zinfandels, a massive wine with 17 percent alcohol that has as many detractors as it has enthusiasts.

PAUL MASSON
MONTEREY
CHARDONNAY
1983

ESTATE
BOTTLED

Output: 7,000 cases

Leading Wines:
Cabernet Sauvignon,
Chardonnay, Chenin
Blanc, Muscat Canelli,
Sauvignon Blanc, White
Zinfandel, Zinfandel

Output: 5,000 cases

Leading Wines:
Cabernet Sauvignon,
Chardonnay, Merlot,
Sauvignon Blanc

Output: 7,000 cases

Leading Wines:
Cabernet Sauvignon,
Chardonnay, Pinot Noir,
Sauvignon Blanc,
Zinfandel

M

MAZZA VINEYARDS
North East, Lake Erie

Output: 6,500 cases

Leading Wines:
Cayuga, Commemorative
Red, Dutchess, White
Riesling, Seyval Blanc,
Vidal Blanc

On the edge of Lake Erie in Pennsylvania's northwestern corner, Mazza produces light, fruity wines generally finished with some residual sweetness (even if labeled "dry"). All grapes are purchased for 20 labrusca, French-American hybrid, and vinifera varietals and blends.

McDOWELL VALLEY VINEYARDS
Hopland, San Francisco Bay North

Output: 50,000 cases

Leading Wines:
Cabernet Sauvignon,
Chardonnay, Chenin
Blanc, French Colombard,
Fumé Blanc, Grenache,
Petite Sirah, Zinfandel

The McDowell Valley is a vineyard area which had been known for its sympathetic microclimate in the mid-19th century. McDowell began planting here in the early 1970s and its vineyards extended to include all the plantable land within the valley, 360 acres in all. After selling grapes to other northern California wineries for several years, McDowell built its own winery in 1979.

In 1982, McDowell Valley Vineyard's petition for recognition of McDowell Valley as a Viticultural Area was approved by BATF, making the estate vineyards and the Viticultural Area virtually co-terminous. Geographically the valley is distinct from surrounding areas, as is its microclimate. Temperature records show that as a consequence of marine air flow, McDowell Valley is cooler in summer and warmer in the spring, making the region relatively frost-free at this critical period of the growing season.

To date, the winery has demonstrated fine consistency with a wide range of grapes. There is very much a feeling of evolution about the wines of McDowell Valley Vineyards, and the critical success that will put this potential-laden winery on the map has yet to emerge.

McLESTER WINERY
Inglewood, South Coast

Output: 2,000 cases

Leading Wines:
Cabernet Sauvignon,
Runway Red, Runway
White, Sauvignon Blanc,
Suite 13, Zinfandel,
Zinfandel Rosé

Founded in 1979, Cecil McLester's winery produces several vintage-dated, vineyard-designated wines from Central Coast grapes. Early specialties were Cabernet Sauvignon and Zinfandel made from grapes grown in San Luis Obispo and Amador counties. In 1984 Sauvignon Blanc and Merlot were added to the line, which is produced in this 8,500-gallon facility close to the Los Angeles airport. Three proprietary blends—Runway White (Thompson Seedless, French Colombard, and Muscat); Runway Red (Ruby Cabernet and Barbera); and Suite 13 (a sweet Muscat dessert wine with 13 percent residual sugar and 13 percent alcohol)—round out the line.

M

MEIER'S WINE CELLARS
Silverton, Ohio

Output: over 500,000 cases

Meier's is by far the largest of Ohio's 40-odd wineries and one of the oldest, with roots in the remnants of Nicholas Longworth's early 19th century Cincinnati wine empire. Although the main winery remains in the Cincinnati suburb of Silverton, Meier's has expanded operations with vineyards and winery facilities in northern Ohio. The estate vineyards are on Lake Erie's Isle St. George, including one of the largest plantings of European vinifera varieties in the eastern United States. With the longest growing season anywhere in the interior Northeast, the island promises very ripe fruit, suggesting a big, rich, California wine style to Meier's cellarmen. But, as yet, harsh winters and viticultural problems have plagued the project.

Leading Wines: Chardonnay, Chateau Reim Champagne, Cocktail Sherry, Cream Sherry, Gewurztraminer, Johannisberg Riesling, Pink Catawba, Sauternes, Vermouth

The winery's sherries have been more successful — among the best examples of the transformation of labrusca grapiness into smooth, rich fruit. Meier's native grape table wines include a soft, light Catawba with more delicacy than the variety generally achieves. Lonzbrusco is a sweet, fruity Concord wine in the style of Lambrusco.

The first part of the name refers to the old Lonz Winery in northern Ohio, purchased by Meier's in 1980. The nearby Mon Ami and Mantey wineries, also dating back to the last century, were bought at the same time. All three have become satellite facilities sharing aspects of production and marketing.

MEREDYTH VINEYARDS
Middleburg, Virginia

Output: 10,000 cases

When the Smith family began planting grapevines in 1972 (at the start of Virginia's wine renaissance), they were regional pioneers as no one knew which varieties suited the Atlantic Piedmont. Fifty-four acres have been planted with two dozen French-American and vinifera varieties. Most of these are made into small lots of vintage varietals that have gone a long way toward mapping out northern Virginia's vinicultural landscape.

Leading Wines: Cabernet Sauvignon, Chardonnay, De Chaunac, Harvest Red, Marechal Foch, October Harvest, Riesling, Rougeon Rosé, Seyval Blanc, Villard Blanc, Villard Noir

Meredyth's wine style tends to let the area's lush growing seasons and rich, red soil run riot in the wines, producing big, intense reds and full-bodied whites. Its red wines are fermented extensively on the skins, often in new barrels, to extract maximum body, color, and tannin. They are routinely aged for a year or more in American oak to soften and mature, but still have plenty of keeping power. Harvest Red is the notable exception, made without skin or wood contact for a fresh, fruity, early wine. Meredyth's whites often show oak aromas and flavors within rich, ripe fruit. The regular Chardonnay has tighter structure and more finesse than the intense, barrel-fermented, California-style Special Reserve. Meredyth Seyval Blanc is a muscular, mature fruit version of the variety. A lush, late-harvest Seyval with moderate residual sugar is labeled October Harvest.

M

Merlot

The predominant grape of St. Emilion, this red vinifera was originally planted in California in the 1970s for blending, to soften Cabernet Sauvignon, which it resembles in aroma and flavor. But many wineries found that it makes an interesting varietal in its own right. There are 2,100 acres in California, 1,300 of which are in San Francisco Bay North. Elsewhere, in Washington and certain eastern regions this grape is only occasionally produced as a varietal, with little marked success as yet.

MESA VERDE
Rancho California, South Coast

Output: 4,000 cases

Leading Wines: Cabernet Sauvignon, Chardonnay, Chenin Blanc, Sauvignon Blanc, White Riesling

Eighty-nine acres of vineyards are owned by Mesa Verde. Vineyard-designated Sauvignon Blanc comprises nearly half the current output. But expected soon are a Johannisberg Riesling and a Chenin Blanc with an Orange County appellation, probably the first since the destruction of the Anaheim vineyards by Pierce's Disease in the 1880s.

Approximately half of Mesa Verde's 100,000-gallon storage capacity is devoted to custom work for other wineries.

MESSINA HOF WINE CELLARS
Bryan, Texas

Output: 7,000 cases

Leading Wines: Cabernet Sauvignon, Chenin Blanc, Papa Paulo Porto, Sweet Bianco, Vino Di Amore, White Zinfandel

In the humid, eastern part of Texas, Messina Hof stands apart from the rest of the state's new wineries. The high likelihood of vine disease in this climate led the Bonnarigo family to hedge its bets and plant a cross-section of old Texas, vinifera, and French-American hybrid varieties. Grapes are also purchased from the western part of the state, bringing more diversity into the product line.

There is a stronger sense of Italian family roots than of Texas pioneering and the wines often carry family names for house blends. Blending is an important part of the cellar strategy here, including varietally labeled wines—Messina Hof has no fetish for pure varietal character. Red wines are modeled after Bordeaux, with plenty of tannin and staying power and prominent oak. The whites lean toward a German style with some residual sugar. Zinfandel is a specialty in offbeat styles, such as a nouveau and a semidry white.

THE MERRY VINTNERS
Santa Rosa, San Francisco Bay North

Output: 6,000 cases

Wine: Chardonnay

Merry Edwards, who guided Matanzas Creek through their first six vintages, established her own winery with the 1984 crush to produce Chardonnay in two styles. One is a light, fruity, tank-fermented version, intended primarily for restaurant sales and for early release. The second Chardonnay will be partially barrel-fermented, and vinified in the relatively full-bodied style which characterized the well-received Chardonnays Merry Edwards made at Matanzas Creek.

Méthode Champenoise

The classic (and only permissable) method used to produce sparkling wine in the French Champagne district and the way America's best sparkling wines are made is indicated on American labels as "*Méthode Champenoise*" or "Fermented in This Bottle." In this process the wine undergoes its second fermentation (which produces effervescence) in the bottle. Sediment from that fermentation is removed by disgorging and the wine is topped up with a *dosage*. Keeping the wine in the bottle from start to finish retains more of the qualities imparted by the second fermentation than the transfer process or bulk fermentation, including creamy texture and small bead (bubbles). But the amount of individual handling in *méthode champenoise* sparkling wines is reflected in higher prices.

MICHIGAN

The mass of Lake Michigan, plunging toward the nation's midsection, shelters the largest vineyard district outside west and east coast states. Nearly all Michigan's vineyards lie along the east shore of the lake, where prevailing northwest winds cool the land in summer, warm it in winter, prolong fall ripening weather, and pile up insulating snow in winter. Temperatures rarely exceed 90°F or drop below –10°F, remarkable for the Midwest, permitting the cultivation of relatively hardy wine varieties, mainly whites.

Grapes have been grown on the lake's shores since the mid-1880s, but all its wineries have opened since Prohibition. Beginning in the 1970s, experiments with French-American hybrid and vinifera varieties narrowed Michigan's focus to Vidal Blanc, Vignoles, and Riesling. These are varieties that respond best to long, cool growing seasons by accumulating fruity esters. Michigan whites show bright fruit with more roundness than delicacy. There are some good sherries and country reds. Most of the 14,000 acres of vineyards are concentrated in the southwestern corner of the state, including those devoted to Concord grapes not used for wine. The Leelanau and Old Mission peninsulas to the north grow only wine grapes.

MID-ATLANTIC COAST

The relatively new wine district arcing from New Jersey across southeastern Pennsylvania and Maryland into northern Virginia has acquired the name Mid-Atlantic Coast, for want of a better term. Some part of Virginia logically falls within this district, in terms of growing conditions and wine styles, but Virginia has developed its own wine identity and is treated separately in this book.

M

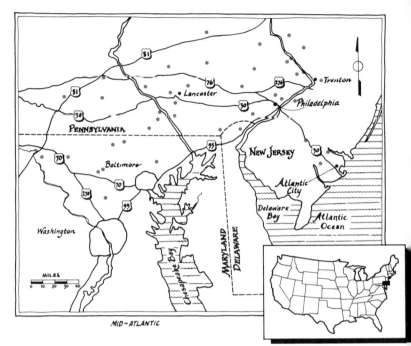

MID-ATLANTIC

In its brief tenure, the Mid-Atlantic region has begun to emerge as the East's first serious red wine district, while also producing many fine white wines. Climate is the key to this. The vineyards are far enough south and sufficiently within the maritime influence of the Atlantic to grow more tender varieties than the Finger Lakes, for example, and to bring grapes to fuller, fatter maturity. Higher sugars at harvest often translate into bigger wines with more alcohol than those made to the north. But the climate here is still continental, so that acids for balance and structure are still retained in the wines. Consequently, acids and sugars are closer in proportion to wines of Bordeaux than to north coast California wines.

In fact, cold damage is a nagging problem for Mid-Atlantic winegrowers, and surprisingly this chilling effect diminishes as one moves north through the district. Wildly fluctuating winter temperatures and spring frosts often reduce crops, creating more economic damage than quality problems.

Most vineyards are planted in rolling terrain where eastern spurs of the Appalachian Mountains descend to relatively flat, coastal land. Hillsides improve soil and frost drainage and lift vines above the heaviest humidity, but rot and mold are still a constant challenge to the production of clean wines, calling for major vineyard spray programs.

Nearly all the vineyards in this region have been established since the mid-1970s. Early plantings of French hybrid varieties have shifted to an emphasis on European vinifera grapes, particularly in Virginia and Maryland. Cabernet Sauvignon has done well on the best sites, producing wines with strength and finesse. Chardonnay and Sauvignon Blanc also show good varietal adaptation. Among French hybrids, Seyval, Chambourcin, and Marechal Foch stand out. There were about 60 wineries in the Mid-Atlantic region in 1985.

MILANO VINEYARDS AND WINERY
Hopland, San Francisco Bay North

Since its launching in 1977, Milano has specialized in producing flavorful, full-bodied Chardonnays from its Mendocino County location. Seventy-five percent of the production of this 40,000-gallon winery is Chardonnay. Grapes for all its wines are purchased from vineyards in Mendocino and Sonoma counties.

Output: 10,000 cases

Leading Wines:
Cabernet Sauvignon,
Chardonnay,
Late-Harvest Zinfandel,
White Zinfandel,
Zinfandel

MILL CREEK VINEYARDS
Healdsburg, San Francisco Bay North

Mill Creek, with 70 acres of vineyards in the Dry Creek Valley Viticultural Area, was founded in 1975. The 50,000-gallon winery is noted for its Cabernet Sauvignon, Merlot, and Cabernet Blush, a trademarked name for smoked salmon-colored Blanc de Noirs from Cabernet Sauvignon. This is the only winery in California that is legally allowed to call the popular, light-colored wine from red grapes 'blush wine'.

Output: 10,000 cases

Leading Wines:
Cabernet Blush, Cabernet
Sauvignon, Gamay
Beaujolais,
Gewurztraminer, Merlot,
Pinot Noir, Sauvignon
Blanc

Leon Millot

A close relative of the red French-American hybrid Marechal Foch, Millot (Leon is sometimes left off labels) is similar to Foch but with somewhat fuller body and heavier flavors that can develop a chocolatey quality.

MIRASSOU VINEYARDS
San Jose, San Francisco Bay South

With five generations having continuously run the winery since it was founded by Pierre Pellier in 1854, the Mirassous can claim to be America's oldest winemaking family. But it was not until 1966 that their winery distributed under the family name; until that point, Mirassou wines were sold in bulk to other wineries.

Besides marketing under their own name, the current generation of the Mirassou family has made several other innovations at the winery. In the late 1950s urbanization of the area around the winery in the Santa Clara Valley persuaded them to look for acreage elsewhere, and Mirassou became one of the pioneers of Monterey County. A consequence of this move was that the winery and vineyards were two hours apart. But after several years of experimentation, Mirassou introduced first the practice of mechanical harvesting and, more recently, field-crushing to ensure the freshness of the grapes. (Field-crushing is still a controversial practice but one that is winning more converts with each vintage.) Mirassou's *méthode champenoise* sparkling wines established a good reputation when they were introduced in the late 1960s. Recent vintages have not been up to the early standards, however, and lack the complexity of their predecessors.

Output: 300,000 cases

Leading Wines:
Cabernet Sauvignon,
Chardonnay, Chenin
Blanc, Fumé Blanc,
Gamay Beaujolais,
Johannisberg Riesling,
Monterey Riesling, Petite
Sirah, Pinot Blanc, Pinot
Noir, Zinfandel; Sparkling
Wines: Au Naturel, Blanc
de Noir, Brut

Special lots of Mirassou Chardonnay, Fumé Blanc, Cabernet Sauvignon, and Pinot Noir are labeled as Harvest Reserve. This designates wines made from specially selected barrels which are determined by the winemaker to merit extra care and aging. In the case of Chardonnay, it also means that the wine was barrel-fermented.

Mirassou occupies an unusual position among California's large producers of premium wines. Not only does it offer a wide range of well-made wines at attractive prices, but it also manages to produce the occasional wine of top quality. This was perhaps accomplished more regularly in the 1960s than it is today, but a 1977 Anniversary Selection Zinfandel was one of the outstanding wines produced from that grape in recent memory.

Mission

Brought to California by the Franciscan missionaries at the end of the 18th century, this red vinifera formed the basis of their viticulture and the earliest commercial vineyards in California. (The Mexicans call this variety Criolla, and it is still widely planted in Mexico.) There are just over 3,000 acres of Mission remaining in California. Although occasionally made as a varietal and more often as a sweet white dessert wine, its chief use now is as a blending grape.

MISSOURI

Although Missouri's days of glory were before Prohibition, the state has developed a modest, modern wine industry. German immigrants planted the first vineyards along the Missouri River west of St. Louis in the 1830s. By the end of the Civil War, and into the 20th century, the state ranked second in wine production.

Particularly devastating to Missouri vintners, Prohibition left a legacy of huge stone cellars and native American grape vineyards. Those old varieties — Catawba, Concord, Niagara, Delaware — continue to dominate Missouri wine with their sweet, grapey flavors. But French-American hybrids now play a role in most cellars, and half a dozen wineries — led by Mt. Pleasant, Stone Hill, and Hermannhof — are committed to making dry, European-style wines. Seyval and Vidal Blanc have been the leading varietals.

Mid-continent extremes of climate regularly put Missouri vineyards to the test: spring frosts, drought, blistering summer heat waves (40 days over 100°F in 1980), and winter lows down to –25°F. Only hardy varieties produce dependably, and vintages can fluctuate wildly in size and character. Favorable microclimates and deep-soil sites give some growers a critical edge, especially those located along the Missouri River.

In the early 1980s, total vineyard acreage in the state was approximately 1,100 acres; wine production ranked ninth in the nation. Only about half the grape crop is used for wine.

MOGEN DAVID WINE
Westfield, Lake Erie

Mogen David is the home of Concord wine. The urgent, raw grape flavor of Concord is ameliorated by heating the must, then diluting and blending it with California wine. Sparkling wines are carbonated. Most of Mogen David's wines are finished with sweetness; many are fortified with brandy; 30 percent are kosher. The winery was moved from Chicago in 1967 to be closer to the source of grapes, which are purchased from Chautauqua County growers.

Output: Over 3 million cases

Leading Wines: Blackberry Royal, Golden Chablis, Concord, Cream Red Concord, Cream White Concord

MONARCH WINE COMPANY
Brooklyn, New York

Although it is one of the largest winemaking facilities in the United States, covering a 7-square block area of Bush Terminal on New York Harbor, Monarch's name rarely appears on labels. Its major brand is Manishewitz, under a royalty agreement made with the famous kosher food company when Monarch opened for business following Prohibition. A number of other brand names are also used, and Monarch does a thriving business in private labels. All wines are kosher, although only about 15 percent of Monarch's market is Jewish.

Grapes—primarily Concord, but also Niagara, Catawba, Delaware, and some French-American hybrids—are purchased in the Lake Erie area, where they are pressed and stored as juice. Tank trucks shuttle the juice year-round to Brooklyn for fermentation and finishing. Blending wines come from California to moderate labrusca flavors. Other fruits and fruit bases (blackberry, cherry, loganberry, and elderberry) come from as far afield as Ireland, Holland, and Austria, as well as New England and the Northwest.

All Monarch wines are fermented dry, then sweetened to varying degrees. Monarch's sparkling wine production is one of the largest in the nation, much of it private labeled, and all bottle-fermented (transfer process).

Output: Over 4 million cases

Leading Wines: Champagne, Cold Duck, Concord, Cream White Concord, Sparkling Burgundy, Tina Coconetta

ROBERT MONDAVI WINERY
Oakville, San Francisco Bay North

A great innovator and ambassador of the California wine industry, Robert Mondavi is one of the leading figures in American winemaking. Since his departure from Charles Krug in 1966 to open his family-owned winery, the first to be built in the Napa Valley following Repeal, Robert Mondavi has consistently produced wines that combine critical success with popular appeal.

From the beginning the new winery demonstrated Mondavi's forward-looking commitment. His Mission-style building included temperature-controlled, stainless steel fermentation tanks which had not been used

Output: 1.4 million cases

Leading Wines: Cabernet Sauvignon, Chardonnay, Chenin Blanc, Fumé Blanc, Johannisberg Riesling (Late-Harvest, Botrytis and Special Selection), Moscato d'Oro,

Pinot Noir;
Sauvignon Blanc,
Robert Mondavi
Vintage Red,
White, and
Rosé Wines

1983
Napa Valley
FUMÉ BLANC
Dry Sauvignon Blanc
ALCOHOL 13% BY VOLUME
PRODUCED AND BOTTLED BY
ROBERT MONDAVI WINERY
OAKVILLE, CALIFORNIA

before in the Napa Valley, and other advanced equipment. The Oakville facility was also the first to use a centrifuge for clarification after fermentation, replacing the slower method of settling by gravity and racking. Mondavi also introduced small French oak barrels for aging his red wines and some whites on a scale larger than had been seen up to that time in California.

But Mondavi's most influential innovation is probably Fumé Blanc, introduced in 1967. For it Mondavi took a previously undistinguished grape — Sauvignon Blanc — and styled it to resemble the Pouilly-Fumé of the Loire Valley. Through the success of this wine Mondavi single-handedly created a new market for California wines made from this grape and demonstrated both his skill as a winemaker and the extent of his influence.

From its first crush of only a few hundred cases the winery has grown rapidly. There are now nearly 2 million gallons of storage capacity at Oakville and another 6 million at the Woodbridge winery Mondavi purchased in 1979. Formerly belonging to a growers' cooperative, the Woodbridge facility produces the popular multi-varietal blends: Robert Mondavi Vintage Red, White, and Rosé.

Although no longer small, Mondavi has retained the ability to treat each lot of wine differently, to ferment individual lots of grapes, and to bring them to maturity separately. Winemaker Tim Mondavi (Robert Mondavi's son) has the option to barrel-ferment some Chardonnays and Fumé Blanc, for example, or to induce malolactic fermentation in those wines that would benefit from the added complexity this would impart.

Perhaps the most important recognition of the winemaking talents of the Mondavi family was the invitation of Baron Phillippe de Rothschild, proprietor of Chateau Mouton-Rothschild, to cooperate in a joint venture to produce a California-French wine in 1975.

After nearly ten years of preparation and of fermenting, aging, and bottling, the first vintages of that joint venture were introduced in 1984. Called "Opus One," the vintages of 1979 and 1980 were released simultaneously. These first vintages, blends of Cabernet Sauvignon and Cabernet Franc, were made in the Oakville winery by the combined winemaking efforts of Tim Mondavi and Lucien Sionneau, winemaker at Chateau Mouton.

Opus One is just another piece in a very familiar Mondavi pattern. The winery has always stood for innovation and high quality, and has always been remarkably prescient in setting and anticipating new trends. Mondavi is a major force in the California wine industry, both in its line of so many remarkably consistent wines in the marketplace, and in the influence it has exerted on countless other California wineries.

R. MONTALI WINERY
Berkeley, San Francisco Bay South

Overlooking Aquatic Park in Berkeley, Montali is part of what appears to be a growing phenomenon — the urban winery. (There are now half-a-dozen in Berkeley and an equal number in the greater Los Angeles area.) Montali draws upon such distant viticultural locations as Santa Maria Valley in the south and from the closer Napa Valley and Amador County for their grapes. Founded in 1982, Montali has 200,000 gallons of storage capacity.

Output: 60,000 cases

Leading Wines:
R. Montali Label:
Cabernet Sauvignon,
Chardonnay,
Gewurztraminer, Pinot
Noir, Sauvignon Blanc,
Zinfandel

MONTBRAY WINE CELLARS
Westminister, Mid-Atlantic Coast

A pioneer in the Mid-Atlantic states, Montbray began in 1964 with 600 vines and a mission to identify the varieties that would excel in this rolling part of central Maryland, near the Pennyslvania border. Vineyard and winery are the endeavor of G. Hamilton Mowbray, a former research psychologist at Johns Hopkins University. His 1966 Seyval (labeled Seyve-Villard after the hybridizer's nursery) was the first varietal wine from that grape. Seyval remains a specialty and one of the best examples of the variety, made in the dry style of an upper Loire Valley wine. Montbray also made the area's first Chardonnay, Riesling, and Cabernet Sauvignon. The winemaking style is traditionally French, relying on oak cooperage.

Output: 2,400 cases

Leading Wines:
Cabernet Sauvignon,
Chardonnay, Johannisberg
Riesling, Marechal Foch,
Seyve-Villard

MONT ELISE VINEYARDS
Bingen, Washington

Mont Elise Vineyards, near Bingen, is in a special microclimate at the point where the Columbia River cuts through the towering Cascade Mountains on its way to the Pacific. Temperate west and arid eastern climates collide, often tumultuously, along the gorge, and growing conditions change rapidly within short distances.

Mont Elise is in one of the few Washington microclimates suited to Pinot Noir. In the late 1960s, owner Charles Henderson experimentally planted 20 different grape varieties in the Bingen region in cooperation with Dr. Walter Clore and others from Washington State University's agricultural research center. Pinot Noir and Gewurztraminer showed best, and in 1972 Henderson planted his vineyards to them. Eighteen-acres are now bearing; 15 more have been planted.

In 1986, Mont Elise will release its first bottle-fermented sparkling wine. Made in a Brut style, the wine will spend at least two years on the yeast.

Output: 4,000 cases

Leading Wines:
Chenin Blanc,
Gewurztraminer,
Pinot Noir

M

MONTEREY PENINSULA WINERY
Monterey, Central Coast

Output: 12,000 cases

Leading Wines:
Barbera,
Cabernet Sauvignon,
Chardonnay,
Late-Harvest Chenin
Blanc, Malvasia Bianca,
Muscat Canelli,
Petite Sirah, Pinot Blanc,
White Zinfandel,
Zinfandel

A 100,000 gallon winery, Monterey Peninsula specializes in making small lots of 100 percent varietals from selected vineyards, including the 50 to 75-year-old vines of Ferrero Vineyards in Amador County and Dusi Vineyard of Paso Robles. Because of this emphasis, Monterey Peninsula may produce five to seven lots of Zinfandel, for example, in any year, each of which is fermented, matured, and bottled separately.

Monterey Peninsula is probably best-known for its Zinfandels in a full-bodied uncompromising style. Generally, fermentation lasts for 10 to 20 days, extracting the maximum of color and flavor from the skins to produce the "big" red wines for which the winery is noted. Extended aging in small oak barrels follows, during which the wines are clarified by settling and racking. Chardonnay and Pinot Blanc are barrel-fermented in French oak and then aged in the same barrels for a year or more.

For its size, Monterey Peninsula produces an enormous range of wines. A late-harvest Zinfandel is produced in both dry and sweet styles. In those years in which Botrytis mold develops on the grapes, Late-Harvest Johannisberg Riesling and/or Late-Harvest Chenin Blanc is made. In addition, several fruit wines (plum and apricot, for example) and Malvasia Bianca and Muscat Canelli are made in a dessert style.

THE MONTEREY VINEYARD
Gonzales, Central Coast

Output: 125,000 cases

Leading Wines:
Cabernet Sauvignon,
Chardonnay,
Chenin Blanc,
Classic Dry White,
Classic Red, Fumé Blanc,
Gewurztraminer,
Johannisberg Riesling,
Petite Sirah, Pinot Blanc,
Riesling,
Sauvignon Blanc,
Zinfandel

VINTAGE 1978

SAN LUIS OBISPO COUNTY
BOTRYTIS SAUVIGNON BLANC
DESSERT WINE
SPECIAL SELECTION

PRODUCED AND BOTTLED BY THE MONTEREY VINEYARD • B.W. 4674
GONZALES, MONTEREY COUNTY, CA. USA • ALCOHOL 15.5% BY VOL.

One of the largest early wineries in Monterey, The Monterey Vineyard has passed through some difficult times since it was founded in 1974. Starting with high hopes for Monterey varietals, it began making wine just as demand was slackening and its more than 2 million gallons of storage capacity had to be turned over to production for other wineries. Briefly owned by the Coca Cola Company, in 1983 Seagram took control of The Monterey Vineyard.

Northern Monterey County, where the Monterey Vineyard is located, is the coolest grapegrowing region in the United States. Harvest dates are 6 to 8 weeks later than for the same varieties in the Napa Valley, for example. This posed problems at first for Monterey grapegrowers. Warm climate varieties such as Cabernet Sauvignon were not ripening properly, and left a green, vegetative taste in the wines. However, pioneers like Dr. Richard Petersen at Monterey Vineyards began to match grape varieties with locations to take advantage of this cool microclimate. The correct grapes ripen to more balanced sugar/acid ratios, and have a varietal intensity not usually found in other regions. This is further enhanced by the low yields of 1½ to 3 tons per acre in the upper Salinas Valley. In the past, Monterey Vineyards have taken advantage of the long, cool, dry growing season to allow grapes to hang on the vines well past usual harvest dates to produce a Thanksgiving Riesling and a December Harvest Zinfandel.

Botrytis develops every year in their vineyards and this has made it possible to produce botrytised Sauvignon Blanc, a wine similar to the naturally sweet Sauternes of Bordeaux. In 1978 there was even a botrytised Pinot Noir.

MONTEVINA WINES
Plymouth, Sierra Foothills

Output: 30,000 cases

Leading Wines:
Barbera,
Cabernet Sauvignon,
Chardonnay,
Chevrier Blanc,
Sauvignon Blanc,
White Zinfandel,
Zinfandel

Launched in 1973, this 250,000 gallon winery has been in the forefront of the revival of Amador County and Sierra Foothills as grape-growing and winemaking regions. From its Shenandoah Valley vineyards Montevina produces full-bodied Zinfandels of great varietal intensity, and powerful Cabernet Sauvignons whose deep color belies a softness in the mouth and are among the best examples from this region.

Montevina was among the first wineries to experiment with Zinfandels in the "nouveau" style by carbonic maceration but these unusually fruity wines have been discontinued. The winery was also one of the earliest producers of the now-ubiquitous White Zinfandel. Success with Sauvignon Blanc, however, has resulted in the addition of this varietal, in a Fumé Blanc style to their line.

Montevina's vineyards are planted in rocky soil, which is mainly decomposed granite. A thin layer of top soil over a subsoil that is rich in minerals provides conditions not conducive to high yields and the vines yield about half the average California tonnage per acre. This, in combination with their cool, 1,700-foot elevation, tends to impart more definite varietal intensity to their grapes.

The output of Montevina's own vines has been supplemented with purchased grapes to produce a Chardonnay, while Semillon, under the name Chevrier Blanc, has recently been added to their line.

MOORE-DUPONT WINERY
Sikeston, Missouri

Output: 15,000 cases

Leading Wines:
Catawba, Chambourcin,
Sparkling Catawba,
Riesling, Seyval Blanc,
Vidal Blanc

Two growers in the southeastern part of the state formed this white wine specialty house in 1982. Catawba is the major product—fresh, semidry, still and sparkling. Dry and off-dry French hybrid varietals are well-made light table wines. The recent involvement of investors from California—a professor of enology and a viticultural consultant—suggests Moore-Dupont is a winery to watch.

J.W. MORRIS WINERY AND VINEYARD
Healdsburg, San Francisco Bay North

Output: 25,000 cases

Leading Wines:
Cabernet Sauvignon,
Chardonnay,

Founded in 1975, Morris made only port-style wines until 1979 when the line was expanded to include table wines. In 1983 Morris was purchased by the owners of Black Mountain Vineyard in the Alexander Valley, then the principal sources of their wine grapes.

Morris's two vintage ports are one-third Cabernet Sauvignon, one-third Zinfandel, and one-third Petite Sirah blend, from the 70 year-old vines in the Black Mountain Vineyard. The vintage-dated ports, produced in the Portuguese manner, are bottled after only two years of wood-aging. The late-bottled vintage port spends a minimum of five years in wood prior to bottling. The non-vintage Founders Port is made predominantly from Pinot Noir, which Morris Winery believes is the same grape as the Tinta Francisca, one of the traditional grapes grown in the Douro Valley in Portugal.

In 1985, Morris will add a Black Mountain label under which it will bottle Chardonnay, Cabernet Sauvignon, and Zinfandel made from selected lots of grapes. These wines will be fermented and aged separately from the J.W. Morris varietals and bottled after aging in small oak barrels.

Storage capacity at J. W. Morris Winery is 135,000 gallons.

Sauvignon Blanc,
Founders Port,
Red Reserve Port,
Vintage Port,
Late-Bottled Vintage Port,
White Private Reserve

MOUNT BAKER VINEYARDS
Everson, Washington

From its first crush in 1982, Mount Baker Vineyards was the largest producer of wine from western Washington grapes. Most of the wineries in the metropolitan areas west of the Cascades bring in grapes from the Columbia Valley east of the mountains.

In contrast to the sunny, warm, and dry climate of Columbia Valley, western Washington is cool and moist, and the suitable grape varieties are necessarily different. Mount Baker's emphasis is on little-known, cool-climate vinifera varieties. Stratton is experimenting with five different rootstocks for Chardonnay to reduce vegetative growth and foster early ripening. Mount Baker also experiments with the vines, which are trained to an overhead canopy; not, as the training method was designed, as a sun shield, but for protection against the rain.

Output: 8,000 cases

Leading Wines:
Chardonnay,
Gewurztraminer,
Madeleine Angevine,
Muller-Thurgau,
Okanogan Riesling,
Precoce de Malingre

MOUNT EDEN VINEYARD
Saratoga, San Francisco Bay South

A small 12,000-gallon winery with a relatively colorful history, its vineyards were first planted 2,000 feet above the Santa Clara Valley by Martin Ray in the 1940s. Ray made wines of great character and intensity for many years until his death in 1976 and his tradition was carried on in a limited production of full-bodied, estate-bottled Chardonnay, Cabernet Sauvignon, and Pinot Noir. A second Chardonnay is produced from Ventana Vineyards grapes, and sold under the MEV label.

Winery storage capacity is 12,000 gallons. Its small output is produced in tiny lots, some of only a few hundred cases—a reflection of the low yields from the 23 acres of old vines. The largest lots are those produced from Ventana grapes, which account for nearly half of the winery's total output.

Output: 2,700 cases

Leading Wines:
Cabernet Sauvignon,
Chardonnay,
Pinot Noir

Both Chardonnays are barrel-fermented in French oak and undergo a full malolactic fermentation. Mount Eden's red wines are vinified and aged in a 'traditional' manner, producing full-bodied, flavorful wines that can take lengthy aging.

MT. HOPE ESTATE AND VINEYARD
Cornwall, Mid-Atlantic Coast

This elegant estate of an early 19th century Pennsylvania ironmaster was reborn with vineyards and a winecellar in 1980. Mt. Hope is associated with Mazza Vineyards on Lake Erie, a source of grapes to supplement its small vineyard. Both generic and varietal wines are made from French-American hybrids, and late-harvest wines, Ravat and Vidal Ice Wine, have become a specialty.

Output: 9,000 cases

Leading Wines:
Burgundy, Chablis, Ravat, Seyval, Vidal

MT. PLEASANT VINEYARDS
Augusta, Missouri

A long bend of the Missouri River 35 miles west of St. Louis creates a sheltered microclimate around the town of Augusta that before Prohibition was home to 13 wineries. All were put out of business, but Mt. Pleasant was revived in 1968.

Dry, light, wines make up most of Mt. Pleasant's product line, led by a bone-dry Seyval Blanc with tart, grassy fruit reminiscent of a Loire Valley Sauvignon. Vidal is made slightly rounder, but still dry and brisk. The Munch grape—bred by Mt. Pleasant's founder in the late 19th century—survives here in commemorative red, white, and rosé bottlings. The winery strikes a balance between holding onto its legacy and spearheading a new, European-style generation of Missouri wines. The latter include limited bottlings of Chardonnay and Sauvignon Blanc.

Output: 25,000 cases

Leading Wines:
Blanc de Blancs, Cordon Rouge, Cynthiana, Munch Red, Pleasant Rosé, Seyval Blanc, Stark's Star, Vidal Blanc

MOUNT VEEDER WINERY
Napa, San Francisco Bay North

This 25-acre winery, founded in 1973, makes only two varietals: a barrel-fermented Chardonnay and a Cabernet Sauvignon. The latter contains enough Cabernet Sauvignon (75 percent) to be so labeled, but it is a Bordeaux-style blend, with some Cabernet Franc, Merlot, Petit Verdot, and Malbec. It is aged for two years in French oak before bottling and release.

Mount Veeder's vines are planted at an elevation of 1,000 to 1,600 feet on well-drained soil, consisting primarily of shale and volcanic ash. Although growing season temperatures are cooler than those on the Napa Valley floor, the grapes usually ripen a week earlier. The vineyards are not irrigated, and this, in combination with the other growing conditions in the Mount Veeder vineyards, results in small berry size and low yields

Output: 4,500 cases

Leading Wines:
Cabernet Sauvignon, Chardonnay

M

of approximately 2 tons per acre for the red varieties and less for the Chardonnay. As might be expected, the grapes tend to be intensely varietal, and the Chardonnay from this 15,000-gallon winery benefits from added balance given by the blend.

MULHAUSEN VINEYARDS
Newberg, Oregon

Output: 8,000 cases

Leading Wines:
Chardonnay,
Gewurztraminer,
Pinot Noir, Riesling,
Sylvaner

Having developed an interest in wine while in Europe, Zane Mulhausen planted a vineyard in the Chehalem Mountains in the northern Willamette Valley in 1973. A winery was bonded in 1979 and Mulhausen began to work full-time in the vineyard and winery. The expanded vineyard now comprises 40 acres.

As is common practice in Oregon, Mulhausen ages Chardonnay in French oak barrels, but he ferments the wine at relatively cool temperatures in stainless steel to preserve the cleanliness and fresh fruit of the grape.

Mulhausen is virtually the only Oregon winery producing a Sylvaner. An unusual wine, Mulhausen's version is both Riesling-like and earthy. Future plans call for the production of sparkling wine from Chardonnay and Pinot Noir grapes.

Muscadine

The specie of grapevine native to the southeastern states is classified as *Vitis rotundifolia* (for its large, round berries), popularly called Muscadines. Varieties within this species—Scuppernong, Carlos, Noble, Magnolia—are appearing more frequently on southern wine labels, but the term Muscadine itself is sometimes used to label wine from any of those grapes. The Muscadines share family characteristics of intense aromas and musky fruit flavors which are very distinct within the lexicon of wine types: the flavor of Muscadines is nearly as jarring to Catawba drinkers as it is to devotees of Chardonnay. This was the taste of the first American wine made at Spanish outposts four-and-a-half centuries ago, cultivated in rural southern tradition.

Muscat Blanc

Also known as Muscat Canelli and Muscat Frontignan, this white Vinifera makes aromatic wines finished anywhere between a light, dry style to fortified dessert wines. There are 1,600 acres of this grape planted in California. Interest is apparently increasing in light sweet wines made from it and labeled as Muscat Canelli. When labeled Muscat Frontignan, the wines are usually sweet and contain 18-20 percent alcohol.

NAPA CELLARS
Oakville, San Francisco Bay North

Output: 10,000 cases

Founded in 1976, Napa Cellars is now owned by the DeScheppes family of Belgium. Currently, winery capacity is 45,000 gallons and beginning with the 1984 vintage, Napa Cellars has bought grapes only from Napa Valley growers. The winery will continue to ferment a portion of Chardonnay in stainless steel for the sake of fruitiness, and a portion in French oak barrels for complexity and body.

Leading Wines:
Cabernet Sauvignon,
Chardonnay,
Sauvignon Blanc,
Zinfandel

NAPA CREEK WINERY
St. Helena, San Francisco Bay North

Output: 15,000 cases

Founded in 1980, since 1983 Napa Creek has produced a range of varietals from purchased grapes, some of which are vineyard-designated.

Storage capacity now stands at 70,000 gallons; much of it is in stainless steel. Sauvignon Blanc is made in a Fumé Blanc style; and Cabernet Sauvignon and Chardonnay are aged in small oak barrels. The Chardonnay is also barrel-fermented.

Leading Wines:
Cabernet Sauvignon,
Chardonnay,
Chenin Blanc,
Johannisberg Riesling,
Gewurztraminer,
Sauvignon Blanc

NASHOBA VALLEY WINERY
Concord and Bolton, New England

Output: 5,000 cases

Starting out in a suburban Boston basement in the late 1970s, Nashoba Valley grew rapidly into one of a small group of American wineries bringing a new status to fruit wines. Owner Jack Partridge aims to revive the New England fruit wine tradition with modern winemaking equipment and techniques.

The wines are finished at all levels of sweetness from bone-dry apple and oak-aged blueberry (one of the best, resembling a Beaujolais but with a Maine accent) to an intense, ripe. After Dinner Peach. Many awards in wine competitions attest to Nashoba Valley's rigorous standards and distinctive style.

Leading Wines:
dry and semisweet Apple,
Sparkling Apple,
Blackberry, Dry
Blueberry, Orchard Run,
After Dinner Peach, Pear

N

Natural

The driest category of sparkling wine. Sometimes spelled "Naturel," it identifies a wine which received no dosage of sugar. The word "Natural" on still wine labels has no particular meaning.

NAYLOR WINE CELLARS
Stewartstown, Mid-Atlantic Coast

Output: 10,000 cases

Leading Wines: Eau De Chaunac, Niagara, Rosé

Traditional eastern American wines are alive and well-made in the enthusiastic care of this small, southeastern Pennsylvania producer. Naylor grows several of the native labrusca grape varieties as well as many French-American hybrids and a smattering of vinifera, supplemented by purchased grapes and other fruit for a product line of more than two dozen wines. The prevailing style here emphasizes simple, fresh fruit flavors usually with at least some sweetness and moderate alcohol.

Nebbiolo

Interest is increasing in California in this red vinifera which yields the big, dark wines of northern Italy. There are now 380 acres planted in California, over 200 of which are in Stanislaus County in the Central Valley. But experimental plantings are being made in San Luis Obispo and elsewhere, and a few wineries have made successful varietals from Nebbiolo in limited quantities.

NEVADA CITY WINERY
Nevada City, Sierra Foothills

Output: 5,000 cases

Leading Wines: Cabernet Sauvignon, Douce Noir (Charbono), Petite Sirah, Pinot Noir, Zinfandel

In the Sierra Foothills of Nevada County, this 25,000-gallon winery produces an ambitious list of moderately priced varietals. Grapes are purchased in several viticultural regions—El Dorado, Shasta, Monterey, and Nevada counties. Included in its list of wines is the first sparkling wine commercially made in the Sierra Foothills in this century.

NEW ENGLAND

Of the six New England states, only Vermont has no winery, as most of the region's 20-odd producers hug the coastline for maritime protection against the extremes of Northeastern winters. Two are even situated on islands, where they feel secure enough to grow viniferas exclusively. Most vineyards, however, mix vinifera and French-American hybrids, yielding to the latter on inland hillsides; there is relatively little acreage planted in native American grapes. At the same time, a rich heritage of New England fruit wines has been revived by cellars in Massachusetts and Maine.

Stony, well-drained, high-acid, relatively infertile soils in much of New England fit the classic European principal of difficult ground to suppress yields and enhance grape quality. In that vein, viniculture seems a natural (though not an easy) choice for this land. Plantings have been small: in 1984, approximately 400 acres were under vine.

New England wines are predominantly white, often with firm acidity. There is a regional effort to make wine that complements seafood, with dry, lean flavors and restrained fruit. But, as in other young wine districts, this is a rule with a multitude of exceptions: vintages vary dramatically, and warm years do fatten up the wines.

Seyval, Chardonnay, White Riesling, and Vidal Blanc are the principal varieties. Some worthy reds have come out of inland as well as coastal wineries, made from Marechal Foch and Pinot Noir, the latter a *cause célèbre* for several producers.

NEWTON VINEYARD
St. Helena, San Francisco Bay North

Output: 20,000 cases

Leading Wines:
Cabernet Sauvignon,
Chardonnay,
Merlot,
Sauvignon Blanc

Peter Newton, one of the founders of Sterling Vineyards, started this 50,000-gallon winery in 1979 on 62 acres of vineyards on the steps of Spring Mountain. Four varietals are planted on some of the steepest and most extensively terraced slopes in the state. The soils are all volcanic in origin, but vary in composition from one location to another within relatively short distances. The range of soil composition and solar exposure, which also varies widely as a result of the steepness of the slopes, are thought by Newton to contribute to the complexity of its wines. Chardonnay is the only grape that Newton purchases because of the history of Chardonnay-destroying disease in the area. But Merlot, one of Newton's innovations at Sterling, is its leading varietal and is one of the best versions of wine in the Napa Valley.

Niagara

For preserving the simple grape flavor in wine, no other variety equals Niagara: it has a remarkable capacity for retaining through the process of winemaking the immediate sensation of eating fresh grapes. Not surprisingly, Concord is one of this white hybrid's genetic parents. Like wine from that grape, Niagara relies upon some sweetness to support its pungent and powerful fruit. New York vineyards in 1980 totaled 2,250 acres. Another several hundred acres are divided among Ohio, Pennsylvania, Michigan, Missouri, and Arkansas.

NIEBAUM-COPPOLA ESTATE
Rutherford, San Francisco Bay North

Output: 3,000 cases

In 1978, film director Francis Ford Coppola acquired the 18th-century mansion and estate of Gustav Niebaum, the founder of Inglenook. Coppola has built a small, 42,000-gallon winery in one of the old buildings on the property and in 1985 will release his first wine, a 1979 vintage Cabernet Sauvignon (with some Cabernet Franc) produced entirely from grapes grown in the 85-acre vineyard on the estate.

Wine:
Cabernet Sauvignon

NISSLEY VINEYARDS
Bainbridge, Mid-Atlantic Coast

Output: 15,000 cases

Leading Wines:
Aurora Bainbridge
White, Chancellor,
Chardonnay,
De Chaunac, Riesling,
Seyval Blanc, Vidal Blanc

In a stone addition to a tobacco barn the Nissley family have built one of southeastern Pennsylvania's biggest farm wineries. Grapes and fruit are purchased from several local growers to supplement expanding estate vineyards for a full line of French-American, native American, vinifera, and cherry and apple wines. The winemaking style favors fresh, fruity flavors in light whites, and medium-bodied reds. Nissley's profusion of well-made dry and sweet varietals and blends is more likely to please every taste than to leave a strong impression of individual style.

Norton, See Cynthiana

NOVITIATE WINES
Los Gatos, San Francisco Bay South

Output: 35,000 cases

Leading Wines:
Altar wines, Angelica,
Black Muscat, Black Rosé
Champagne, Black Rosé
Table Wine, Burgundy,
Cabernet Sauvignon,
Chablis, Chardonnay,
Chenin Blanc, Cream
Sherry, Grenache Rosé,
Muscat Frontignan, Petite
Sirah, Pinot Blanc, Tinta
Port, Zinfandel

The Jesuits in Los Gatos have been supporting the training of Jesuit fathers and brothers since 1888 by making wines at this Santa Cruz Mountain winery. Winemaking at the site was begun by Brother Louis Olivier, who sent home to southern France for cuttings to start a vineyard.

Today the Novitiate owns no vineyards but buys grapes to make a full line of table, aperitif, and dessert wines as well as eight different styles of altar wine. Novitiate is probably best known to consumers for its dessert wines, particularly Black Muscat.

Oak

The preferred wood for tanks and barrels to store wine is white oak, because of its structural properties and limited effect on wine chemistry. Half-a-dozen varieties of oak from regional forests in France — Nevers, Limousin, Alliers, Troncais, Bourgogne, and Vosges — are used in France, and, increasingly, in American wine cellars. Most winemakers and connoisseurs find the flavors they impart to wine more refined than those from American or other varieties of oak, but this is a matter of preference and some debate. The flavors oak cooperage gives to wine are often described as vanilla, cedary, and...oaky.

OAK KNOLL WINERY
Hillsboro, Oregon

Output: 20,000 cases

Leading Wines:
Chardonnay, Loganberry,
Pinot Noir, Raspberry,
Rhubarb, Riesling

The home winemaking hobby of Ron and Marjorie Vuylsteke led to the opening of a commercial fruit and berry winery in 1970. Fruit and berry wines still comprise the majority of Oak Knoll's production but the output of vinifera wine is up to half the annual output. Oak Knoll garnered special note for its 1980 Oak Knoll Vintage Select Pinot Noir, which was praised by André Tchelistcheff as one of the finest he had ever experienced.

   Vuylsteke's experience with fruit and berry wines has influenced his grape winemaking methods. While still taking advantage of the textural and flavor transformations of barrel-aging, the fruit of the grape takes precedence over the oak.

OBERHELLMANN VINEYARDS
Fredericksburg, Texas

Output: 4,000 cases

Leading Wines:
Cabernet Sauvignon,
Chardonnay,
Domaine Blanc,

Oberhellmann began as a grapevine nursery to select the varieties suited to its central Hill Country microclimate. Its results narrowed the winery's emphasis to Pinot Noir (Pommard clone), Chardonnay, Cabernet Sauvignon, and Johannisberg Riesling.

O

Ebelblume,
Johannisberg Riesling,
Pinot Noir, Traminer

The Cabernet is softened with Merlot and ages in American oak. Chardonnay is aged in French Nevers oak puncheons for moderate buttery-oak overtones. The German sweet reserve method of back-blending with juice produces a light, Kabinett-style Riesling. A secondary, Oberhof label identifies nonvintage proprietary blends using estate-grown and purchased grapes. A food technician by training, owner-winemaker Robert Oberhelman makes an effort to substitute scrupulous sanitation for sulfur dioxide and other preservatives. First vintage was in 1982.

OREGON

Oregon's history of vinifera wine production dates to the 19th century, when wineries populated the state from the southern California border to the northernmost end of the Willamette Valley near Washington. Prohibition destroyed the premium grape wine industry, and Oregon was unable to recover after Repeal. In the decades that followed, Oregon wine became synonymous with fruit and berry wine.

The modern grape winemaking industry dates to 1961, when Richard Sommer, trained in agronomy and viticulture at U.C. Davis, came to Oregon in search of a cooler winegrowing climate. He purchased acreage in Oregon's Umpqua Valley near Roseburg, planted vinifera grapes, and bonded the Hillcrest winery two years later. Sommer focused his efforts on Riesling, and the grape remains a mainstay of the Oregon wine industry.

David Lett, another Davis graduate, came to Oregon in 1965 looking for a climate suited to the Burgundian grape varieties. Lett bypassed the Umpqua Valley to settle in an even cooler growing area in the nothern Willamette Valley, southwest of Portland, and concentrated on what has become Oregon's most famous varietal, Pinot Noir. Dick Erath and others came shortly thereafter, and the northern Willamette Valley rapidly became Oregon's viticultural heartland.

Although there has been recent vineyard development along the Columbia River Gorge and in eastern Oregon, virtually the entire Oregon wine industry is located in the western part of the state, in a long strip of land running north to south from the Washington to California borders. The growing area is delimited on the west by the Coast Range, and on the east by the foothills of the Cascade Mountain Range. Less mountainous than the Cascade Range, the Coast Range only partly blocks the wet, cool marine air, still allowing it to temper the winegrowing climate.

In climate, viticultural practices, winemaking methods, and philosophy, Oregon is the most traditionally European of America's western winegrowing states. Nearly all Oregon wineries are estate wineries, with the winery and typically the winemaker's home adjacent to the winery's principal vineyard. Most Oregon wineries are relatively small: none produce more than 50,000 cases a year.

As in Europe's best winegrowing regions, Oregon vintages vary considerably from year to year, and those that are less good are almost

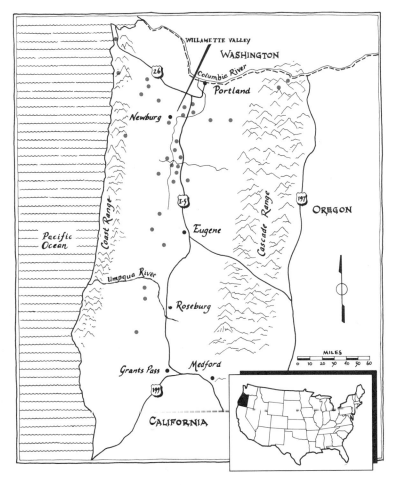

always so because the year was too cool, rarely because the year was too warm or the grapes were overripe or ripened too soon. Like the Europeans, Oregon winegrowers believe a growing climate which ripens the grapes rapidly, early, and easily is also a growing climate that robs the grapes of complexity and nuance. It is not merely out of tradition, they argue, that Pinot Noir is not grown in Bordeaux, where it would produce big wines and ripen easily every year. In Europe's best winegrowing regions, grape varieties are not planted where they will ripen most easily, but where the ripening of the grapes coincides with the end of the growing season.

The shape of the Willamette Valley describes an elongated 'V', with its widest part at Oregon's northern border on the Columbia River and narrowing southward until at Eugene, halfway down the state, the valley ends in the convergence of the foothills of the Cascade and Coast Ranges. Most vineyards are in the northern part of the valley, on south-facing slopes along the western perimeter, to take advantage of the rain shadow effect of the coastal mountains. Nearly all of Oregon's Pinot Noir comes from this area, with Riesling and Chardonnay as the two other major varieties. Gewurztraminer, Sauvignon Blanc, Pinot Gris, Merlot, and Cabernet Sauvignon are among other varieties grown in smaller quantities. The climate is generally too cool for Cabernet Sauvignon, and Merlot suffers from poor berry set in the valley's cool wet springs.

South of Eugene, the Umpqua Valley near Roseburg is home for several wineries, including Hillcrest, Oregon's oldest continuously operating premium grape winery. The Umpqua Valley is much narrower, smaller, and more convoluted than the Willamette, and although the climate is generally drier and warmer, grape selection is more varied and depends more on the microclimates of individual vineyards and interests of the winegrower. The same three grape varieties — Riesling, Pinot Noir, and Chardonnay — predominate, but none is dominant, some finding favor at one winery to the near exclusion of others. Cabernet, still a minor variety, is more widely grown here than in the Willamette.

Near the California border, the Applegate and Illinois valleys and other growing sites in the area are the warmest and driest regions in western Oregon. Cabernet Sauvignon is the major red wine grape; Merlot, Pinot Noir, Chardonnay, Gewurztraminer, and Semillon are among other varieties grown in the area.

As in most of Europe, and unlike most of Washington, Idaho, and California, Oregon vines are cane-pruned and not pruned and trained into cordons. Cane-pruning requires much more care and labor, but is necessary in Oregon's climate to insure, among other things, consistent and adequate harvest tonnages and reliable ripening. In the cooler, less intensely sunny Oregon climate, the vines do not produce the high tonnages of ripe fruit more common in Washington's Columbia Valley and most of California.

Berry size is generally smaller, and the grapes become ripe and flavorful at lower sugar levels in Oregon. For sparkling wines, grapes must have lower sugar for a successful second fermentation, and in warmer climates this means that they are picked when far from ripe or flavorful. But in Oregon, particularly in cool vintages when the grapes may not be ideal for still wine, low sugar levels at ripeness mean that more and more winegrowers are making fine sparkling wines.

Winter cold is not a problem for Oregon winegrowers, and spring frosts are a concern only in southern Oregon, where winters are harder and summers are warmer. Like many European winegrowing regions, rain during harvest can be a problem in some years, particularly in the Willamette Valley, offering the risks of mildew, dilution of fruit concentration, delays in final ripening and harvest, and difficulty moving equipment through muddy vineyards. Except for those in the southernmost part of the state, few Oregon vineyards are irrigated as the natural rainfall provides sufficient moisture throughout the growing season.

Riesling is one of Oregon's most widely planted varietals. The grape acquires its varietal character early in the ripening process, and makes good wine even in poor years. Most winegrowers do not try for botrytis because of frequent rainfall during harvest season, but the few that take the risk have produced excellent versions. Oregon Chardonnays are very successful, sometimes seemingly quite Burgundian yet at other times with their own style. Typically they are delicate but full-flavored, with a softness that comes from moderate alcohol levels and fairly major malolactic fermentations, while displaying crisp balancing acidities.

Pinot Noir, which rarely does well outside its native Burgundy, is undoubtedly Oregon's major success story. Produced in all of Oregon's growing regions, it has found a special home in the Willamette Valley. This is not to say that all Oregon Pinot Noirs are outstanding. Pinot Noir is a difficult and demanding grape for grower and winemaker alike, but in Oregon the results are now reliably good, and a few are excellent to outstanding. Low cropping and older vines have been key factors.

Typically, Oregon Pinot Noir displays more forward, spicy fruit than most Burgundies, but less of the pleasant, Burgundian, earthy dankness, although these differences narrow as the wines age. Ironically, many winemakers have been releasing Pinot Noir at acid levels far below those of typical Burgundies, perhaps to appeal to what they view as the popular palate. Sadly, these wines have not aged well; but others made with adequate acidity, even the more delicate examples from less good years, have aged superbly. Recent releases suggest that more winemakers are attentive to these lessons, and further successes seem likely for this already excellent Oregon grape.

The standard disclaimer that poor wines can be made in good vintages and good wines in poor vintages is especially applicable to Oregon. The years 1977, 1978, and 1980, for example, were all poor or mediocre for Oregon Pinot Noir, yet at least one winery in each of those years produced a Pinot Noir of exceptional quality.

1977   A cool, wet year that resulted in a poor vintage.

1978   A hot year with high sugars and some excellent Chardonnays in a riper style were produced but in many cases, the heat was too much of a good thing. Pinot Noir suffered from overripeness, producing big wines lacking in acid, fruit, and finesse.

1979   A warm year that produced high yields of fruit with good sugars. The red wines are uniformly very good. For the new wineries just coming into production, an easy year to make good Pinot Noir.

1980   A cool year which produced lower than normal sugars in the grapes. Volcanic ash from the Mount St. Helen's eruption combined with rains in the spring caused some vine damage in the northern Willamette Valley. Overall, but with a few notable exceptions, the wines are light and lacking in intensity.

1981   A cool wet spring with poor berry set resulted in a low crop. Midsummer was warm and dry with some very hot spells but rain returned in the weeks prior to harvest. As a result, quality was variable in most varieties. But Riesling, benefitting from higher than normal sugars, fruit intensity, and botrytis, produced wines of exceptional quality.

1982   The ideal conditions for flowering and berry set were augmented

O

by periodic rainfall in the weeks and months prior to harvest, and together resulted in exceptionally high yields and a record crop. The wines are generally good, though sometimes lacking the concentration of the best years.

1983   Poor berry set caused a reduced crop. Early summer was cool and rainy, but a dry late summer and a sunny, warm fall produced grapes with adequate sugars, high acids, small berries, and intense varietal fruit. Perhaps the best ever vintage for Pinot Noir.

1984   A cool wet spring delayed bud break and flowering. Summer was dry but cool, and the final ripening period was very cool and wet so that generally sugars were very low, except in southernmost regions.

ORLEANS HILL
Woodland, Sacramento Valley

Output: 7,500 cases

Leading Wines:
Cabernet Sauvignon,
Chardonnay,
Chenin Blanc,
French Colombard,
Sauvignon Blanc,
White Zinfandel,
Zinfandel

Orleans Hill is the first major winery to be founded in Yolo County. Established in 1980, the winery is small, with 20,000 gallons of storage capacity. Plans call for the addition of a varietal called Orleans. Wine has not been produced from this rarely grown variety in California since the 1880s: Orleans produces a wine which is described as Riesling-like in character.

P

PAPAGNI VINEYARDS
Madera, Central Valley

Madera, in the hot Central Valley, may appear to be an unlikely area in which to produce dry table wines. However, Papagni believes that high-quality grapes with good varietal flavor can be grown in this region with the right care for the vines, especially in their pruning and irrigation.

To a large extent the wines are the most eloquent argument in support of its belief. Papagni's line of inexpensive varietals continues to win friends. The surprise wine on the list is the Alicante Bouschet, which has been largely ignored by commercial winemakers in the post-Repeal era. Papagni's version is big and darkly-colored, but well-balanced with flavor and acidity.

Papagni's wines are no longer looked upon as Central Valley curiosities. After nearly ten years of providing sound, dry, vintage-dated, estate-grown varietals at attractive prices, this 3 million-gallon winery is regarded as a pioneer, and its wines take home awards from major California wine judgings.

Output: 120,000 cases

Leading Wines: Alicante Bouschet, Barbera, Bianca di Madera, Charbono, Chardonnay, Chenin Blanc, Fu Jin, Fumé Blanc, Gamay Rosé, Muscat of Alexandria, various bulk process sparkling wines

PARDUCCI WINE CELLARS
Ukiah, San Francisco Bay North

The oldest winery in Mendocino County, Parducci Wine Cellars dates from 1931 and was the first to plant fine grape varieties in the region. Until the 1960s Parducci wines sold in bulk to other wineries around California and in jugs to local residents. Since that time this 1.5 million gallon winery has established a reputation for good, reliable wines at attractive prices.

Grapes come from its own 450 acres and other Mendocino County locations. Those wines that are exceptional from any vintage are bottled under Cellar Masters Selection.

Parducci's line of varietals shows most consistent quality in the whites, which are for the most part light, fruity, not overly oaked, and attractively priced wines. The reds are a little more disparate. Several years ago they included some enormous Zinfandels and Petite Sirahs; now they tend to be lighter and for early consumption.

Output: 350,000 cases

Leading Wines: Burgundy, Cabernet Sauvignon, Carignane, Chablis, Charbono, Chardonnay, Chenin Blanc, French Colombard, Gamay Beaujolais, Gewurztraminer, Muscat Canelli, Petite Sirah, Sauvignon Blanc, Vintage Red and White

P

PARSONS CREEK
Ukiah, San Francisco Bay North

Output: 10,000 cases

Leading Wines:
Chardonnay,
Johannisberg Riesling,
sparkling wine

Since its founding in 1979 Parsons Creek has made only white wines, all from purchased grapes harvested, crushed, and pressed in the field by its own equipment. Parsons Chardonnays have caught most attention and come with Anderson Valley or Sonoma County appellations. Both are briefly aged in small American oak barrels. A Johannisberg Riesling and a Mendocino County appellation sparkling wine—a Brut made from a blend of Pinot Noir and Chardonnay—round out its line.

PAT PAULSEN VINEYARDS
Cloverdale, San Francisco Bay North

Output: 15,000 cases

Leading Wines:
Cabernet Sauvignon,
Chardonnay,
Muscat Canelli,
Sauvignon Blanc

Pat Paulsen, the television comedian, planted this vineyard in 1971, and built the accompanying winery in 1980. Paulsen now has 40 acres of producing vineyards in the Alexander Valley, and 60,000 gallons of storage capacity. Paulsen has received favorable critical attention for his white wines, the majority of his output, in particular his lively Muscat Canelli.

PEDRIZZETTI VINEYARDS
Morgan Hill, San Francisco Bay North

Output: 35,000 cases

Leading Wines:
Cabernet Sauvignon,
Chardonnay,
Chenin Blanc

This family-run 1.5 million gallon winery dates back to the early years of the century. In 1968, Pedrizzetti bulk and jug wines were replaced by cork-finished varietals and generics. All grapes are purchased in San Luis Obispo and Monterey counties and Clarksburg in the Sacramento River Delta.

PENN SHORE VINEYARDS
North East, Lake Erie

Output: 12,000 cases

Leading Wines:
Baco Noir, Chablis,
Chancellor, Delaware,
Free Spirit, Ravat Blanc,
Rosé, Seyval Blanc,
Vidal Blanc

Three Pennsylvania farms in the heart of the Lake Erie grape belt feed this partnership winery with a range of American and French-American hybrid varieties. Established as a market outlet in 1968, Penn Shore spent its first decade struggling for a style and identity. The bulk of production has evolved into a line of low-alcohol wines highlighting the fresh fruit flavor of American grapes. Sold under the Free Spirit label, they are cold-fermented and under 10.5-percent alcohol—simple, easy-drinking wines priced and packaged for everyday use.

Penn Shore's Signature Vintage label is reserved for small lots from vineyard blocks singled out each year for fruit quality. The style for white wines is Germanic, emphasizing fruit and acid. Ravat Blanc and Seyval Blanc are Penn Shore's best wines, the Ravat made in an unusual, flinty dry, Chablis style aged in steel.

PERDIDO VINEYARDS
Perdido, Alabama

Alabama's first and only winery since Prohibition produces wines with the strong southern accent of the region's native Muscadine grapes. The desire here is to capture the full, wild grape flavors traditional in wines of the Deep South. Cold fermentation and (usually) some sweetness play up fresh fruitiness, which survives hot, humid growing seasons because these varieties are adapted and ripen late in the season. Perdido's unpretentious, easy-drinking style is summed up in its Rosé Cou Rouge — "red neck rosé."

Output: 14,000 cases

Leading Wines:
Apple, Ecor Rouge,
Magnolia, Magnolia Vat 6
Dry Reserve, Mardi Gras
Red, Rosé Cou Rouge

Petite Sirah

Although this grape is now thought not to be the Syrah of the northern Rhône but another Rhône grape, the Duriff, Petite Sirah has demonstrated that it can make elegant and complex wines in California. Previously used as a blending grape in generic reds, it is produced as a varietal by over 75 wineries. There are nearly 6,000 acres of Petite Sirah in California, still largely in the Central Valley.

JOSEPH PHELPS VINEYARDS
St. Helena, San Francisco Bay North

Within a very short time after producing its first wine, a Johannisberg Riesling, in 1973, Phelps had established an enviable reputation first for whites and now for almost all its line of high-quality varietals.

Phelps owns 340 acres of vineyards in several Napa Valley locations, including 175 acres surrounding the winery which are planted Gewurztraminer, Johannisberg Riesling, Cabernet Sauvignon, Zinfandel, Scheurebe, and Syrah.

Of the eight varietals that are produced by Phelps, two are distinctive for California: Scheurebe and Syrah. Scheurebe is a botanical cross of Riesling and Sylvaner. Syrah is also rare and not to be confused with Petite Sirah, a grape that is widely planted in California. The true Syrah accounts for much of the acreage of the northern Rhône, and the famous wines of Hermitage and Côte-Rotie are produced from this variety. In early vintages Phelps tried to produce an Hermitage by co-fermentation with Chenin Blanc but the winery now uses partial carbonic maceration. Phelps produces a house wine called Insignia, a Bordeaux-style blend of Cabernet Sauvignon with Merlot and Cabernet Franc. This wine is an important example of the new generation of California high-quality proprietary wines. Phelps also produces a generic claret, which is a blend of 92 percent Cabernet Sauvignon and 8 percent Cabernet Franc, aged for 16 months in Nevers oak barrels.

Phelps has been startlingly successful with a wide range of grape varieties, achieving critical acclaim for everything from Cabernet Sauvignon to late-harvest dessert wines. There are few other large wineries in California with a higher rate of success across-the-board.

Output: 80,000 cases

Leading Wines:
Cabernet Sauvignon,
Chardonnay,
Gewurztraminer,
Johannisberg Riesling,
Sauvignon Blanc,
Scheurebe, Syrah,
Zinfandel

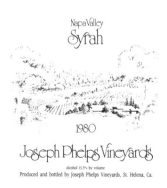

Napa Valley
Syrah

1980

Joseph Phelps Vineyards
Alcohol 13.9% by volume
Produced and bottled by Joseph Phelps Vineyards, St. Helena, Ca.

P

Phylloxera

In the 1860s, cuttings of American grapevines shipped to France carried a stowaway bug, an aphid called phylloxera that feeds on vine roots. Native American vines had developed natural resistance to phylloxera, but the soft, fleshy roots of European vinifera vines were extremely vulnerable. The insect multiplied rapidly, destroying vine after vine, then vineyard after vineyard. Within 20 years it had affected or killed virtually every vineyard in France, and was spreading through the rest of Europe. The European wine industry was suddenly fighting for its existence. The first response was to replant with resistant American vines, but their wine quality was too strange. But two alternative strategies did use American vines to defeat phylloxera, and European vineyards were either grafted with American grape varieties to create bug-resistant vines that made European style wine or, less commonly, planted with French-American hybrids.

PIEDMONT VINEYARDS
Middleburg, Virginia

Output: 4,500 cases

*Leading Wines:
Chardonnay,
Semillon, Seyval Blanc*

Virginia's first commercial European grape vineyard was started at Piedmont in 1973, with the consultation of New York State's vinifera guru, Dr. Konstantin Frank. Chardonnay takes up about two-thirds of the 30-acre vineyard, located in the fox hunt country of the Blue Ridge foothills; Semillon and Seyval Blanc are the only other varieties grown. All three are cold-fermented bone-dry to hold onto varietal fruit flavor and acids that have survived the area's steamy summers. All wines are aged in American oak, less extensively in recent vintages than in the early years of very woody Piedmont wines. Seyval is the lightest wine. Small lots of Semillon have been made experimentally in a sweet Sauterne style.

PINDAR VINEYARDS
Peconic, Long Island

Output: 20,000 cases

*Leading Wines:
Cabernet Sauvignon,
Chardonnay,
Gewurztraminer,
Nouveau, Riesling, late-
harvest Riesling,
Winter White*

Pindar's 120 acres makes it easily the largest on Long Island, and it emphasizes light fruit in its wines, reflecting the youth and high productivity of the vineyard. Pindar grows vinifera for the most part, but has the island's only hybrid vineyard (Seyval and Cayuga White). Winter White is a blend of French-American hybrid and vinifera wines released early after each harvest with fresh, semidry fruit and a slight spritz. The Cabernet Sauvignon from Pindar's early vintages is made for drinking after 1 to 2 years. A Nouveau from Pinot Noir has appealing, cherry-like flavors and is bright and clean.

Pinot Blanc

A white vinifera that yields medium-bodied fruity wines, Pinot Blanc is often compared to, and mistaken for, Chardonnay. There is some controversy as to whether all acreage in California called Pinot Blanc is the true varietal. There are about 2,200 acres of Pinot Blanc reportedly planted in the state, of which 1,300 are in Monterey.

Pinot Noir

This vinifera is responsible for the great reds of Burgundy. (Whereas Bordeaux's Cabernet Sauvignon is always blended with other grapes, Pinot Noir stands alone in Burgundy.) Pinot Noir is an extremely finicky grape, with far more elusive aromas and flavors than most other red wine grapes. Many factors have to be exactly right to produce a great Pinot Noir, and historically it has proved very difficult to reproduce its Burgundian heights in other winegrowing regions.

Great Pinot Noir has been a holy grail for California viniculture for years, but it appears that breakthroughs are finally being made. Better selection of vineyard sites, better selection of its many clones, and better understanding of the sometimes quirky Burgundian techniques have all led to improved wines.

In the cool climate of Oregon's Willamette Valley Pinot Noir is showing promise at several wineries. While some examples lack the complexity of the classic French versions, in the best years the region produces fruity wines that also have good acid/sugar balance, indicating strong aging possibilities.

Wines made from Pinot Noir can be majestic. The exciting cherry flavors of youth eventually give way to sublime combinations of earth and spice, and the velvety texture of a great Pinot Noir is unforgettable. California Pinot Noirs have traditionally been thin and less complex, but the better side of this grape is clearly emerging in areas as diverse as Edna Valley, Monterey, San Benito, Santa Cruz, and Los Carneros. There are about 8,800 acres in California, over 5,000 of which are in San Francisco Bay North.

Pinot St. George

Apparently not related to Pinot Noir, this red vinifera is used to make simple varietal table wines by a handful of California wineries. There are nearly 200 acres planted in California.

P

PIPER SONOMA
Windsor, San Francisco Bay North

Output: 70,000 cases

Leading Wines:
Blanc de Noirs,
Brut, Tete de Cuvée

Founded in 1980, Piper Sonoma is a joint venture in which Champagne house Piper Heidsieck of Reims is involved, specializing in sparkling wines. Grapes come from 1,200 acres in the Alexander Valley for this highly-automated *méthode champenoise* winery, where everything from riddling to disgorging and dosage is performed by machine.

Three styles of sparkling wines are made at Piper. The flagship wine is Tete de Cuvée, an equal blend of Chardonnay and Pinot Noir which spends 2 to 3 years on the yeast. The Brut is a crisp blend of about 75 percent Pinot Noir with about 25 percent Chardonnay, which is aged on the yeast for an average of 20 months. Piper Sonoma Blanc de Noirs is 100 percent Pinot Noir.

PLANE'S CAYUGA VINEYARD
Ovid, Finger Lakes

Output: 5,000 cases

Leading Wines:
Cayuga, Chancellor,
Chardonnay, Duet,
Ravat Vignoles,
Riesling

Before its first vintage in 1980, Plane's began to establish a reputation with its vineyard designation on the labels of other Finger Lakes wineries. Known by local standards for very ripe, fat fruit which yielded round, earthy wines, this style has continued with Plane's own label. The barrel-aged Chardonnay has a smoky fullness and softer, more mature fruit than most other examples of this variety from the Finger Lakes. Cayuga and Ravat are made fairly dry, with moderate acid. A blend of the two varieties called Duet is better than either one separately, and is one of the best examples of crisp, citrusy Finger Lakes country white wine. Plane's Chancellor ranks among the region's few good reds.

PONZI VINEYARDS
Beaverton, Oregon

Output: 5,000 cases

Leading Wines:
Chardonnay, Pinot Gris,
Pinot Noir, Riesling

Dick and Nancy Ponzi first planted their vineyard in 1970 on sandy benchland near the Tualatin River in the northern Willamette Valley. The 11-acre estate vineyard is planted equally to Pinot Noir, Chardonnay, Riesling, and Pinot Gris. An additional 25 acres are under contract from two nearby vineyards.

Ponzi was among the first Oregon wineries to work with Pinot Gris, a grape variety with its origins in Alsace and northern Italy. As yet very little Pinot Gris acreage is planted in Oregon, but the grape, a genetic relative of Pinot Noir, may someday become one of Oregon's more important varieties, filling a role alongside Chardonnay as a premium white dinner wine. Unlike most in Oregon, Ponzi Riesling is made in a dry style to accompany food. Some Oregon Pinot Noirs are released with overly low acidity, but Ponzi's Pinot Noirs have adequate balancing acidity to complement food and develop with age.

POPLAR RIDGE VINEYARDS
Valois, Finger Lakes

"Wine Without Bull" is the motto of Poplar Ridge, reflecting owner-winemaker David Bagley's easygoing approach to winemaking and his stint as cellarmaster at Bully Hill Vineyards. In keeping, the Poplar Ridge style is clean, fruity, uncomplicated, and approachable. Cayuga White is the best example, loaded with fruit-salad flavors. Lemony, semidry Vidal Blanc is another specialty. These are wines for hot summer afternoons. Marechal Foch is more of a food wine, but still fresh, fruity, made for quaffing. Bagley's choice of varieties and superb site on Seneca Lake's east shore permit high yields and low prices, appropriate to Poplar Ridge's populist ethic.

Output: 7,000 cases

Leading Wines:
Cayuga White,
Johannisberg Riesling,
Marechal Foch,
Ravat, Seyval,
Valois Blanc and Rouge,
Vidal Blanc

POST WINERY
Altus, Arkansas

Post is one of two big family wineries that date back to the late 19th-century settlement of Arkansas hill country by Swiss and German immigrants. Now in its fifth generation, the winery is being modernized and diversified from a traditional emphasis on sweet, fortified wines — though they still account for nearly half Post's production.

Few of Post's table wines are completely dry, but the trend is toward drier French-American hybrids with low alcohol and tannin, for early consumption in local markets. In the cellar, old redwood vats have been replaced with stainless steel tanks to lighten the wines and preserve more fruit and acid. Some Chardonnay and Riesling have been added to the 150-acre vineyard, along with Muscadine varieties and Niagara.

Output: 40,000 cases

Leading Wines:
Catawba, Cynthiana, Ives
Noir, Muscadine, Niagara,
Seyval Blanc, Villard
Noir, White Delaware

PRESQUE ISLE WINE CELLARS
North East, Lake Erie

One of the pioneers of small-scale, high-quality wine using new varieties to the east, Presque Isle broke out of a big Concord vineyard in the traditional heart of the Lake Erie grape belt. Douglas and Marlene Moorhead planted a wide range of vinifera and French-American hybrid grapes in the early 1960s to test their lake-protected site.

Presque Isle makes wine to evaluate its line of equipment and to explore what can be done with grapes suitable to the Northeast. Many varieties have come and gone in the vineyard and small cellar to arrive at the Moorheads' current selection. The reds all get prominent oak aging, most successful with supple, tightly structured Cabernet Sauvignon and Cabernet Franc. Riesling is another specialty, while Presque Isle's labrusca wines are among the most refined examples of these varieties.

Output: 1,000 cases

Leading Wines:
Cabernet Franc, Cabernet
Sauvignon, Chardonnay,
Chelois, Delaware,
Dutchess, Marechal Foch,
Riesling, Seyval Blanc,
Steuben

P

PRESTON VINEYARDS AND WINERY
Healdsburg, San Francisco Bay North

Output: 12,000 cases

Leading Wines:
Cabernet Sauvignon,
Cuvée de Fumé
(Sauvignon Blanc),
Zinfandel

Situated in the Dry Creek Valley Viticultural Area, Preston Vineyards was founded in 1975. Currently Preston owns 120 acres of vineyards and has 50,000 gallons of storage capacity. The winery is perhaps best-known for its fruity but clean Sauvignon Blanc, a wine reminiscent of some white wines from the Loire Valley, and its full-bodied Zinfandel.

PRESTON WINE CELLARS
Pasco, Washington

Output: 50,000 cases

Leading Wines:
Chardonnay, Chenin
Blanc, Gewurztraminer,
Merlot, Riesling,
Sauvignon Blanc

The Preston winery and vineyards are situated in the vast open spaces of the Columbia Basin near Pasco, in the broad 'U'-shaped area where the Columbia and Snake rivers converge. In 1972 Bill Preston planted one of Washington's first commercial vinifera vineyards in the modern era adjacent to the Preston home, releasing his first wines from the 1976 vintage. Later plantings have expanded the estate vineyards to 181 acres, making Preston the largest family-owned winery in the state.

Produced and Bottled by

These words preceding the winery name on the label confirm that the wine was made (fermented and finished) by the winery, and not purchased from another source. Federal regulations allow this phrase to be used when the winery carried out the production for at least 75 percent of the wine in the bottle; so there is still some allowance for blending. But in most cases, "produced and bottled by" means all the wine was made at the winery named.

QUADY WINERY
Madera, Central Valley

Output: 3,000 cases

Leading Wines:
Bastardo, Essencia,
Elysium,
Tinta Amerela,
Tinta Cao, Touriga,
Zinfandel ports

Since 1975 Quady has produced non-vintage ports from Amador County Zinfandel, and from traditional Portuguese grapes, and vintage ports from both Zinfandel grapes and Portuguese varieties The wines are bottled within two years after fermentation, and require extended aging to reach maturity.

Quady also makes two specialty wines from members of the muscat family. Essencia, made from the Orange Muscat grape, has a delicate scent of orange blossoms and a wispy citrus flavor. Elysium is made from the Black Muscat grape, and has an aroma and flavor reminiscent of black raspberries and black cherries.

QUAIL RIDGE WINERY
Napa, San Francisco Bay North

Output: 8,000 cases

Leading Wines:
Cabernet Sauvignon,
Chardonnay,
French Colombard,
Merlot

Located in the old Hedgeside Caves which were hand-hewn in 1885, Quail Ridge makes a small range of luscious, well-balanced wines that has a considerable cult following.

Chardonnay is the leading wine. It is barrel-fermented and allowed to undergo malolactic fermentation — two processes that invariably create complexity — and is aged for 7-9 months in French oak. Quail Ridge also produces an unusual barrel-fermented French Colombard.

QUAIL RUN VINTNERS
Zillah, Washington

Output: 33,000 cases

Leading Wines:
Aligote,
Cabernet Sauvignon,
Chardonnay,

Quail Run was the first winery of substantial size established in the Yakima Valley. Founded in 1982, it is a partnership of twenty owners, headed by Stan Clarke. Clarke graduated from U.C. Davis with a degree in viticulture and worked for several California vineyards and Chateau Ste. Michelle before coming to Quail Run.

Q

Gewurztraminer,
Lemberger,
Morio Muscat, Riesling

The two Quail Run vineyards, comprising 175 acres, are owned separately by two of the partners, and grapes are sold to the Quail Run partnership. Both vineyards were planted in 1980 with unusually dense spacing. Clarke prefers this spacing so that less demand is put on individual root systems, so that the vines ripen grapes readily and produce consistent yields with good fruit intensity and balance, while enabling the vines to maintain sufficient reserves to combat the winter cold.

Winemaker Wayne Marcil, an enology graduate from U.C. Davis, styles his wines to display the fruit and natural acidity of Yakima Valley grapes. Rieslings are the mainstay, but Quail Run also makes interesting wines from some lesser-known varieties including Morio Muscat — a genetic cross of Sylvaner and Pinot Blanc. The linalool component in Sylvaner is amplified by the cross, giving a distinct Muscat character. Besides Morio Muscat, Quail Run makes Aligote, from the lesser white grape of Burgundy, and a Lemberger made in a fruity Beaujolais style. In the coming years, the dry red and white varieties will receive increasing emphasis.

Rack

Racking is the process of syphoning clear wine off the sediment formed after fermentation or as the wine clarifies.

RAPIDAN RIVER VINEYARDS
Culpeper, Virginia

Output: 4,500 cases

Leading Wines:
Chardonnay,
Gewurztraminer,
Pinot Noir, White Riesling

A German influence is evident everywhere at Rapidan River. Owned by a surgeon living in Hamburg, the estate was researched and developed by viniculturists from Germany's prestigious Geisenheim Wine Institute. Immaculate, high-density vineyards, early harvesting, rigidly controlled cold processing, and sterile filtration result in clean, fresh wines with light varietal character.

While the Riesling grape might not have seemed the logical choice for the long, hot growing seasons of central Virginia, this was to be a Riesling estate. It is a tribute to the skills applied in vineyard and cellar that Rapidan's dry and semisweet Rieslings seem to be cool-climate wines, with floral aromas and delicate fruit. Rapidan's Gewurztraminer, a much fuller-bodied wine with moderate spice, is equally successful. This and the winery's Chardonnay and Pinot Noir are made in smaller quantities, the latter varieties briefly aged in French and German oak but still relatively light versions emphasizing fruit. Major expansion of the 25-acre vineyard is under way.

Ravat

J.F. Ravat, a French grape breeder, hybridized this variety in the late 19th-century scramble to replant Europe's phylloxera-stricken vineyards. It has found a home in the eastern United States, where it makes what many believe to be the best of the French-American varietal white wines; at least it seems unique among the white hybrids in its capacity to develop complexity with bottle age.

Ravat matures with abnormally high acid levels, even when harvested late with plenty of sugar, and most winemakers respond to this by leaving

R

at least some sweetness in the wine to balance high acidity and some astringency. This provides a sturdy frame for Ravat's forceful fruit flavors of grapefruit, peach, and lemon, with earthy undertones. The variety's tight, thick-skinned grape clusters are susceptible to botrytis, evident in the honeyed quality of many Ravats. Acreage is about 100 but increasing, most of it in New York, Pennsylvania, and Michigan.

RAVENSWOOD WINERY
Sonoma, San Francisco Bay North

Output: 5,000 cases

Leading Wines:
Cabernet Sauvignon,
Zinfandel

This small winery, with 10,000 gallons of storage capacity, was founded in 1976 to specialize in Cabernet Sauvignon and vineyard-designated Zinfandels. Grapes are purchased to make fairly full-bodied, tannic wines.

Rayon D'or

Vineyard acreage of Rayon d'Or is minimal and widely scattered east of the Rocky Mountains from Connecticut to Texas. The grapes mature with high sugar, and the wines typically have abundant orange-lemon fruitiness and at least some residual sweetness. In style they resemble the wines of the middle Loire Valley in France (Vouvray, Saumur), where there is considerable acreage of this white French-American hybrid.

Regions I-V, U.C. Davis

In an attempt to classify the grape growing areas of California by climate and to recommend those varieties most suitable for each, the University of California Department of Viticulture and Enology at the Davis campus has identified five distinct viticultural regions. These regions are defined according to a heat summation scale based on accumulated "degree days" during the growing season. Degree days are measured from a base of 50°F, since grapevines do not grow very much or mature their fruit at lower temperatures. The average number of degrees above this temperature multiplied by the number of days it reached this figure will give the total of degree days.

Region I, for example, includes the coolest areas—under 2,500 degree days—which are similar to the climate of Alsace or Germany; at the other extreme, Region V—(4,000 degree days or more)—includes the long, hot growing season of the San Joaquin Valley. The university recommends grape varieties whose viticultural requirements for optimum fruit quality match each region. These recommendations made a substantial contribution to the quality revolution in California wine by guiding new vineyard plantings in the 1960s and 1970s. But they offer a somewhat simplistic scheme for matching grapes to growing conditions, and they have not been widely used outside California. Moreover it is generally acknowledged that other factors, such as soil composition, should be considered in planting vineyards.

R

Residual Sugar

The natural sugar of the grape that is left in wine after fermentation is termed "residual sugar." Wines with perceptible sweetness have at least 0.8 percent residual sugar, ranging up to 16 percent or more in very sweet, late-harvest or dessert wines. (The threshold of perception varies between individual wine drinkers.) Even dry wines almost always have some small fraction of residual sugar, which can slightly soften the flavor without actually tasting sweet. Residual sugar (from the grape) is always distinguished from cane sugar added to wine to make it sweet or sometimes to mask flaws.

REX HILL VINEYARD
Newberg, Oregon

Owned by husband and wife Paul Hart and Jan Jacobsen, Rex Hill was begun in 1983 with 18 acres of grapes in the northern Willamette Valley. Winemaker David Wirtz produced Rex Hill's first wines from purchased Chardonnay and Pinot Noir that same year. (Wirtz was formerly cellarmaster and later winemaker for the now-defunct Charles Coury and Reuter's Hill wineries.) Release of Rex Hill's first wines is imminent.

Output: 6,000 cases

Leading Wines: Chardonnay, Pinot Noir, Riesling

RIDGE VINEYARDS AND WINERY
Cupertino, San Francisco Bay South

Founded on historic vineyard acreage on Monte Bello Ridge 2,300 feet above the Santa Clara Valley (vineyards were first planted there in the 1890s), Ridge makes some of the most highly-acclaimed red wines in all of California.

First Ridge wines were made in 1962 but since 1970 its full-bodied, big style has been associated with winemaker Paul Draper. From his experience in France and Italy Draper practices what he describes as "traditional" winemaking, that is, using the finest grapes and interfering with the wine as little as possible. Fermentations at Ridge use only natural yeast present on the skins of the grapes and in the winery. Unlike most commercial winemakers in California who kill off native yeasts at the crush and innoculate with a commercial yeast culture, Draper feels that fermentations with a number of wild yeasts simultaneously make wines of greater complexity. Other unusual techniques include a latticework to keep the "cap" in place during fermentation, long skin contact, and the inclusion of press wine in the developing must. All Ridge wines are barrel-aged: one year for Zinfandel and two years for Cabernet Sauvignon, mainly in American oak. Filtration is used only if necessary for stability. However, light fining with fresh egg whites or silver leaf gelatin is employed for approximately 70 percent of the wines, adding to their clarity and reducing tannins slightly.

Output: 30,000 cases

Leading Wines: Cabernet Sauvignon, Chardonnay, Zinfandel

Ridge output is almost equally divided between Cabernet Sauvignon and Zinfandel. Cabernet Sauvignon is produced with Monte Bello and York Creek appellations (generally less complex). Some Merlot and Cabernet Franc are often included in both to round out the wine. Some Petite Sirah and a small amount of Chardonnay are also made each year.

The Monte Bello wines are produced from the winery's own 500 acres, supplemented by an additional 15 acres that are leased on the mountain. A further two-thirds of Ridge's grapes are purchased from selected vineyard locations: Santa Cruz Mountains, Napa County, Sonoma County, Fiddletown, Paso Robles, and Howell Mountain. Ridge has shown astuteness in its choice of vineyards for its Zinfandel and regularly produces some outstanding individual bottlings. (Ridge was the first winery to include the appellation, the date of bottling, and precise alcohol readings together with the winemaker's assessment of the wine's aging potential.)

One measure of the success of this 200,000-gallon winery, and the success of the winemaker in producing fine wines by traditional, natural methods, is that Ridge's Zinfandels have been largely responsible for elevating the status of this varietal from that of material for blending in ordinary wines to premium quality on a level with Cabernet Sauvignons. At the same time, Ridge's Cabernets are among the most sought-after in California.

ROLLING VINEYARDS
Hector, Finger Lakes

Output: 2,500 cases

Leading Wines:
Chelois, Marechal Foch,
Riesling, Seneca Lake Red,
Seyval Blanc, Vidal Blanc,
White, and Rosé

A very small winery with a relatively big and diversified vineyard, Rolling Vineyards vinifies the grapes that ripen best each year and sells the rest to other wineries, large and small. This keeps the product line of half-a-dozen wines in flux, but semidry Seyval and Vidal Blanc are impressive and usually available. Chelois from this vineyard has produced red wine of unusual depth and breed for the Finger Lakes. The location, on a steep slope above Seneca Lake, promises good things from new vinifera plantings.

ROSE BOWER VINEYARD & WINERY
Hampden-Sydney, Virginia

Output: 2,000 cases

Leading Wines:
Briery Lake White,
Cabernet Sauvignon,
Chardonnay,
Hampden Forest Claret,
Marechal Foch,
Seyval Blanc

A "cottage" winery in southern Virginia, Rose Bower endeavors to make wine in the 18th century spirit of its country house, pictured on the label. Vinifera and French-American varieties are clarified with natural agents such as egg whites or gelatin, siphoned instead of pumped, minimally filtered (when feasible), and all aged in lightly toasted oak barrels.

Hampden Forest Claret spends time in barrels made from local Virginia trees. A nouveau Marechal Foch is released each year at Halloween, as early as any current vintage wine can be had. Well-aged Cabernet Sauvignon and barrel-fermented Chardonnay are leading varietals.

ROSENBLUM CELLARS
Emeryville, San Francisco Bay South

This is another of the small urban wineries located in San Francisco East Bay and founded in 1978. Grapes are purchased from Napa and Sonoma county vineyards which are usually identified on its labels.

Rosenblum's specialty is a Gewurztraminer produced by *méthode champenoise* in which unusually the second fermentation in the bottle is initiated by the addition of sweet reserve Riesling juice to the still wine.

Output: 3,000 cases

Leading Wines:
Cabernet Sauvignon,
Chardonnay, sparkling
Gewurztraminer,
Petite Sirah, Zinfandel

ROUDON SMITH VINEYARDS
Santa Cruz, San Francisco Bay South

A small Santa Cruz winery founded in 1972, Roudon Smith makes a range of varietals from growers in several different vineyard areas: Santa Cruz Mountains, Sonoma County, Mendocino County, Edna Valley, San Luis Obispo, and Santa Barbara County.

Production in this 42,000-gallon winery emphasizes Chardonnay which is barrel-fermented and, in a practice unusual in California, encouraged to undergo malolactic fermentation. All wines see some barrel-aging.

Output: 12,000 cases

Leading Wines:
Cabernet Sauvignon,
Chardonnay, Petite Sirah,
Pinot Noir, Zinfandel,
White Zinfandel

ROUND HILL VINEYARDS
St. Helena, San Francisco Bay North

When this winery was founded in 1977, it acted as a *négociant* — buying, finishing, bottling, and distributing wines. But Round Hill now also produces its own wines at its 120,000-gallon winery under two labels: Rutherford Ranch and Round Hill. Rutherford Ranch wines generally require some aging. Ready to drink, Round Hill wines in general represent good value for the money.

Output: 90,000 cases

Leading Wines:
Burgundy,
Cabernet Sauvignon,
Chablis, Chardonnay,
Chenin Blanc

ROYAL KEDEM WINERY
Milton, Hudson River Valley

The Hudson River Valley's largest producer, Royal has extended its line of mostly sweet, native grape wines with a number of dry French-American varietals. Its Seyval gives a good, light fruity account of the variety. The American grape wines have been made lighter in recent years, including its kosher specialty, Cream Concord. The winery was established in 1949 on the bank of the Hudson River, where it ships over 30 table and fruit wines, sparkling wines, and coolers throughout the Northeast. In addition to using grapes from its own 140-acre vineyard, Royal is the major purchaser of grapes in the valley.

Output: 500,000 cases

Leading Wines:
Aurora, Burgundy,
Chablis, De Chaunac,
Cream Concord,
Seyval Blanc, Tokay

R

Ruby Cabernet

Perhaps the most successful new variety created by Harold Olmo at U.C. Davis, Ruby Cabernet is intended to combine the character of Cabernet Sauvignon with the yield of Carignane. There are now 12,000 acres of Ruby Cabernet in California, nearly all in the Central Valley. Made as a varietal, it has some of the characteristics of Cabernet Sauvignon's aroma and flavor, but usually lacks the finesse and elegance which the latter is capable of achieving.

RUTHERFORD HILL WINERY
Rutherford, San Francisco Bay North

Output: 100,000 cases

Leading Wines:
Cabernet Sauvignon,
Chardonnay,
Gewurztraminer,
Johannisberg Riesling,
Merlot,
Pinot Noir,
Sauvignon Blanc,
Zinfandel

Originally the Pillsbury-owned Souverain winery of Rutherford, in 1976 this winery was taken over by some of the Freemark Abbey partners and renamed. With the advantage of having several owners who control extensive vineyard acreage, winemaker Phil Baxter has been able to choose his grapes and established a consistent record for Rutherford's wines across a wide range of varietals. Rutherford Hill's Cabernet Sauvignon and Pinot Noir have received most attention, but the Merlot, Chardonnay, and Sauvignon Blanc also have first-rate reputations.

RUTHERFORD VINTNERS
Rutherford, San Francisco Bay North

Output: 15,000 cases

Leading Wines:
Cabernet Sauvignon,
Chardonnay
Johannisberg Riesling,
Merlot,
Pinot Noir

Run by the former winery manager of Louis Martini Winery, this 84,000-gallon winery produces a range of varietals from its Cabernet Sauvignon and Riesling-planted vineyard as well as purchased grapes. Cabernet Sauvignon is produced in two styles, both estate-bottled.

S

Sacramento Valley

The northern section of California's great Central Valley is often spoken of as the Sacramento Valley. This region includes the northern portion of the large river delta through which the Sacramento and San Joaquin rivers drain into San Francisco Bay. The counties of Sacramento, Butte, Colusa, Glenn, Shasta, Tehama, Yolo, and Yuba make up the region.

Growing season temperatures are warmest at this northern end of the valley, which is classified as a Region IV. The Sacramento River flows south through the center of the valley and exerts some moderating influence generally, but of more importance are the onshore flows of marine air through the river delta, which reduce temperatures in the delta significantly below those in the other northern reaches of the valley.

Fully one half the vineyards (3,800 acres out of a total of 7,600) planted in the region are growing on the broad, fertile, alluvial plains of the Sacramento River. The most heavily planted grape in the region is Chenin Blanc, with over 1,000 acres devoted to this variety, half of which are in Sacramento County. The variety appears to do well in the delta, which has gained a small measure of fame in recent years for Clarksburg and Meritt Island Chenin Blancs. Both appellations, which have been approved by the BATF for use on wine labels, are just across the Sacramento County line in Yolo County. Second in importance in terms of acreage is French Colombard, followed by Zinfandel and Cabernet Sauvignon.

ST. CLEMENT VINEYARDS
St. Helena, San Francisco

Output: 10,000 cases

Leading Wines:
Cabernet Sauvignon,
Chardonnay,
Sauvignon Blanc

Founded in 1975, this winery was expanded to 25,000 gallon capacity in 1979 and moved to a native stone building set into the base of Spring Mountain. Only two acres of vineyards are owned and most grapes are purchased for its very likable line of ripe-fruit wines that avoid being ponderous. To date, the winery has been more successful with whites than with reds.

STE. CHAPELLE VINEYARDS
Caldwell, Idaho

Output: 120,000 cases

Leading Wines:
Cabernet Sauvignon,
Chardonnay,
Chenin Blanc,
Gewurztraminer,
Merlot,
Riesling

IDAHO 1984
Johannisberg Riesling

Produced and Bottled by Ste. Chapelle, Inc.
Caldwell, Idaho. BWID-8. Alcohol 10.2% by Volume.

The rapid success of Ste. Chapelle Vineyards is made more remarkable for being the first winery in the modern era in a new and untested wine-growing region. Yet within a few years of its first commercial crush in 1976, Ste. Chapelle became one of the Northwest's major wineries. Owned jointly by Bill Broich, the winemaker, and the Symms family, long-time Idaho orchardists, Ste. Chapelle began its plantings in the early 1970s, in the Snake River Valley.

Ste. Chapelle also purchases Washington grapes to augment local grape production, releasing the Washington wines under a separate label. For the consumer this allows some interesting comparisons between Washington and Idaho grapes. Some wines, however, such as Cabernet Sauvignon and Merlot, are made only from Washington grapes.

Ste. Chapelle's vineyards are planted at an elevation of 2,500 feet, higher than any other major Northwest vineyard. Cold winters and spring frosts are problems, while the bright winter sunlight reflecting off the snow can create a 50°F to 60°F difference between day and night temperatures in the vineyards.

Ste. Chapelle's first wine in 1976 was a Riesling; this was followed in 1978 by a full-bodied Chardonnay, and later by Chenin Blanc and Gewurztraminer. Each new wine more firmly established Idaho as a premium wine region capable of successfully producing a range of varietals. But as yet, neither Idaho nor Ste. Chapelle has a red wine, although Pinot Noir may be the grape. At present, Ste. Chapelle makes a popular Pinot Noir Blanc, and Pinot Noir is the basis for a bottle-fermented sparkling wine.

Finished with residual sweetness, Ste. Chapelle's Rieslings are full-flavored and low alcohol, in their own way more closely resembling the fuller-bodied wines from the Rheingau than wines from Mosel. The Chardonnays too are fuller-bodied and fuller-flavored, and little like the traditional steely wines of Chablis that some might expect from an Idaho Chardonnay. Without botrytis as a factor, Ste. Chapelle's late-harvest Rieslings are made from exceptionally ripe, late picked grapes. It is one of the few wineries of its size that does not subject its wines to cold stabilizations, and this is sometimes visible in the harmless tartrate crystal deposits on their corks.

Ste. Chappelle is the Northwest's largest producer of sparkling wines, and in late 1984 the winery celebrated its first release of 25,000 cases of sparkling Riesling made by the charmat process.

St. Emilion

Also known as Ugni Blanc and Trebbiano, St. Emilion's chief use has been as a blending grape in generic whites. In recent years, interest has developed in St. Emilion as a base wine for sparkling wines, apparently because of its rather neutral character. There are 1,500 acres in California.

ST. FRANCIS VINEYARD AND WINERY
Kenwood, San Francisco Bay North

Beginning as grape growers, the owners of St. Francis built a modern winery in 1979 and began a program of estate-bottled varietals supplemented by occasional bottlings of small lots from nearby vineyards with high reputations.

Outstanding among its varietals has been its Gewurztraminer. The wine is produced in a dry style and, though it is a bit softer than Alsatian Gewurztraminers, it often shows the spicy Gewurztraminer character that is usually associated only with the Alsatian versions.

Output: 18,000 cases

Leading Wines:
Chardonnay,
Gewurztraminer,
Johannisberg Riesling,
Merlot,
Pinot Noir

ST. JULIAN WINE COMPANY
Paw Paw, Michigan

The largest and oldest winery in Michigan, St. Julian produces over three dozen wines—the most diverse line of table, sparkling, dessert, fruit, and specialty wines of any American winery outside California.

Half the product line consists of table wines in three groups: varietal, generic, and Frankenmuth wines. Seyval is made in the style of French Graves: fruity, cold-fermented wine back-blended with heavily oaked batches. Chancellor is medium-bodied, aged for over two years in American oak—often one of the best examples of the variety. Reserve varietals from Vidal, Seyval, and Vignoles are cold-fermented with Steinberg yeast and sweetened with preserved juice, in the German style, lowering the alcohol content. Excepting the regular Seyval, all St. Julian whites have some sweetness and prominent fruit. Friar's Noir and Friar's Blanc are consistently well-made French-American hybrid blends.

The generic table wines blend hybrid and labrusca varieties to show more grapey flavors. St. Julian's semisweet Frankenmuth wines are made from grapes grown in the Saginaw Bay area of eastern Michigan, where the winery's branch facility has helped initiate a new vineyard district. All grapes for this and the main winery are purchased from area growers, though some California wine has been used for blending.

St. Julian has one of only three sherry soleras in the eastern United States, helping to sustain the East's tradition of fruity, offbeat sherries.

Output: 100,000 cases

Leading Wines:
Chancellor Noir,
Frankenmuth May Wine,
Friar's Blanc,
Friar's Noir,
Seyval Blanc,
Vidal Blanc,
Vignoles,
various sherries

SAINTSBURY
Napa, San Francisco Bay North

Located in the heart of the Carneros Viticultural Area, Saintsbury was founded in 1981. It specializes in two varietals, Chardonnay and Pinot Noir, thought to do particularly well in this cool region where a long growing season yields grapes with relatively high acidity. As a result of these growing conditions and of harvesting at a moderate maturity level of 22°F to 23°F Brix—that is, without a great deal of sugar—Saintsbury's Chardonnay and Pinot Noir show fresh, varietal character and good balance.

Output: 12,000 cases

Leading Wines:
Chardonnay,
Garnet,
Pinot Noir

S

SAKONNET VINEYARDS
Little Compton, New England

Output: 10,000 cases

Leading Wines:
America's Cup White,
Chardonnay,
Compass Rosé,
Rhode Island,
Riesling,
Spinnaker White,
Vidal,
Sparkling Vidal

In its first decade, Sakonnet Vineyards developed a style of dry, austere fruit, relatively high acid wines designed for New England seafood. Notable among these are the America's Cup White blend of Seyval and Vidal Blanc with light oak finish, a serious, well-balanced rosé, and a tinder-dry, tart Vidal reminiscent of a sharp Muscadet.

Sakonnet's Chardonnay is a flinty fruit version with enough French oak aging to add some depth but not enough to taste. As with other New England wineries, vintages do vary considerably at Sakonnet. Riesling is the clearest barometer, ranging from light and off-dry to a honeyed, Auslese-style in the best years. Rhode Island Red is a smooth, medium-bodied blend of Chancellor, Foch, and Leon Millot well-aged in oak casks, better for being such a mellow surprise in a white wine stronghold. All wines are estate-bottled from the 45-acre vineyard in Rhode Island's picture-book coastal countryside.

SALISHAN VINEYARDS
La Center, Washington

Output: 2,000 cases

Leading Wines:
Cabernet Sauvignon,
Chardonnay,
Chenin Blanc,
Pinot Noir,
Riesling

Salishan's growing site is outside Washington's viticultural mainstream, and there are few other vineyards in the area, and no other wineries. Its climate is very similar to Oregon's nearby northern Willamette Valley, and except for Chenin Blanc, the vines are cane-pruned as they are in Oregon, rather than cordon-pruned as in California and most of Washington. The climate is excellent for Pinot Noir, and Salishan is virtually the only Washington winery producing consistently successful wines from this varietal.

SANFORD AND BENEDICT
Lompoc, Central Coast

Output: 10,000 cases

Leading Wines:
Cabernet Sauvignon,
Chardonnay,
Johannisberg Riesling

Founded in 1972, this small winery has become known for Burgundian style Pinot Noir and Chardonnay. Fermentation procedures are patterned after those in Burgundy as is the character of the limestone soil Sanford and Benedict chose as their vineyard site.

SANFORD WINERY
Buellton, Central Coast

Output: 6,000 cases

Leading Wines:
Chardonnay,
Pinot Noir,
Pinot Noir-Vin Gris,
Sauvignon Blanc

Formerly a partner in Sanford and Benedict, Richard Sanford started this winery in 1981. He continues to work in a Burgundian style with Pinot Noir and Chardonnay with success and has added Sauvignon Blanc.

All wines see barrel-aging, including a rosé from Pinot Noir. Called Vin Gris, it is one of the most complex and varietally-correct "blush wines" produced in California.

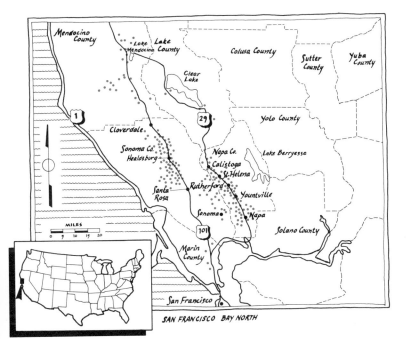

SAN FRANCISCO BAY NORTH

SAN FRANCISCO BAY NORTH

Encompassing Napa, Sonoma, Mendocino, and Marin counties and the western vineyard areas of Solano and Lake counties, this region includes many of the outstanding winegrowing regions and wineries in California. Here are located the Napa, Sonoma, Dry Creek, and Alexander valleys, Los Carneros, and Chalk Hill Viticultural Areas. It was here also that the production of fine California wines began in the 19th century after Agoston Haraszthy brought an estimated 100,000 European cuttings of dozens of vinifera varieties to Sonoma in 1862.

The region encompasses a wide variety of growing conditions (microclimates, solar exposure, heat units, soils), but there is however a weather pattern during the growing season which has an effect on the entire region. In fact, one of the key arguments for approval of the North Coast Viticultural Area was this weather phenomenon. From mid-April to mid-October, but particularly during the summer months of June, July, and August, the entire region is blanketed almost daily by an incursion of marine air. After sunset the low-lying fog bank which hovers a few miles off-shore throughout the summer months moves inland as far as 30 miles, but usually has retreated by 10 o'clock the following morning. This cooling flow of marine air has the effect of moderating temperatures throughout the region during the growing season, allowing the grapes to ripen and still maintain a good acid/sugar balance that tends to produce more complex wine.

The geology of the region defies generalizations. Its shape was created by the uplifting of the North American continent from the ocean floor, and subsequent volcanic activity and alluvial action. This bending and cracking of the sedimentary crust created a rugged terrain with numerous valleys and canyons in which microclimates vary markedly from one to another. While thousands of years of rainfall have washed the volcanic mineral deposits to the valley floors, creating very fertile soils, these soils are very uneven in composition, ranging from light sandy loams to relatively heavier clay loams and clay. But most are well-drained and grapes grow well throughout the region.

Rainfall is usually confined to the winter months and it is rare for a harvest to be beset with problems arising from precipitation during the harvest period. However, winter rainfall can be heavy, ranging from 20-inches in the valley to over 50-inches in the mountains. In most years harvest occurs from early September to mid-October.

According to U.C. Davis systems for measurement of heat units, San Francisco Bay North ranges from Region I, in the areas nearest the Bay and those affected by the marine influence such as Los Carneros, to Region III at the northern end of the Napa Valley and the areas surrounding Geyserville in Sonoma County.

During the so-called 'wine revolution' of the late 1960s and early 1970s, vineyard acreage in the regions more than doubled. Most of the wineries are less than ten years old although growth in the region — in the wineries and acreage — has slowed almost to a halt. In excess of 70,000 acres are now planted to wine grapes and more than a third of these are of the two varietals acknowledged to produce the 'best' wines in California, Cabernet Sauvignon and Chardonnay. Substantial acreage is also planted to Zinfandel, Pinot Noir, and White Riesling; while plantings of Merlot and Sauvignon Blanc are increasing. (New plantings tend to be in the whites.) Together these five varietals account for approximately 60 percent of the vineyard acreage in San Francisco Bay North.

1980   In one of the coolest seasons in many years, crops were large and acid levels were unusually high. Chardonnay and Sauvignon Blanc were generally excellent, although some Chardonnays are very high in alcohol. Cabernets and Zinfandels were hard and are only now softening to drinkability, with the former showing its age best. Some fine botrytised wines were produced.

1981   Despite the heat, acids remained high in Chardonnay and Sauvignon Blanc in Napa and Sonoma. Cabernets in all areas are light to medium in body but lacking in fruit. Zinfandel especially from Mendocino attained good acid/sugar balance.

1982   A long cool season benefited Chardonnays and Sauvignon Blancs. Late rains also resulted in botrytised Rieslings and Sauvignon Blancs. Cabernets show good fruit but have sufficient tannins to age well. With one or two robust, tannic exceptions Zinfandels were light.

1983   A wet winter and harvest rains followed by a cool summer resulted in some excellent botrytised wines but damaged much of the Chardonnay crop. Cabernet and Zinfandel fared poorly and are generally low in color and alcohol. Sauvignon Blanc generally survived the adverse weather and there are some excellent examples from the Napa Valley.

1984   Record temperatures resulted in high yields in cool areas but reduced crops in warmer regions. In cooler areas acid levels and varietal character were good, especially for Sauvignon Blanc and Chardonnay. Virtually everywhere sugar and alcohol were higher than desirable, and in the Napa Valley and Mendocino reds display excessive tannins that will require lengthy aging to soften.

SAN FRANCISCO BAY SOUTH

Vineyard areas located south, east, and southeast of San Francisco Bay are included in this region, covering the counties of Alameda, Contra Costa, Santa Clara, San Mateo, and Santa Cruz. San Francisco Bay South is home to such famous names as Paul Masson, Almadén, Mirassou, Concannon, and Wente. But urban sprawl and rising tax rates at the end of World War II prompted wineries to look for vineyard land elsewhere. Now the vineyards of Almadén, Paul Masson, and Mirassou are mainly located farther south in Monterey and San Benito Counties.

The low, rolling hills of the Coastal Range dominate the region's topography. Vineyards have historically been planted in the valleys, but in recent years new plantings have climbed the hillsides of the Santa Cruz Mountains. Soils and growing conditions differ considerably from one vineyard to another. In the Livermore Valley, an hour's drive east of San Francisco, the gravelly soils reminded pioneer planters of Graves in Bordeaux. To the south, in the Santa Clara Valley, soils are deep and fertile, suitable for a variety of orchard crops as well as grapes. However, under the pressure of urbanization, most of the orchards and vineyards have disappeared from Santa Clara. In the early 1950s 9,000 acres of vineyards were planted in Santa Clara Valley; today, no more than 1,500 acres of vines remain in the valley itself, and approximately 3,000 survive in Santa Clara and Alameda counties, 1,700 of which belong to Wente Brothers in Livermore.

Temperatures during the growing season are moderately cool along the coastline, particularly on the slopes of the Santa Cruz Mountains, but warmer inland. On the Davis scale for heat summation, the area ranges from Region I to II.

No single grape variety predominates in the vineyards of San Francisco Bay South. Less than a thousand acres are planted to Cabernet Sauvignon, Chardonnay, Sauvignon Blanc, Semillon and Pinot Noir combined.

1980   Cool weather held crops below normal, concentrating flavors in Cabernets. Unusually high acidity indicates a long life for this varietal. Zinfandels were also hard but many lacked depth.

1981   An early harvest in Livermore Valley, but in the Santa Cruz Mountains Cabernet ripened later than usual. Sugar levels and alcohol in Cabernets were generally low and color is slightly weak. Chardonnays showed good acid and fruit, and were of high quality. The Zinfandels are unexceptional.

S

1982   An uneven year in which some botrytis developed in Rieslings and Semillon in the Livermore. These and the whites across the region were generally better than the reds, which sometimes showed too much acid.
1983   Those vineyards that escaped damage from rain during harvest produced good wines, especially some rich Chardonnays from the Santa Cruz Mountains. Livermore Cabernets show better balance than the light, Santa Cruz versions produced this year.
1984   The heat wave was moderated in the Livermore Valley to the west, but in the Santa Clara Valley and eastern Santa Cruz Mountains temperatures were high. Some very well-balanced Cabernets and Sauvignon Blancs from the warmer areas and excellent Santa Clara Chardonnays were produced.

SAN MARTIN VALLEY
San Martin, San Francisco Bay South

Output: 250,000 cases

Leading Wines:
Cabernet Sauvignon,
Chardonnay,
Chenin Blanc,
Fumé Blanc,
Johnnisberg Riesling,
Soft Chenin Blanc,
Soft Gamay Beaujolais,
Soft Johannisberg Riesling

San Martin was founded as a growers' cooperative in 1906. In the 1970s, it was known principally as a producer of fruit and berry wines running the gamut from apple wine to raspberry wine. Since then, the emphasis has moved to grape wines, and in 1979 it was purchased by the Somerset Wine Company, a Norton Simon subsidiary.

Under the direction of Ed Friedrich, the winemaker from 1973 to 1982, San Martin pioneered the concept of "soft wines." These wines contain extremely low alcohol levels of under 10 percent, and met with tremendous success among consumers looking for lighter, low-alcoholic beverages.

SANTA CRUZ MOUNTAIN VINEYARD
Santa Cruz, San Francisco Bay South

Output: 3,500 cases

Leading Wines:
Cabernet Sauvignon,
Chardonnay,
Duriff, Merlot,
Pinot Noir

Founded in 1974 to produce Pinot Noir wines, this 17,000 gallon winery has since diversified, producing several varietals from estate and purchased grapes including one from Duriff, a Rhône grape that may be the same as Petite Sirah. Pinot Noir, however, remains the focus. Characterized by their enormous fruit and rich extracts, they are not to everyone's liking, but they are true California curiosities.

SANTA YNEZ VALLEY WINERY
Santa Ynez, Central Coast

Output: 10,000 cases

Leading Wines:
Blanc de Cabernet,
Chardonnay,
Gewurztraminer,
Johannisberg Riesling,
Merlot,
Sauvignon Blanc

Starting as the first commercial vineyard in the cool Santa Ynez Valley, grapes from Santa Ynez's 110-acre plantings were sold until 1976, when a 35,000-gallon winery was built. The winery is best-known for its Chardonnay and in particular for its Sauvignon Blanc. The Sauvignon Blanc is fermented in small French oak barrels and aged for four months, also in small oak, following the completion of fermentation; in some vintages a small amount of Semillon is added.

SANTINO WINERY
Plymouth, Sierra Foothills

Although a relatively recent addition (founded 1979) to the growing list of wineries producing in the Shenandoah Valley, Santino has already established a reputation for fruity, full Zinfandel. Grapes are purchased in two vineyard areas, Fiddletown and Shenandoah. Fiddletown has long been known as the source of some of California's richest Zinfandels, and Shenandoah enjoys equal fame for this grape variety.

Output: 18,000 cases

Leading Wines:
Cabernet Sauvignon Blanc,
Sauvignon Blanc,
White Zinfandel,
Zinfandel

SARAH'S VINEYARD
Gilroy, San Francisco Bay North

Founded in 1978, this small winery has stirred up a great deal of attention for its elegant, hand-crafted wines. Typically, they are lean-structured and delicate, with high acidity and excellent varietal definition. The Chardonnay has been especially successful.

Output: 2,000 cases

Leading Wines:
Chardonnay,
Johannisberg Riesling

SAUCELITO CANYON VINEYARD
Arroyo Grande, Central Coast

Founded in 1982, Saucelito Canyon produces small quantities of three wines: Cabernet Sauvignon, Zinfandel, and White Zinfandel. The latter two are produced from the output of three acres of vines planted near the winery site in 1880. The white Zinfandel is barrel fermented to create an unusually complex blush wine.

Output: 1,000 cases

Leading Wines:
Cabernet Sauvignon,
White Zinfandel,
Zinfandel

SAUSAL WINERY
Healdsburg, San Francisco Bay North

This group of Alexander Valley growers produced the first release under their own label in 1979—a 1974 Zinfandel made from grapes harvested from 65 to 70-year-old vines. Three 100 percent varietals are produced from grapes grown in Sausal partners' vineyards, two blanc-de-noir wines, and a proprietary blend called Sausal Blanc (French Colombard and Chardonnay).

Output: 8,000 cases

Leading Wines:
Cabernet Sauvignon,
Chardonnay,
Pinot Noir Blanc,
Sausal Blanc,
White Zinfandel,
Zinfandel

Sauvignon Blanc

This white vinifera slumbered in California until Robert Mondavi offered a dry-finished Fumé Blanc in the late 1960s; this marketing concept spurred a great increase in the planting of Sauvignon Blanc, and today it is often considered California's second white wine, after Chardonnay. There are a number of distinct styles: crisp and grassy like the Loire versions; softer and fruitier like the Bordeaux wines; and—California's own variation—rich and complex due to either barrel-fermentation or oak aging. All these wines may be labeled either Sauvignon Blanc or Fumé Blanc; the name that the winery has chosen is not a reliable guide to the style. There are now around 13,700 acres planted in California.

SCHARFFENBERGER CELLARS
Ukiah, San Francisco Bay North

Output: 10,000 cases

Leading Wines:
Blanc de Noir,
Chardonnay,
Eaglepoint:
Sauvignon Blanc,
Scharffenberger Brut

Scharffenberger was founded in 1981 to specialize in *méthode champenoise* sparkling wines.

Most of Scharffenberger's grapes are sold to other wineries (it has appeared on vineyard-designated Fetzer wines, for example). But Pinot Noir and Chardonnay grapes for its sparkling wines are purchased from the Anderson, Ukiah, and Redwood valleys. Some still wines are also produced and bottled under the Eaglepoint label.

SCHRAMSBERG VINEYARDS
Calistoga, San Francisco Bay North

Output: 38,000 cases

Leading Wines:
Blanc de Blancs,
Blanc de Noirs,
Cremant Demi-Sec,
Cuvée de Pinot,
Reserve

NAPA VALLEY
CRÉMANT

VINTAGE 1982   DEMI-SEC
PRODUCED AND BOTTLED BY
SCHRAMSBERG VINEYARDS   ALCOHOL 12.0% BY VOLUME
CALISTOGA, CALIFORNIA   CONTENTS 750 MLS

The old winery, founded in 1862 by Jacob Schramm, was extensively refurbished and brought back into production of high quality sparkling wines with great success by Jack and Jamie Davis in 1965. Since its first releases in the 1960s, Schramsberg has built up an enviable reputation and is perhaps California's leading producer of *méthode champenoise* wines. Schramsberg's use of traditional grape varieties, a practice it introduced to the Napa Valley, and Champagne techniques, and extended aging on the yeast have resulted in a series of wines of great complexity and balance.

A Pinot Noir, Chardonnay, and Pinot Blanc blend in a Reserve bottling that receives four years on the yeast is probably Schramsberg's leading wine. But the traditional Blanc de Noirs, of Chardonnay and Pinot Noir, is its most constantly praised, and a brut Blancs de Blancs is its most popular. Schramsberg was the first winery to use Flora (a variety developed by Harold Olmo at U.C. Davis by crossing Semillon and Gewurztraminer) to make a dessert style sparkling wine called Cremant Demi-Sac. As in Champagne district, Cremant has about half the effervescence of other sparkling wines.

In 1982 a joint venture of Schramsberg with Remy Martin was announced to produce brandy in a Cognac style in the Carneros district of the Napa Valley.

SCHUG CELLARS
Calistoga, San Francisco Bay North

Output: 8,500 cases

Leading Wines:
Chardonnay,
Pinot Noir

Founded in 1980, Schug Cellars features three vineyards on their wines. Heinemann Mountain on the eastern slopes of Spring Mountain produces Pinot Noir, and Ahollinger Vineyard and Beckstoffer Vineyard in the Carneros area supply both Pinot Noir and Chardonnay to Schug Cellars.

The Chardonnay is barrel-fermented in the 100-year-old caves at the restored Grimm winery. The techniques for producing the Pinot Noir are a blend of traditional Burgundian practices and the winery's creative approach to winemaking. A portion of the grapes go through a standard fermentation and some are subject to whole-berry fermentation similar to the technique of carbonic maceration employed in producing Beaujolais nouveau before blending.

Scuppernong, See Muscadine

SEA RIDGE WINERY
Cazadero, San Francisco Bay North

This winery was founded in 1980 primarily to produce Pinot Noir and Chardonnay following Burgundian techniques. Both wines receive malolactic fermentation and are aged in oak.

Output: 5,000 cases

Leading Wines:
Chardonnay
Gewurztraminer

SEBASTIANI VINEYARDS
Sonoma, San Francisco Bay North

Sebastiani Vineyards is one of the oldest and largest family-owned wineries in California, dating back to 1889. In the years after Prohibition it operated as a bulk winery, its wines ending up with such well-known labels as Paul Masson and Beaulieu, but from 1944 it began selling wines under its own name. Until 1980 Sebastiani's reputation was primarily as a producer of inexpensive jug wines (mainly reds) and a full line of varietals. But with the third generation, Sebastiani appears to be placing greatest emphasis upon its high-quality wines: the top-of-the-line Proprietor's Reserve, its Vintage Varietal Red, and its Vintage Classic wines.

Modernization, begun earlier, has continued in this 6 million-gallon winery: small oak barrels have been added to the redwood tanks and oak ovals for wood development and in 1985, a *méthode champenoise* sparkling wine was added to the line.

But its full-bodied, vigorous Barbera, for which Sebastiani has long been noted, continues to be a hallmark of the winery. This and its Cabernet Sauvignon and Zinfandel are also produced in the longer-aged Proprietor's Reserve, which shows some promise of adding a reputation for fine varietals to Sebastiani's image.

Output: 4.5 million cases

Leading Wines:
Proprietor's Reserve:
Barbera,
Cabernet Sauvignon,
Chardonnay,
Sauvignon Blanc,
Pinot Noir,
Zinfandel;
Vintage Classics:
Gewurztraminer,
Pinot Noir Rouge,
Gamay Beaujolais,
Pinot Noir Blanc,
Muscat Canelli;
Vintage Varietals:
Barbera,
Cabernet Sauvignon

Semillon

A white vinifera that is dry, medium-bodied with a distinctive aroma of figs as a varietal. Although there are 3,400 acres of this variety growing in California, Semillon's use has been primarily as a blending grape with Sauvignon Blanc. Interest now appears to be increasing in it as a varietal, sometimes as a dessert wine in the style of the Sauternes of Bordeaux.

Seyval Blanc

Seyval is the French-American hybrid variety most responsible for defining a new eastern American wine style. It is the most widely grown white hybrid (currently approaching 1,000 acres), and one that is remarkably adaptable to different regions and climates. If a winery produces any French-American hybrid wine, it probably produces a Seyval.

The versatility of the wine is matched by the wine, but two principal styles have emerged. First, a light wine with citrusy, appley fruit and relatively high acid (often balanced with residual sugar) made to be consumed young with a prominent fresh fruit flavor. This is the predominant style for Seyval in the Finger Lakes, Michigan, and other northern districts, though there are many exceptions. The alternative style typically begins with very ripe, lower acid grapes, often uses warmer fermentation temperatures to increase extract and phenolics for more body, and ferments or ages in wood to develop bouquet. This is the Seyval Blanc style in southern Pennsylvania, Maryland, Virginia, again with a few notable exceptions.

Seyval Blanc is similar to Sauvignon Blanc in its grassy quality and its adaptability to both dry and crisp-fruit styles, but it is less assertive and has more obvious fruit. The only significant cultural challenge with the vines is their determination to overproduce, requiring rigorous cluster thinning to prevent the wine turning out thin and sharp.

SHAFER VINEYARD CELLARS
Forest Grove, Oregon

Output: 6,000 cases

Leading Wines:
Chardonnay,
Gewurztraminer,
Pinot Noir,
Riesling,
Sauvignon Blanc

First planted in 1973, Shafer's 20-acre vineyard is located in the narrow Gales Creek Valley at the northernmost part of the Willamette Valley. At first intended only as a vineyard, the enterprise evolved into a winery out of a desire to see the grapes through to completion as wine.

The first three vintages were made at other wineries, but beginning with the 1981 vintage, all the wines are made at Shafer's own winery. Chardonnay and Pinot Noir are specialties. Shafer's Chardonnay is fermented and aged in Limousin and Nevers oak barrels. The Pinot Noir is fermented in small bins and the cap punched down by hand, before aging in Allier oak barrels. Unusual for the Willamette Valley, Shafer also produces a Sauvignon Blanc, demonstrating that the grape can ripen better and sooner in this cool region than viticultural texts would suggest.

SHAFER VINEYARDS
Napa, San Francisco Bay North

Output: 14,000 cases

Leading Wines:
Cabernet Sauvignon,
Chardonnay,
Merlot

Shafer is a family-run winery, founded in 1980, on a 50-year-old vineyard. Sixty-five acres of Shafer Vineyards are planted to Cabernet Sauvignon, Cabernet Franc, Chardonnay, Merlot; some Chardonnay grapes are purchased from the sparkling wine producer S. Anderson Winery.

CHARLES F. SHAW VINEYARD AND WINERY
St. Helena, San Francisco Bay North

Founded in 1979, this winery specializes in Beaujolais-style wines made from the variety known as the Napa Gamay. This variety may not in fact be related to the Gamay grape of Beaujolais, but nevertheless it can produce wines of that style. Of its two styles of Gamay, one is made as a "Nouveau," using the carbonic maceration employed in Beaujolais to produce Nouveau wines; the second is produced in a conventional style, rendering it a wine for longer keeping.

Output: 20,000 cases

*Leading Wines:
Chardonnay,
Fumé Blanc,
Gamay "Nouveau,"
Napa Valley Gamay*

SHENANDOAH VINEYARDS
Edinburg, Virginia

The 40-acre vineyard at this Shenandoah Valley winery is evenly divided between French-American hybrid and vinifera varieties used for proprietary blends and varietals respectively. Another third of the grapes used at Shenandoah are purchased from independent Virginia growers.

The style for whites and rosés is light and fruity except for Chardonnay and Seyval Blanc, which have fuller-body and are briefly aged in barrels for a light oak finish. Red wines are made for at least a few years of aging, routinely beginning with two years or more in French and American oak. Since opening in 1979, Shenandoah has delivered its most consistent quality with off-dry Riesling and Vidal, Seyval Blanc, and a big, woody Chambourcin. With vintage 1983 it began production of a bottle-fermented sparkling wine blend from Pinot Noir and Chardonnay.

Output: 10,000 cases

*Leading Wines:
Cabernet Sauvignon,
Chambourcin,
Johannisberg Riesling,
Pinot Noir,
Ravat,
Seyval Blanc,
Shenandoah Blanc,
Vidal Blanc*

SHOWN AND SONS VINEYARDS
Rutherford, San Francisco Bay North

Richard Shown began the 80-acre "Las Agualitas" vineyard in 1971, and produced high-quality grapes (Cabernet Sauvignon, Johannisberg Riesling, and Chenin Blanc) which he sold to neighboring wineries. Since 1978 Shown has produced its own wines and although Las Agualitas was sold to Joseph Heitz in 1984 the new emphasis on only two varietals holds some promise.

Output: 10,000 cases

*Leading Wines:
Cabernet Sauvignon,
Chardonnay*

SIERRA FOOTHILLS

Although the vineyards of the Sierra Foothills are situated in the foothills which name the region, most are planted on relatively flat land in the valleys which pocket the area. Vineyards planted on the western slopes of the Sierra Nevada Foothills during the Gold Rush days of the 1850s dwindled during the Prohibition era. In the 1960s and 1970s the region received renewed attention, especially for the planting of Zinfandel. The counties of Alpine, Amador, Claveras, El Dorado, Nevada and Placer are included in the region.

S

Temperatures during the growing season are moderately warm, declining at higher altitudes.

Zinfandel is clearly the most important variety in the Sierra Foothills with nearly 1,300 acres planted to this variety. Ninety percent of this is in Amador County—a total of 1,100 acres.

SIERRA VISTA WINERY
Placerville, Sierra Foothills

Output: 3,000 cases

Leading Wines:
Cabernet Sauvignon,
Chardonnay,
French Syrah,
Sauvignon Blanc,
White Zinfandel

Aptly named, Sierra Vista is located on an El Dorado County ridge against a dramatic backdrop of the Sierra Nevada Mountains. At 2,800 feet in elevation, Sierra Vista's 15 acres of vineyards are among the highest in the state and benefit from the cooling breezes off the towering Sierras to the east.

First vintages, beginning in 1977, were produced in leased space. A 28,000-gallon winery was completed in 1984.

SILVER MOUNTAIN VINEYARDS
Los Gatos, San Francisco Bay South

Output: 2,000 cases

Leading Wines:
Chardonnay,
Zinfandel

Established in 1979 primarily to produce barrel-fermented Chardonnay, Silver Mountain has 10 of its 17 acres of vineyards planted to this variety in the Santa Cruz Mountains Viticultural Area.

SILVER OAK WINE CELLAR
Oakville, San Francisco Bay North

Output: 15,000 cases

Leading Wine:
Cabernet Sauvignon

Silver Oak Wine Cellar was founded in 1972 to make Cabernet Sauvignon exclusively. Storage capacity of 115,000 gallons consists primarily of American oak barrels, as all vintages are aged for five years prior to release. Some wines are estate-bottled but grapes are also purchased in the Alexander and Napa valleys. They are labeled as either Napa Valley, Alexander Valley, or Bonny's Vineyard (wines aged in French oak from one of the partner's vineyards).

SILVERADO VINEYARDS
Napa, San Francisco Bay North

Output: 20,000 cases

Leading Wines:
Cabernet Sauvignon,
Chardonnay,
Merlot,
Sauvignon Blanc

Silverado Vineyards were begun in 1976 by Lillian Disney, widow of the famed Walt Disney, and her daughter and son-in-law, although a 150,000-gallon winery was not built until 1981.

Silverado produces four varietals from its 180 acres: Chardonnay, Sauvignon Blanc, Cabernet Sauvignon, and Merlot, a recent addition to the list. All wines see some oak before bottling.

SIMI WINERY
Healdsburg, San Francisco Bay North

Simi has a long and distinguished history dating to 1876, when it was founded by Pietro and Giuseppe Simi. One of the few wineries open during Prohibition, producing sacramental wine, it enjoyed great popularity immediately after Repeal. After passing out of family ownership in 1972, Simi had a succession of proprietors until Moët-Hennessy took control in early 1981.

The recent history of Simi includes two of California's first and most eminent women winemakers, first Mary Ann Graf, and since 1979, Zelma Long. Under Long's guidance, Simi has undertaken extensive remodelling and expansion of the original 19th century stone cellar. At the same time, Simi is exploring innovative winemaking techniques. For example, Long is trying out a gentler method of cap management during fermentation to extract greater color and aroma in the wines without increasing the tannins. Another program is being conducted to supplement laboratory measures of sugar and acid levels as determinants of ripeness in the vineyards.

Storage capacity at Simi is now 1 million gallons. The winery now owns 100 acres of vineyards; raw land was purchased in the up-and-coming Chalk Hill Viticultural Area in the Alexander Valley in 1982 and planted to Cabernet Sauvignon and Merlot.

Simi has forged itself an enviable position in the marketplace and is as capable of making a top-quality Chardonnay or Cabernet Sauvignon prized by connoisseurs as it is a delightfully fresh Chenin Blanc or Rosé of Cabernet Sauvignon to be drunk by picnickers.

Output: 150,000 cases

Leading Wines:
Cabernet Sauvignon,
Cabernet Sauvignon
Reserve,
Chardonnay,
Chardonnay Reserve,
Chenin Blanc,
Sauvignon Blanc,
Rosé of Cabernet
Sauvignon

SIMI

Rosé of
Cabernet Sauvignon

1 9 8 4

SISKIYOU VINEYARDS
Cave Junction, Oregon

Situated in the Illinois Valley in southernmost Oregon, Siskiyou's climate is much warmer and drier than most of western Oregon, and the principal grape varieties are accordingly different. Planted in 1974, the shallow soils and warm, dry climate make irrigation a necessity. Although the quality of the first wines has been uneven, the warmer climate varieties, Cabernet Sauvignon, Sauvignon Blanc, and Semillon, seem suited to this area.

Output: 6,000 cases

Leading Wines:
Cabernet Sauvignon,
Gewurztraminer,
Pinot Noir,
Sauvignon Blanc,
Semillon

SMITH AND HOOK
Soldad, Central Coast

Founded in 1980, Smith and Hook produces Cabernet Sauvignon with dedication and commitment to experimentation. All wines are estate-bottled from its 250 acres, which include Merlot and Cabernet Franc. Grapes from its separate slopes are hand-picked, hand-selected, and vinified separately before blending, to control quality and monitor the different effects of solar exposure, irrigation, and so on.

Output: 10,000 cases

Leading Wine:
Cabernet Sauvignon

S

SMITH-MADRONE VINEYARDS AND WINERY
St. Helena, San Francisco Bay North

Output: 6,000 cases

Leading Wines:
Cabernet Sauvignon,
Chardonnay,
Pinot Noir,
Riesling

This 27,000-gallon winery was founded on the side of Spring Mountain, 1,700 feet above the Napa Valley, in 1977. All its wines are estate-bottled from the surrounding 38 acres. In these vineyards yields are extremely low, only one to two tons per acre, assuring pronounced varietal character. This feature was obviously prized by the small neighboring wineries who bought Smith-Madrone grapes in the early years before it had a winery of its own.

Cabernet Sauvignon, Pinot Noir, and Chardonnay are fermented in stainless steel and aged in French oak barrels; the Chardonnay is partially barrel-fermented. Most successful of its wines is the Riesling, which is vinified in the German style, producing a lower-alcohol wine with distinct Riesling character. The very first vintage of this wine (1977) won first place in a tasting staged by Gault-Millau in Paris, in 1979. Pinot Noir, a wine with which California winemakers have had checkered results in the past, also shows promise at Smith-Madrone.

SNOQUALMIE WINERY
Snoqualmie Falls, Washington

Output: 35,000 cases

Leading Wines:
Chenin Blanc,
Gewurztraminer,
Muscat Canelli,
Riesling,
Semillon

Joel Klein, winemaker at Chateau Ste. Michelle, left in 1982 to organize a winery in association with David Wyckoff, a Yakima Valley grape grower. Snoqualmie Winery was formed in 1983 and the first wines were made at Wyckoff's bonded winemaking facility, Coventry Vale, in the Yakima Valley. Later wines will be made at a showcase winery near Snoqualmie Falls, close to Seattle. The initial releases of off-dry to semisweet white wines will be followed by oak-aged Chardonnay, Sauvignon Blanc, Cabernet Sauvignon, and Merlot.

SOKOL BLOSSER WINERY
Dundee, Oregon

Output: 23,000 cases

Leading Wines:
Chardonnay,
Gewurztraminer,
Muller-Thurgau,
Pinot Noir,
Riesling,
Sauvignon Blanc

In 1971, Bill Blosser and Susan Sokol Blosser planted 18 acres of grapes in the Red Hills, in the northern Willamette Valley. In 1977 a limited partnership was formed with Bill and Susan Blosser as general partners and members of Susan Blosser's family as limited partners. Bob McRitchie, then chief chemist for California's Franciscan Vineyards, was hired as winemaker for the first crush that year. At a time when many Oregon wineries were operating from converted farm buildings, Sokol Blosser's construction of a modern winery and visitor facility marked an evolutionary step in the Oregon wine industry.

Sokol Blosser is participating in an experimental program of vine and grape evaluation. The test plot includes many Pinot Noir clones. Blosser, however, plays down the importance of Pinot Noir clonal variation, pointing out that Pinot Noir vines continually mutate throughout their ex-

istence, and that Burgundians generally replant and replace their old vines not with a single clone but with approximately the same ratio of variations already present in the vineyard. Sokol Blosser's Pinot Noirs from the better years are characterized by moderately high tannin and extract and a slightly tarry quality.

In response to consumer demand for white wines, 70 percent of Sokol Blosser's production is of whites, and this proportion is increasing. Of these whites, Chardonnay is the best, showing typically tight structure, restrained character, and crisp balancing acidity that enable it to marry well with food and develop with age.

Sokol Blosser was the first commercial producer of Muller-Thurgau in America. Similar to Riesling, Muller-Thurgau, the grape of Liebfraumilch, is widely grown in Germany. Riesling, in semisweet style, is Sokol Blosser's best selling wine.

SONOMA-CUTRER VINEYARD
Windsor, San Francisco Bay North

Formerly this 800-acre vineyard sold its grapes to other wineries where its designated bottlings won several awards. Since 1981, however, it has made its own Chardonnays with Russian River or Carneros appellations for which the grapes are air-chilled and hand-sorted before the whole clusters are pressed. (Whole cluster pressing has been practiced in Burgundy, but is rarely seen in the United States.)

All the wines are barrel-fermented and aged at the winery for an additional year before release.

Output: 2,500 cases

Leading Wine:
Chardonnay

SONOMA HILLS WINERY
Santa Rosa, San Francisco Bay North

Established in 1983, Sonoma Hills Winery released its first wine, a Chardonnay, in 1984. In contrast to the many lush, complex California Chardonnays, the Sonoma Hills Chardonnay emphasizes leanness and austerity.

Output: 1,000 cases

Leading Wine:
Chardonnay

SOTOYOME WINERY
Healdsburg, San Francisco Bay North

Founded in 1974, Sotoyome produces both Petite Sirah and Shiraz wines. Petite Sirah was long thought to be the same grape as the Syrah of the northern Rhône Valley, but is now identified as the Duriff, which is also a Rhône grape. Petite Sirah is widely planted in California, but acreage of the true Syrah is very low. Shiraz is the name applied to the Syrah in Australia, and is at least a clone of the Rhône grape from which the wines of Hermitage and Côte-Rotie in the northern Rhône are produced.

Output: 1,000 cases

Leading Wines:
Cabernet Sauvignon,
Chardonnay,
Petite Sirah,
Shiraz,
Zinfandel

S

SOUTH COAST

The South Coast includes some of the oldest vineyard areas in California as well as some of the newest. Commercial wine production began in California in Los Angeles in the 1830s. However, there are no longer commercial vineyards in Los Angeles County, and the vineyards of the famed Cucamonga region in San Bernardino County have been declining in acreage and importance in the last 40 years. Smog, freeways, housing tracts, and rising taxes adversely affected the region, but of greater importance has been declining consumer interests in aperitif and dessert wines and a move towards drier table wines that are produced in cooler regions.

As vineyard acreage has declined in San Bernardino County (from more than 20,000 acres at the end of World War II to 6,000 acres today) it has been partially replaced by new plantings in Riverside and San Diego Counties. Currently southwest Riverside County can boast of 2,700 acres of vineyards, with a potential for several thousand more. Less than 200 acres of vineyards are growing in northern San Diego County, most of them in the San Pasqual Valley. Orange County is of but little importance viticulturally, with less than 50 acres of vineyards.

Soils in the South Coast are varied as is the topography. Cucamonga is on the edge of a desert and soils contain considerable amounts of sand. The vineyards of Riverside and San Diego counties lie in the Coastal mountains and are well drained, with varying amounts of pebbles or rocks in some areas and decomposed granite in others.

SOUVERAIN CELLARS
Geyserville, San Francisco Bay North

Output: 150,000 cases

Leading Wines:
Burgundy,
Cabernet Sauvignon,
Chablis,
Charbono,
Chardonnay,
Chenin Blanc,
Colombard-Blanc,
Fumé Blanc,
Gewurztraminer,
Johannisberg Riesling,
Zinfandel

Souverain traces its founding to 1943, when Lee Stewart built a small winery on a hillside near Angwin above the Napa Valley. Since then the winery has passed through several owners and a change of location. The original building is now Burgess Cellars. Souverain is owned by a partnership of growers who purchased the winery from Pillsbury in 1976, and the 3-million gallon winery is located in the Alexander Valley.

Souverain's winemaker draws upon the 10,000 acres of vineyards belonging to the partners to make an extensive list of 16 varietals, 5 generics, and 3 estate-bottled vintage selections. Souverain's wines have a reputation for being light and drinkable and sometimes good value, more often in the reds than whites. Their more expensive "Estate-Bottled Vintage Selection" wines are made only in exceptional years. Of variable success, again the reds seem to offer the best value.

SPRING MOUNTAIN VINEYARDS
St. Helena, San Francisco Bay North

Output: 25,000 cases

Spring Mountain has its beginnings in 1968, in the basement of an old Victorian house north of St. Helena. Early successes with its Cabernet Sauvignon, Chardonnay, and especially Sauvignon Blanc encouraged the winery to move to the 19th century Miravalle Estate on the southeastern slope of Spring Mountain.

The new 145,000-gallon winery draws on 383 acres of vines in the Spring Mountain vineyards. A dry style Sauvignon Blanc first attracted attention to the winery, and although its approach to this varietal is now fairly common, Spring Mountain still maintains a reputation for this wine and for a stylish Cabernet Sauvignon and Chardonnay. Included is a small planting of ten acres of the Pinot Noir clone known as Pinot Noir Petit. This is allegedly the descendant of one given Paul Masson by Louis Latour in 1898, from La Romanée Conti or from Latour's Corton Grancey Vineyards in Beaune. All Spring Mountain Pinot Noirs are produced from this clone.

Falcon Crest, a second label, was established by the winery for selected lots and is a reminder that the television series of the same name uses Spring Mountain as a location.

Leading Wines:
Cabernet Sauvignon
Blanc,
Chardonnay,
Pinot Noir,
Sauvignon Blanc;
Falcon Crest:
Cabernet Sauvignon,
Chardonnay

STAGS' LEAP VINEYARD
Napa, San Francisco Bay North

Founded on the ruins of a 19th century winery and a hotel known as Stags' Leap, first wines were produced in 1972 in leased space. Since 1979 a 60,000-gallon winery has been producing five estate-bottled varietals under the Stags' Leap label, and a generic Burgundy. "Pedregal" is a second label for wines produced from purchased grapes.

The wine which most clearly denotes the Stags' Leap style is the Petite Syrah. Made from 100 percent free-run juice it is big, dark and flavorful, with some complexity.

There exists a certain amount of confusion between Stags' Leap Winery, and the neighboring Stag's Leap Wine Cellars and for a time the wineries were involved in litigation over the use of the Stag's Leap (or Stags' Leap) name. The issue was settled in 1984 and both wineries may continue to use the name. Currently use of the Stags Leap name to designate a Viticultural Area is pending but is opposed by both these wineries.

Output: 12,000 cases

Leading Wines:
Burgundy,
Cabernet Sauvignon,
Chenin Blanc,
Merlot,
Pedregal Chardonnay,
Petite Syrah,
Pinot Noir

STAG'S LEAP WINE CELLARS
Napa, San Francisco Bay North

Since this winery was founded in 1972, the names of Stag's Leap Wine Cellars and Warren Winiarski have become increasingly synonymous with fine Cabernet Sauvignons. The winery and this wine catapulted to fame following the 1976 Paris wine competition (arranged by Stephen Spurrier of L'Academie de Vin), when Stag's Leap Wine Cellars 1973 Cabernet Sauvignon finished ahead of half-a-dozen classified growths of Bordeaux.

Just south of the winery on Silverado Trail are its 45 acres of Cabernet Sauvignon and Merlot, from which Warren makes wines designated as

Output: 30,000 cases

Leading Wines:
Cabernet Sauvignon,
Chardonnay,
Gamay Beaujolais,
Johannisberg Riesling,
Merlot,
Petite Sirah,
Sauvignon Blanc

Stag's Leap Vineyards; each is 100 percent varietal. The Cabernets have demonstrated consistent excellence since the famous 1976 victory; they are rich, luscious wines with uncommon balance and elegance, while the Merlots are far more successful than most examples of this varietal. Since 1976, Stag's Leap has made a stylish Chardonnay from Haynes Vineyards, in the southern Napa Valley. A fruity, vineyard-designated Johannisberg Riesling is made from grapes purchased from Birkmeyer Vineyard, located in Wild Horse Valley, in the southeastern hills of the Napa Valley.

In addition to these vineyard-designated wines, Stag's Leap also produces a Gamay Beaujolais, a second Johannisberg Riesling, and a second Cabernet Sauvignon, made from purchased grapes and sold under its second label, Hawkcrest.

STELTZNER VINEYARDS
Napa, San Francisco Bay North

Output: 3,500 cases

Leading Wines:
Cabernet Franc,
Cabernet Sauvignon,
Merlot

Long famous for the quality of its grapes, Steltzner Vineyards founded its winery in 1977. From 60 acres of vineyards and a 20,000-gallon winery Steltzner produces three varietals. Of these, Cabernet Franc is not usually produced as a varietal in California, but more typically is used as a blending grape to soften Cabernet Sauvignon. It makes a lighter wine than Cabernet Sauvignon, but one with the familiar range of Cabernet Sauvignon aromas and flavors.

ROBERT STEMMLER WINERY
Healdsburg, San Francisco Bay North

Output: 7,500 cases

Leading Wines:
Chardonnay,
Fumé Blanc,
Pinot Noir

Stemmler began with the crush of 1977, producing Chardonnay only that harvest. Most grapes are purchased and the list varies as a result. In general, Stemmler's wines are made in a reserved, elegant style, with limited skin contact before fermentation and moderate levels of alcohol in the finished wines. Stemmler's recent Pinot Noirs have been among the most talked-about wines produced from this grape variety.

STERLING VINEYARDS
Calistoga, San Francisco Bay North

Output: 75,000 cases

Leading Wines:
Cabernet Blanc,
Cabernet Sauvignon,
Cabernet Sauvignon
Reserve,
Merlot,
Sauvignon Blanc

Sterling's dramatic white winery at the crest of a wooded hill near Calistoga was completed in 1972, although wines had been made in temporary facilities since 1969. These first vintages established an early reputation for Sterling, and in 1977 the winery was purchased by the Coca Cola Company. A change of winemaker narrowed the Sterling line.

Sterling supplies much of its grapes from 520 acres of owned and leased vineyards. Most of these are the original vineyards planted on the rich alluvial valley floor around the winery. Additional vineyards on Diamond Mountain are planted on steep slopes, on which soils vary from grey volcanic to fairly rich loams. Although the slopes are steep and difficult to harvest, they are well-drained, frost-free (1,000 to 1,500 feet above the floor of the Napa Valley), and provide a wide variation of solar exposures. Grape varieties have been matched to these conditions; for example, Chardonnay is planted on back-lit slopes while Cabernet Sauvignon and Merlot are planted on slopes that receive full sun. Sterling's list of varietals regularly wins critical plaudits and their Cabernet Sauvignon Reserve is most often singled out for praise. Made from selected lots which are sometimes blended with some Merlot, the Reserve spends two years in Nevers oak which adds further to its ripe complex structure. Sterling's full, rich Chardonnays are partially barrel-fermented in Limousin oak and like Sauvignon Blanc also receive some oak aging before release.

After Seagram acquired Sterling in 1983, plans were announced for construction of a sparkling wine facility at the base of the hill below the winery. The facility will be operated by Mumm's, one of the leading Champagne producers of France.

STEVENOT WINERY
Murphys, Sierra Foothills

Output: 55,000 cases

*Leading Wines:
Cabernet Sauvignon,
Chardonnay,
Chenin Blanc,
Muscat Canelli*

Stevenot Winery, established in 1974, is now the largest winery in the Sierra Foothills with 175,000 gallons of storage capacity. Two hundred acres of vineyards support a list of several wines made from six grape varieties. The winery is perhaps known for its Chenin Blanc, rich with the melony-peachy aromas of this grape variety.

STEWART VINEYARDS
Granger, Washington

Output: 7,000 cases

*Leading Wines:
Cabernet Sauvignon,
Chardonnay,
Gewurztraminer,
Muscat Canelli,
Riesling*

Vineyard owners Dr. George and Martha Stewart bonded their winery in 1983. Grapes come from the Yakima Valley where the winery is situated and from a warmer growing area on the Columbia Valley's Wahluke Slope. In some years, varietals from both growing sites will be bottled separately, providing a basis for comparing the characteristics of the two growing areas. Although a different style may evolve with a recent change in winemakers, the first releases tended toward a riper style in both the dry and semisweet white wines.

STONE HILL WINERY
Hermann, Missouri

Output: 40,000 cases

*Leading Wines:
Seyval Blanc,
Norton,
Missouri Champagne,
Missouri Riesling
(American variety)*

Established in 1847 in a German settlement town on the Missouri River, Stone Hill grew to be the third largest winery in the world by the turn of the century. Prohibition put an end to that, emptying the cavernous, arched-brick cellars for an enterprising mushroom farm during the Depression.

The Held family revived the winery in 1965. The wines recall the old days, many using Missouri's traditional grape varieties, some even from vineyards planted before the Civil War. Most have some sweetness, but with a delicacy and bright fruitiness from modern cellaring techniques such as cold fermentation. Norton is the standout among these old varietals: a big, dark wine stuffed with dry fruit, well-aged in oak but with a long life ahead. The winery's Missouri Champagne is a *méthode champenoise* Catawba with some toastiness and subdued grape flavors from tirage on the yeast, finished semidry. Seyval is Stone Hill's dry white; light, citrusy, with a touch of oak. It and Norton are estate-bottled from the 60-acre vineyard. Most of the grapes used come from growers in the Missouri River Valley and Ozark foothills.

STONEGATE WINERY
Calistoga, San Francisco Bay North

Output: 15,000 cases

*Leading Wines:
Cabernet Sauvignon,
Chardonnay,
Merlot,
Sauvignon Blanc*

This is a small winery, founded on the steep slopes of the Mayacamas Mountains which separate the Napa Valley from Sonoma's Alexander Valley. Most of its grapes come from its own and neighboring steeply terraced vineyards which produce grapes of strong varietal intensity.

STONY HILL VINEYARD
St. Helena, San Francisco Bay North

Output: 4,000 cases

*Leading Wines:
Chardonnay,
Gewurztraminer,
Johannisberg Riesling,
Semillon de Soleil*

Considered by many to be the premier Chardonnay producer in California, Stony Hill Vineyard was founded in 1953 by advertising executive Fred McCrea and his wife Eleanor on a steep Napa Valley hillside. Although not intending to become winemakers they planted grapes around their home. Since their 7,000-gallon winery was completed, wines have been made from their own grapes. Each year the entire output is sold by mail to a list of subscribers, many of whom have waited years to be on the Stony Hill list.

Stony Hill was among the first to mature its Chardonnays in French oak, long before the practice became a fad in California. All wines from its low-yielding vineyard are bottled by hand and receive exceptional care. Stony Hill Chardonnays develop slowly. They are austere at first, realizing their full flavor and power only after several years in the bottle, when they blossom into rich, subtle, fully rounded examples of all that the grape can achieve. So unique is the quality of Stony Hill's Chardonnay that cuttings from its vineyard have been planted in other Napa Valley vineyards and christened as the Stony Hill clone.

Stony Hill also produces some Gewurztraminer, Johannisberg Riesling, and a wine called Semillon de Soleil. Semillon de Soleil is a naturally sweet dessert wine, made in tiny quantities from Semillon grapes which have been allowed to dehydrate in the sun before fermentation.

STORYBROOK MOUNTAIN CELLARS
Calistoga, San Francisco Bay North

Founded in 1980 this is one of two different labels produced at the 19th century site of the Grimm Winery. Partner in this venture is Schug Winery, which produces its own line at the same modern 76,000-gallon facility. Storybrook's grapes come from a surrounding 36-acre estate.

Output: 7,500 cases

Wine:
Zinfandel

RODNEY STRONG VINEYARDS
Windsor, San Francisco Bay North

A major presence in the Sonoma County wine industry, this winery began in the late 1950s as Tiburon Vintners and later was known as Sonoma Vineyards. All wines were originally sold through the winery and eventually through mail-order. Retail distribution came with a change in name, to Sonoma Vineyards, in 1970.

At one time the output of this 3.5 million gallon winery was sold under Sonoma Vineyards and for limited retail distribution and mail-order, under Rodney D. Strong and Windsor labels. Now all wines are sold under Strong or Windsor, either with a general North Coast or Sonoma County appellation. Several of the varietals are made in vineyard-designated lots of a few thousand cases and upward, which have tended to be the most distinctive of its wines. In particular, the Chalk Hill Chardonnay, Le Baron Johannisberg Riesling, and Alexander's Crown Cabernet Sauvignon have been most successful. Others such as River West Zinfandel and Chardonnay are more variable.

Output: 500,000 cases

Leading Wines:
Cabernet Sauvignon,
Chardonnay,
Johannisberg Riesling,
Pinot Noir,
Sauvignon Blanc,
Zinfandel

Sulfur

Since Roman times, sulfur has been used for sanitation in wine cellars. Today it is relied upon more than ever, in the dissolved form of sulfur dioxide (SO_2) to protect wine from oxidation and microbial spoilage. The goal of the winemaker, not always achieved, is to use this stabilizer judiciously in the cellar and never let it show in the finished wine. But sweet wines in particular sometimes betray the burnt-match smell of sulfur that has been liberally added to prevent refermentation.

SUTTER HOME WINERY
St. Helena, San Francisco Bay North

This winery traces its origins to 1874, but its current approach to winemaking dates back to the 1960s when it first released an Amador County Zinfandel. A few years later its other varietals were dropped and today 95 percent of its production is red and white Zinfandel. The balance is made up of a light, sweet wine called Muscat Amabile.

Sutter Home's Amador County Zinfandel was one of the first to redefine this varietal in the intense style now associated with the Amador region. Today, various styles of Zinfandel are produced and the grapes

Output: 100,000 cases

Leading Wines:
Muscat Amabile,
Dessert Zinfandel,
Red Zinfandel,
White Zinfandel,
Zinfandel "Reserve"

S

come from several Viticultural Areas. Where appropriate, single vineyards are identified on the Sutter Home label.

The specialty of specialties at Sutter Home is the Zinfandel made from grapes grown at the 1,700-foot elevation in the Sierra Foothills of Amador County. Labeled Zinfandel Reserve, the grapes come from 100-year-old vines in the Deaver Vineyard, a well-known site for fine Zinfandel grapes. Made only in exceptional years, this wine is aged in small oak barrels for up to two years before release and is a deeply colored wine with a complex, spicy-fruity character.

JOSEPH SWAN VINEYARDS
Forestville, San Francisco Bay North

This small (500-gallon) winery came to recognition with a Zinfandel produced in its first vintage, 1969. Swan's winemaking techniques are somewhat unusual for California but have produced a series of big, long-lived wines that have a devoted following. The Chardonnay, for example, receives extensive skin and stem contact and goes through malolactic fermentation.

After bottling, all Swann wines are cellared for a minimum of one year before release. However, extensive additional aging is recommended before consumption and even Swan's white wines are exceptionally long-lived. The 1973 Chardonnay (Swann's first) is still excellent, and the 1969 Zinfandel is only just reaching its peak.

Sales of these sought-after wines are almost entirely restricted to a mail-order list. In 1985 a Cabernet Sauvignon was added to the line.

SYCAMORE CREEK VINEYARDS
Morgan Hill, San Francisco Bay South

Established in 1976 on the site of a pre-Prohibition winery, Sycamore Creek owns 16 acres of vineyards that include 7 acres of 75-year-old Zinfandel and Carignane vines. Recent wines show some promise.

Sylvaner

Sometimes called Sylvaner Riesling this white vinifera is German in origin. On occasion, it has been used to make a varietal but is declining in popularity. Less than 1,400 acres are planted to this variety, of which about 1,000 are in the Central Coast region.

Syrah (French)

This true Syrah of the northern Rhône is used there to make the classic red wines of Hermitage and Côte-Rotie. Less than 100 acres are planted in California, but growers are experimenting with it as a varietal.

1982 CALIFORNIA
ZINFANDEL

PRODUCED AND BOTTLED BY
SUTTER HOME WINERY BW 1007
ST. HELENA, CALIFORNIA
ALCOHOL 13½% BY VOLUME

Output: 1,200 cases

Leading Wines:
Cabernet Sauvignon,
Chardonnay,
Pinot Noir

Output: 5,000 cases

Leading Wines:
Cabernet Sauvignon,
Carignane,
Pinot Noir,
Zinfandel

Table Wine

Wine made to be consumed with food, hence with a moderate level of alcohol. Federal regulations permit the words "Table Wine" to be used on labels in lieu of the percent alcohol in the wine if it is 14 percent or less.

Tannin

A component of grape skins, seeds, and stems, tannin enters juice and wine in quantity during fermentation on the skins (for red wine). The taste of tannin is bitter or astringent; most often encountered in young red wines. Tannin is a natural preservative in wine (as it is in leather), enabling it to keep well as flavors mature and deepen. The tannin itself gradually oxidizes, contributing to the sediment in old red wine. The trend in recent years has been toward shorter skin fermentations and limited tannin content for softer, earlier maturing red wines.

TAYLOR WINE COMPANY/ GREAT WESTERN WINERY

Hammondsport, Finger Lakes

Output: 4 million cases

Leading Wines:
Baco Noir,
Brut and Blanc de Blancs
and Natural Champagne,
Chablis,
Champagne,
Empire Cream Sherry,
Gewurztraminer,
Great Western
Vidal Blanc,
Johannisberg Riesling,
Rhine,
Seyval Blanc,
Taylor Lake

Taylor and Great Western are marketed as two distinct labels but the wineries have essentially merged into one operation, filling more than 40 buildings across the flatlands south of Keuka Lake — the largest winemaking complex in the United States outside California.

Major expansion began in the 1950s, when the 19th century Taylor family winery went public. In the early 1960s they took over Great Western, the Finger Lakes first winery, which had been founded in 1860. Ownership passed to the Coca-Cola Company in 1977 but the operation failed to meet short-term marketing goals. It was sold to the Seagram wine and spirits conglomerate in 1983.

This corporate shuffling has disheveled the product line, but not without some benefits. Most impressive among these is a growing family of French-American hybrid and vinifera varietals sold under the Great Western label. Although limited in production and distribution, they are

Country Chablis,
White and Gold,
Verdelet

PREMIUM NEW YORK STATE
BACO NOIR

BURGUNDY-STYLE VARIETAL TABLE WINE
FROM FRENCH-AMERICAN GRAPES

ALCOHOL 11% BY VOLUME
PRODUCED AND BOTTLED BY THE GREAT WESTERN WINERY
HAMMONDSPORT, N.Y. 14840 • BONDED WINERY NO. 1

uniformly well-made wines, usually on the light side, emphasizing fresh, crisp fruit. Vidal Blanc, Verdelet, and Gewurztraminer are among the best. Great Western's Baco Noir is perhaps the best example of that variety, benefiting from some judicious blending and aging.

Taylor-labelled wines generally reflect a greater use of labrusca grapes than Great Western wines, which increasingly rely upon French hybrids and vinifera varieties. This much-needed distinction seems to be getting clearer under Seagram's stewardship.

Taylor and Great Western sherries and ports—always good—have benefited from a big investment in oak cooperage for aging.

Sparkling wines have been the most visible product from both Taylor and Great Western. Labrusca grapes still dominate the cuvées, and give the wines forward, fruity flavors that should not be approached with expectations of French Champagne. Taylor's Lake Country series and generic table wines rely still more on the native grapes of the East with at least some sweetness, although Lake Country Chablis stands apart as a near-dry, tart-fruit food wine. It is New York's version of Gallo Chablis Blanc, and an enlightening counterpoint in style.

TEPUSQUET VINEYARDS
San Martin, San Francisco Bay South

Output: 65,000 cases

Leading Wines:
Claret,
Hock,
Tepusquet Vineyard
Reserve,
Vin Blanc

Tepusquet Vineyards, a collection of vineyards in San Luis Obispo and Santa Barbara Counties, is famous as the source of grapes for several leading California wineries including Ridge, Caparona, ZD, and Kalin Cellars. But since 1983 it has begun to make a series of generic blends from a portion of its 1,700 acres.

Claret is a blend of Cabernet Sauvignon and Merlot. Vin Blanc contains Chardonnay, Sauvignon Blanc, and Pineau de la Loire (Chenin Blanc). Hock includes Johannisberg Riesling, Gewurztraminer, and Sauvignon Blanc. Tepusquet Vineyard Reserve is a blend of 65 percent Cabernet Sauvignon and 35 percent Merlot. Generally speaking, these are rich wines made in an attractive, accessible style.

TEWKSBURY WINE CELLARS
Lebanon, Mid-Atlantic Coast

Output: 4,500 cases

Leading Wines:
Apple,
Chambourcin,
Chardonnay,
Chenin Blanc,
Delaware,
Gamay Nouveau,
Gewurztraminer,
Rayon d'Or,

A small wine estate set up in a cluster of 18th century stone barns, Tewksbury has made an auspicious entry into making fine white wine. The rolling, pastoral farmland of northwestern New Jersey is little-known at all, much less for winegrowing, but it quickly proved itself congenial to Chardonnay and Gewurztraminer in particular. Since its first vintage in 1979, Tewksbury has steadily brought both these demanding varieties into stylistic focus. The Atlantic-influenced microclimate seems far enough north to retain abundant acid and fruit, yet warm enough to fully ripen and fill out these grapes with their potential for complexity and spice.

The Gewurztraminer is dry, with clear but elegantly restrained varietal character. The Chardonnay is stuffed with ripe fruit within a firm structure; very clean and direct. Seyval Blanc has also done well here, in the hands of Daniel Vernon, a veterinarian turned winemaker. The 20-acre vineyard specializes in white vinifera, but also grows a hearty Chambourcin. Tewksbury's sweet Delaware is a tribute to the variety's origin in a backyard garden of nearby Frenchtown.

Seyval Blanc,
White Riesling

PAUL THOMAS WINES
Bellevue, Washington

Output: 18,000 cases

Fifty percent of Paul Thomas's production is devoted to Crimson Rhubarb, a wine not totally unlike the currently popular "blanc" wines from red grapes. All Thomas fruit wines (as well as his grape wines) are made in a dry or nearly dry style to complement food. American oak is used with red and white grape wines. The distinct American oak character expresses itself most predominantly in the Sauvignon Blanc, the grassy-herbaceous character of the variety mingling with the forward flavors of the American oak. Long-range plans call for equal production of grape and fruit wines, but in the immediate future, Paul Thomas is focusing on a unique segment of a crowded wine marketplace—dry or nearly dry fruit wines.

Leading Wines:
Bartlett Pear,
Cabernet Sauvignon,
Crimson Rhubarb,
Muscat Canelli,
Riesling,
Sauvignon Blanc

TIJSSELING VINEYARDS
Ukiah, San Francisco Bay North

Output: 45,000 cases

Located in McNab Creek Valley in the Coast Range of southern Mendocino County, Tijsseling Vineyards (pronounced Tyse-ling) was founded in 1981. Family-owned vineyards of 260 acres provide grapes for four estate-bottled varietals and three sparkling wines, first released in 1985.

Leading Wines:
Cabernet Sauvignon,
Chardonnay,
Petite Sirah,
Sauvignon Blanc;
Blanc de Blanc,
Blanc de Noir

Tirage

The aging of sparkling wine in the bottle while it still contains sediment from the secondary fermentation. Extended contact with the sediment gives the wine complex, toasty flavors. Tirage literally refers to the tiers of bottles in storage.

TOYON WINERY AND VINEYARDS
Healdsburg, San Francisco Bay North

Output: 5,000 cases

Until 1979, wines were produced at outside facilities for Toyon. Now its estate and vineyard-select varietals are made at a 12,000-gallon winery in the southern Alexander Valley.

Leading Wines:
Cabernet Sauvignon,
Sauvignon Blanc

T

Sauvignon Blanc grapes are produced only in the vineyard-select program and go through full or partial barrel-fermentation to impart complexities and to soften the herbaceous character of the grape. Six acres of winery-owned vineyards supply grapes for estate-grown Cabernet Sauvignon. Grapes for vineyard designated Cabernets are purchased as far south as the Edna Valley.

Transfer Process

A modern procedure in sparkling wine production by which the secondary fermentation still occurs in the bottle but instead of disgorging (removal of sediment from the bottle), the effervescent wine is pumped through a filter into another bottle. Although the wine may gain complexity from aging on yeast sediment in the original bottle, some complexity may be lost in the filtration and transfer. The label usually reads "Fermented in the Bottle," rather than Fermented in This Bottle (*méthode champenoise*).

TREFETHEN VINEYARDS
Napa, San Francisco Bay North

Output: 50,000 cases

Leading Wines:
Cabernet Sauvignon,
Chardonnay,
Eschol Red and
Eschol White,
Pinot Noir,
White Riesling

Trefethen was founded in 1968, with the restoration of the Eschol Vineyard that had been planted in 1886. The purchase of additional acreage brings the holdings to 600 contiguous acres in the Trefethen Oak Knoll Estate, making it the largest single vineyard in the Napa Valley. In addition, there are 48 acres in Hillside Vineyard, a separate location on the western slopes of Napa Valley. Most of the output from these holdings supplies Domaine Chandon and Schramsburg for their sparkling wines but since 1973 Trefethen has also made its own wines. Altogether, four varietals and two generics are produced at the 280,000-gallon facility. The reputation of the two generics—in their price and quality range—is as strong as the reputation of the more expensive premium wines. At both ends of the spectrum, this is a winery for good value.

TRENTADUE WINERY
Geyserville, San Francisco Bay North

Output: 20,000 cases

Leading Wines:
Aleatico,
Cabernet Sauvignon,
Carignane,
Nebbiolo,
San Giovese

The output from this winery's 175 acres in the Alexander Valley was originally sold to other producers but since 1969 Trentadue has produced some wines of its own. Its list of varietals is generally considered to be stronger in reds than whites and includes several unusual grapes that are not commonly grown in California. Aleatico, for example, is produced as table wine, as are the Italian varieties, Nebbiolo, San Giovese, and Freisia.

TRULUCK VINEYARDS
Lake City, South Carolina

Output: 8,000 cases

Leading Wines:

"A touch of France in the Old South" is Truluck's motto, and it was air force service in southern French wine country that inspired the Truluck family to try growing similar wines in South Carolina. The 100-acre estate vineyard, begun in 1971, probes the possibilities for viniculture in a region of soybeans and tobacco. It includes a range of French-American hybrids, rare Munson hybrids, and vinifera varieties rivaling the collections of some agricultural experiment stations. Native southern Muscadine grapes are also bought on contract from local growers to fill out a diverse line of 15 varietals, 3 blends, and a sparkling wine. A special effort is made to match wines with local foods, including Carolina crayfish raised commercially on the farm.

*Cabernet Sauvignon,
Carolina Red, White,
and Rosé
Carlos,
Cayuga White,
Rosé de Chambourcin,
Champagne,
Munson Red,
Ravat Blanc,
Seyval Blanc*

TUALATIN VINEYARDS
Forest Grove, Oregon

Situated in the northernmost Willamette Valley near Forest Grove, Tualatin is one of Oregon's larger wineries, with an estate of 158 acres, of which 80 are now in grapes. The vineyard was first planted in 1973, concluding a search by Bill Fuller and Bill Malkmus for a location suited to cooler climate, early maturing grape varieties. Malkmus, in charge of business operations and marketing, works from Tualatin's office in San Francisco. Fuller, formerly chief chemist and wine production manager for California's Louis M.Martini winery, is in charge of winemaking and vineyard operations.

Tualatin's microclimate is slightly warmer than much of the surrounding area; grapes ripen earlier, and although the character of the vintage is still the predominant factor, Tualatin's wines often reflect the warmer growing climate. The Pinot Noir has a riper, fuller-bodied quality, sometimes showing best in moderately cooler vintages; the Chardonnay and Riesling also show the stylistic effects of warmer growing conditions.

Pinot Noir is one of Tualatin's major varietals, but the grape is given relatively less emphasis than at other Willamette Valley wineries. Eighty percent of Tualatin's vineyard is planted to white varietals, in particular cooler climate grapes, and more acreage is planted to Riesling than any other grape. Fuller has experimented with other white grapes including early Muscat, a seldom-planted, early maturing variety with distinctive varietal character.

Output: 17,000 cases

*Leading Wines:
Chardonnay,
Early Muscat,
Gewurztraminer,
Pinot Noir,
Riesling*

Tualatin

1984
Oregon
Pinot Noir-Blanc
Willamette Valley

GROWN, PRODUCED AND BOTTLED BY
TUALATIN VINEYARDS, FOREST GROVE, OREGON
BW-OR-55   Alcohol 11% by volume

TUCKER CELLARS
Sunnyside, Washington

The origins of Tucker Cellars date to the earliest days of Washington's vinifera wine industry. In the 1930s, M. F. Tucker was one of the original growers for the now defunct Upland Winery, the first vinifera winery in the state. After Upland's rapid decline, the Tucker family turned from grapes to other crops. But four decades later, in 1980, the Tucker family again planted vinifera grapes on their 500-acre farm in the Yakima Valley. Forty acres are now in vine.

Output: 9,000 cases

*Leading Wines:
Cabernet Sauvignon,
Chardonnay,
Chenin Blanc,
Gewurztraminer,
Muscat Canelli,
Riesling*

T

TUCQUAN VINEYARD
Holtwood, Mid-Atlantic Coast

Output: 2,000 cases

Leading Wines:
Chancellor,
Marechal Foch,
Steuben Rose

Tucquan restored commercial grape growing to Pennsylvania's Lancaster County, once a flourishing vineyard area, after a century-long hiatus. The first vines were planted on the Susquehanna River in 1968; wine production began in 1978. Dry red French-American hybrids are the specialty, particularly a robust, wood-aged Chancellor and a fragrant, well-made Marechal Foch. Tucquan also makes labrusca wines, highlighted by a semisweet Steuben rosé. Owners Tom and Cindy Hampton maintain control over every phase of Tucquan's operation, from the exclusively estate-grown grapes in their 11.5-acre vineyard to sales at the winery.

TULOCAY WINERY
Napa, San Francisco Bay North

Output: 2,000 cases

Leading Wines:
Cabernet Sauvignon,
Chardonnay,
Pinot Noir,
Zinfandel

An emphasis on barrel-aging is the explanation for the full-bodied and oaky wines of this small producer, founded in 1975. With 20,000 gallons of storage capacity, Tulocay produces four varietals, but Pinot Noir is considered by the winery to be their specialty. The Cabernet has also received positive critical attention.

TURNER WINERY
Woodbridge, Sacramento Valley

Output: 220,000 cases

Leading Wines:
Burgundy,
Cabernet Sauvignon,
Chablis,
Chardonnay,
Chenin Blanc,
Fumé Blanc,
Johannisberg Riesling,
Merlot,
Petite Sirah,
Zinfandel

In 1979 Turner Winery revived the 19th century Urgon Winery. Grapes are grown on its 580 acres of vineyards in the Kelseyville area (about 100 miles away in Lake County).

Turner produces a long list of varietals and several generics from its 3.8 million-gallon facility. The vintage-dated Cabernet Sauvignons and Chardonnays receive some oak aging, but the emphasis is on fruitiness, and no Turner wine exhibits strong woody character. Only free-run juice goes into their varietal whites and only free-run wine goes into their varietal reds — a practice that creates intense young wines, not destined for long aging. Press juice and wine are blended for their generics.

VAL VERDE WINERY
Del Rio, Texas

The oldest winery in the South-Southwest and the only survivor of a flourishing 19th century wine industry in Texas and New Mexico, Val Verde celebrated its centennial in 1983.

The original vineyard and adobe winery continue to turn out wines from Lenoir and Herbemont, varieties of an obscure Mediterranean grape species introduced into early New World vineyards. Their aromatic, distinctive character lends itself best to the production of a rich, mellow Tawny Port, aged in barrels, some of which also date to the 19th century. Although tradition lives on at Val Verde, a change of generations in the family operation took the winery into a new phase in the 1970s. A consulting enologist from California helped refurbish the cellar and lighten the wines to show more fruit, while the 12-acre estate vineyard has been supplemented with another 15 acres in the nearby Quemado Valley, growing hybrid and vinifera varieties.

Output: 2,500 cases

Leading Wines:
Don Luis Tawny Port,
Johannisberg Riesling,
Lenoir Herbemont,
Rosé,
San Felipe Del Rio
(Lenoir)

VALLEY OF THE MOON WINERY
Glen Ellen, San Francisco Bay North

This 200,000-gallon winery, which lists 1857 as its founding date, was purchased by the Parducci family in 1944, after a succession of colorful owners.

Valley of the Moon is a beautifully isolated pocket of the Sonoma Valley, as rich in winemaking history as it is in associations with the great American writer Jack London. The Parduccis began producing and bottling varietal wines, instead of the jug generics for which the winery had been known. There are now 200 acres of vineyards.

Output: 40,000 cases

Leading Wines:
Chardonnay,
French Colombard,
Pinot Noir,
Pinot Noir Blanc,
Semillon,
White Zinfandel,
Zinfandel,
Zinfandel Rosé

Varietal

A wine made predominantly from one grape variety and labeled with the name of that variety. The varietal content is often 100 percent, but federal

V

label regulations require only 75 percent for all varieties except labruscas and muscadines. A 51 percent minimum for those native varieties takes into account their strong flavor and the common practice of blending with neutral wine from other grapes. Oregon has established the stricter minimum of 95 percent for all varieties except 75 percent for Cabernet Sauvignon, which is traditionally blended. These minimums attempt to give consumers some guarantee that wines are what the labels say they are, while still giving winemakers flexibility for blending to improve the wine. A wine is said to have "varietal character" when the characteristic flavor of the variety is pronounced.

VALLEY VIEW VINEYARD
Jacksonville, Oregon

Output: 10,000 cases

Leading Wines:
Cabernet Sauvignon,
Chardonnay,
Gewurztraminer,
Merlot, Perry,
Pinot Noir

Most of western Oregon is known for its year-round, moist, temperate climate, but toward the southern part of the state near the California border the climate grows increasingly warmer and drier. This is the location of Valley View Vineyard in the Applegate Valley — the warmest, driest, and sunniest part of western Oregon. Grasses and long needle pines replace the lusher vegetation of the north in the valley and in 1972, the Wisnovsky family planted a 26-acre vineyard here, re-establishing one of Oregon's earliest viticultural areas. John Eagle is Valley View's winemaker, assisted by Rob Stuart.

Because its vineyard is too warm for Gewurztraminer and Pinot Noir, the winery purchases those grapes from cooler region southern Oregon vineyards. But the Cabernet Sauvignon and Chardonnay are Valley View's best wines. The Chardonnay is aged in air-dried American oak, while the Cabernet Sauvignon, tannic and full-flavored, is aged in French oak. Valley View Vineyard also releases Oregon Perry, a locally popular wine made from pears.

VEGA VINEYARDS
Buellton, Central Coast

Output: 5,000 cases

Leading Wines:
Cabernet Sauvignon,
Chardonnay,
Gewurztraminer,
Johannisberg Riesling,
Pinot Noir

First crush at this winery was in 1979; now it draws on 34 acres in two vineyards and purchased grapes. Yields in its own vineyards are low: two tons per acre for Pinot Noir, three per acre for Gewurztraminer, and four for Riesling.

Two estate-bottled Rieslings are made, one exclusively from grapes produced by the oldest vines on the Vega River Ranch Vineyard. Both are Germanic in style, with delicate varietal character. Cabernet Sauvignon and Chardonnay are made from purchased grapes.

V

VENTANA VINEYARD
Soledad, Central Coast

Output: 20,000 cases

Leading Wines:
Cabernet Sauvignon,
Chardonnay,
Chenin Blanc,
Petite Syrah,
Pinot Noir,
Sauvignon Blanc,
White Riesling

Doug Meador, proprietor of Ventana, is known not only as a winemaker, but also as a creative and energetic viticulturalist. Meador began planting his 300-acre vineyard in 1972, and bonded Ventana in a converted barn in 1978.

Meador describes his vineyard as experimental. Some of his research has been instrumental in the war against the "Monterey veggies." Meador believes—as do many others—that a range of factors are at play in this situation, but proper irrigation has emerged as a leading theory.

The grapes grown by Meador in his Ventana vineyard are in wide demand by other wineries, in fact the Ventana name is most often seen on the labels of other wineries. Partly because of this, output each year can fluctuate wildly, as can the list. The winery is best-known for its full-bodied Chardonnays, but several other varietals are produced. An occational bottling of Pinot Blanc has been an outstanding promise of the possibilities for this grape.

VICHON WINERY
Oakville, San Francisco Bay North

Output: 25,000 cases

Leading Wines:
Cabernet Sauvignon,
Chardonnay, Chevrignon

The techniques employed at this 240,000-gallon winery have resulted in some very distinctive wines. The whites spend a period of time on the lees and Cabernet Sauvignon receives extended maceration of the skins following fermentation. Both techniques are unusual for the United States but are more common in France. The on the lees technique is used in Burgundy and in the Loire Valley, where white wines are left in contact with expired yeast cells and grape solids after fermentation to achieve the added complexity that results from yeast autolysis. The two wines thus produced are Chardonnay and Chevrignon, a blend of Semillon and Sauvignon Blanc.

Vichon's Cabernet Sauvignon is made from grapes purchased from Fay Vineyard and the Volker Eisele Vineyard, both known for quality Cabernet grapes. Vichon's Cabernets benefit from extended maceration of the cap, another technique unusual in California. No one is absolutely certain about this, but Vichon management believes that the process increases the proportion of soft tannins in the wine as the hard tannins either precipitate out or change into softer phenols. The result is a more drinkable wine but one also with great aging potential.

In early 1985, an agreement had been reached for the purchase of Vichon by Robert Mondavi Winery. No immediate changes in the Vichon winemaking style were planned; it was expected that Mondavi would continue to produce Vichon wines utilizing both the on-the-lees technique for the whites and extended maceration for the reds.

V

Vidal Blanc

A French-American hybrid gaining favor in eastern wine circles. Vidal is a versatile grape, successful in many vineyard districts where it lends itself to different wine styles. A few hundred acres are planted and the number is growing. Michigan has made a specialty of fruity, semidry and rich, late-harvest Vidals. New England makes it tart and bone-dry for fish, and some wineries age their dry, full-bodied Vidal in barrels for fumé-style wine. In the Finger Lakes and Pennsylvania, Vidal's late-ripening schedule and tough skins have allowed grapes to hang well into December for nectarlike ice wines, made from frozen berries. Perhaps more than any other, this variety is in search of identity, in wine regions open to all the possibilities.

Vidal's versatility may be traced to one of its parent varieties, Ugni Blanc, the most extensively cultivated white wine grape in France, used for Cognac, and grown in Italy under the name Trebbiano.

Vignoles, See Ravat

VILLA MT. EDEN WINERY
Oakville, San Francisco Bay North

Villa Mt. Eden is located on an Oakville Crossroad vineyard first planted in 1881. The property was revived and a 70,000-gallon winery built in 1974. About 75 percent of the output is Chardonnay and Cabernet Sauvignon. The Cabernet has drawn especial attention; it's a tough, tannic wine with great aging potential that also offers attractively forward aromas in its youth.

Output: 20,000 cases

Leading Wines:
Cabernet Sauvignon,
Cabernet Sauvignon
Reserve, Chardonnay,
Chenin Blanc,
Gewurztraminer,
Pinot Noir

Villard Blanc/Villard Noir

These are high-yielding French-American hybrid varieties grown in relatively warm districts of the East. Villard Blanc is often finished with some sweetness; Noir is indeed an inky-dark wine with an astringent edge.

Vinifera

The species of grapevines native to Europe. It includes all the classic varieties which evolved in European vineyards throughout the centuries were brought to colonial America. Vinifera vines found ideal growing conditions in California, where they had been grown exclusively since the late 18th century. Cold winters and humidity discouraged vinifera vineyards in other parts of the country until the 1960s and 1970s, when new fungicides and cultural practices opened many areas to the classic wine varieties.

VINIFERA WINE CELLARS
Hammondsport, Finger Lakes

Dr. Konstantin Frank established Vinifera Wine Cellars in 1963 after working as an experimental viticulturist for Gold Seal Vineyards. His own winery was dedicated to production of the European vinifera wines grown at Gold Seal for the first time in the eastern United States. The 60-acre vineyard on Keuka Lake grows more varieties of Vitis vinifera than many agricultural experiment stations.

Of the dozen vinified as varietal wines, Riesling stood out early and remains this winery's hallmark. Relatively dry but with considerable body and rich flavors, Dr. Frank's Johannisberg Rieslings have testified to remarkable vineyard skills, bringing the grapes to full ripeness in a marginal site. Luscious Muscat Ottonel dessert wine and rich, smoky Gewurztraminer have also been specialties. Some Chardonnays have the lean fruit and stylish austerity of French Chablis, but this variety has been more variable.

In the 1970s Frank's wine quality became increasingly inconsistent both between vintages and lots within vintages. Lackluster marketing let wine accumulate in inventory and older vintages were late coming on the market. Some of the wines put the extra years of bottle age to good use, but other didn't (watch color and ullage). In 1984 Frank's son took over the winery and began rehabilitating the cellar, selling off old wines and marketing a fresher, more consistent product. A new vineyard on Seneca Lake promises more changes in wine style, and will add Chardonnay, Pinot Noir, and Pinot Meuier grapes for sparkling wine production.

Among Vinifera's red wines, Pinot Noir and Gamay have filled out in good years with spicy, berry-fruit flavors. In other years they are thin and short. The new generation at Vinifera Wine Cellars promises exciting developments in the bottle.

Output: 10,000 cases

Leading Wines:
Chardonnay, Gamay,
Gewurztraminer,
Johannisberg Riesling,
Muscat Ottonel,
Pinot Noir, Rkatsiteli

Vintage

The year of harvest, and wine made from that harvest. Federal regulations require at least 95 percent of wine in the bottle to be from the vintage on the label. The remaining 5 percent is an allowance for topping up tanks or barrels with wine in inventory from other years. Vintage wines reflect the virtues or shortcomings of each individual growing season. The best wines are vintage wines from the best years. Nonvintage wines, blended from more than one year's production, offer more consistency.

VIRGINIA

Winemaking in the United States began in Virginia — vintage 1609 at the Jamestown colony. Made from wild grapes, the planting of vinifera grapevines shipped from Europe soon followed. In the next three centuries Virginians struggled to grow classic varieties for European-style wine, but insects, climate, and vine diseases defeated every effort. Thomas Jefferson was among the most determined and dejected of these early crusaders.

Native grapes — notably the Norton or Virginia Seedling — supported a modest wine industry in the state by the end of the 19th century, but without enough steam to survive Prohibition. Revival did not come until the wine boom of the 1970s, when small French-American hybrid vineyards began to grace the elegant farms of the eastern Blue Ridge foothills. Successful vinifera vineyards soon followed and exceeded the acreage in hybrids as it became clear that advances in cultural practices and vineyard sprays had changed the picture for viticulture. Virginia is the only eastern state with more acreage in vinifera than in hybrid vines.

High humidity, mildew, rot, and spring frosts challenge Virginia growers more than the cold winters that worry their neighbors to the north. With careful spray programs, vines grow lush and prolific, producing wines with plenty of body and ripe fruit flavors, softer than most eastern wines but still firm by California standards. These characteristics have attracted winery investors to the Charlottesville area from Italy, Germany, France, and California. Vineyard acreage is growing faster than anywhere else in the East, almost exclusively in vinifera varieties; the total acreage in 1984 was 1,300. Major varieties are Chardonnay, White Riesling, Cabernet Sauvignon, Seyval, Vidal Blanc, Chambourcin, Chancellor, and Villard Noir.

Viticultural Area

Federal labeling regulations issued in 1983 provided for the establishment of official "Viticultural Areas" loosely modeled after the geographically defined grape growing districts of Europe. The intent is to regulate and guarantee the accuracy of appellations or places of origin listed on labels. Dozens of areas have been approved by the Federal Bureau of Alcohol, Tobacco & Firearms, based on geographical, climate, and historical factors that suggest a cohesive wine district. Some are well-known, such as Napa Valley and the Finger Lakes. Many are unfamiliar names of areas new to wine with little meaning to consumers. Boundaries can be generously drawn (and hotly debated) to accommodate commercial interests. In a wine country as formative as the United States, any attempt to define specific viticultural districts is a clumsy first step, at best, toward a useful perspective on what is in the bottle.

VOSE VINEYARDS
Napa, San Francisco Bay North

Output: 13,000 cases

Leading Wines: Cabernet Sauvignon, Chardonnay, Zinblanca (White Zinfandel)

From 30 acres on the slope of Mount Veeder in the Mayacamas Mountains, which separate the Napa and Sonoma valleys, this 45,000-gallon winery began producing estate-bottled wines in 1977. So far, the wines have tended towards a ripe, oaky, tannic style.

WAGNER VINEYARDS
Lodi, Finger Lakes

Output: 20,000 cases

Leading Wines:
Aurora, Champagne,
Chardonnay,
De Chaunac, Delaware,
Gewurztraminer,
Johannisberg Riesling,
Port, Seyval Blanc,
Sparkling Rosé,
Wagner's Seyval

Wagner's 1980 Chardonnay was the first single wine since Dr. Konstantin Frank's 1961 Trockenbeerenauslese Riesling to send ripples out from the Finger Lakes through national wine circles. The big, powerful Chardonnay with complex, mouth-filled flavor showed that the Finger Lakes could produce a wine astonishingly like California's best. Wagner's 100-acre vineyard lies in the lee of Seneca Lake's deepest basin, benefiting from its tempering effect both winter and summer. Grape sugars run high, and the wines typically show good color and extract. Chardonnay and Seyval Blanc are barrel-fermented, then aged in steel and glass to keep varietal character prominent. Wagner's Seyval is the label used for a semidry, fresh-fruit version of the French-American variety. Riesling also does extremely well here, with spicy fruit and firm acid, often tinged with the honey scent of botrytis. All these wines, even the big vintages, tend to peak young and show signs of decline after 3 or 4 years.

The vineyard has been expanded in recent years with Gewurztraminer, Pinot Noir, and Ravat. Older acreage planted when Wagner grew grapes for Taylor produces the red French-American variety De Chaunac in abundance. Short demand and accumulating stocks in barrel have resulted in the continuing release of soft, lactic red wines identified with lot numbers. Wagner Champagne is made from Seyval Blanc.

WALKER VALLEY VINEYARDS
Walker Valley, New York

Output: 2,000 cases

Leading Wines:
Autumn Red, Cayuga,
Chardonnay, Foch,
Leon Millot, Ravat,
Rayon d'Or, Riesling,
Seyval

Walker Valley vineyard and winery are the labor of love of one-time physical education teacher Gary Dross. He cleared and planted 10 acres, built the winery, and handles all phases of the operation.

White wines predominate, notably oak-aged Seyval and Chardonnay, and a luscious, ripe-fruit Rayon d'Or. A number of other varietals and blends vary in style in an effort to appeal to different tastes. Three-quarters of the grapes are estate-grown, the rest purchased from the Finger Lakes and Long Island, further dispersing wine styles until Walker Valley's young vineyard comes into full bearing, when wine production will level out at 8,000 gallons (70 percent French hybrid, 30 percent vinifera).

WASHINGTON

Washington is second only to California in quantity of vinifera wines, yet less than two decades ago the state produced virtually no premium wine. Although many wineries came into being immediately following the repeal of Prohibition, protectionist state liquor laws and the lack of any tradition of making or consuming fine wines confined the industry to indifferent wines, often fortified, for sale in taverns. The few vinifera grapes grown in the state were haphazardly blended with winter-hardy native American varieties, including those often least suited for fine wine, such as the ubiquitous Concord. Not until the mid-1960s, when removal of the protectionist laws seemed inevitable, was there significant commercial interest in premium Washington wine. The Washington wine renaissance began on two fronts in the late 1960s with commercial releases of vinifera wines by Associated Vintners, now known as Columbia Winery, and by American Wine Growers, under its new label, Ste. Michelle. The advice and catalytic encouragement of Leon Adams, André Tchelistcheff and others helped set the stage for what was to be a revolutionary transformation and subsequent meteoric growth in the state's wine industry.

Columbia Valley, Washington's principal grape growing area, has a remarkable capacity to produce exceptionally high yields with good fruit intensity and excellent sugars and acids. Like the Vosge Mountains in Alsace and the coastal mountains of Oregon and California, it lies in the rain shadow of a mountain range. But no other major wine producing region is influenced as dramatically as is the Columbia Valley.

Not far from the Pacific Ocean, the Cascade Mountain Range peaks thrust more than 12,000 feet above sea level, interrupting the flow of marine air for hundreds of miles, and dividing Washington State into two radically different climates. West of the mountain range, it is temperate year-round, cool and often rainy, and the land is lushly vegetated. East of the Cascade Range, in the climatic rain shadow that embraces the vast Columbia Valley, the weather is hot during the summer months. Winters are sometimes extremely cold, and the land is semi-arid. Much of the area receives less than ten inches of rain a year, and irrigation is a necessity.

Because increases in grape sugar depend on both warmth and sun, the Columbia Valley's long, warm, sunny days insure adequate sugars at harvest. Decreases in acidity, however, primarily depend on temperature, and the unusually cool nights, especially during the final fall ripening period, insure ample acidities even in the warmer growing sites.

The growing cycle is later than the more southerly American winegrowing climates. Harvest typically begins in late September and carries through October and even into November and December for the late-harvest varieties. Final ripening of the grapes takes place in rapidly moderating fall temperatures.

This northerly American winegrowing climate is well suited to cool climate white wine varieties, but contrary to popular expectation, a broad spectrum of premium wine grapes grows well in Washington. Columbia Valley ranges from Region I to Region V on the U.C. Davis scale, although all Washington's vineyards are located in climatic Regions I, II, III. The traditional Davis method for categorizing growing sites, however, does not adequately capture the Columbia Valley's climatic environments and their effect on the grapes and wine.

Encompassing a third of the state, the Columbia Valley contains many separate valleys and growing areas. The Yakima Valley, a major growing area on the western edge of the Columbia Valley drainage basin, was the first BATF-approved Viticultural Area in the state. Other major growing areas are situated along the Columbia River's path, and include sites near the communities of Paterson, Pasco, and Mattawa. The Walla Walla Valley, encompassing a portion of Oregon, is the state's second approved Viticultural Area, but as yet it is home to few vineyards and most of the wineries in the area purchase grapes from other Columbia Valley growers. The Columbia Valley itself is Washington's third BATF-approved Viticultural Area. The BATF Columbia Valley appellation includes land in Oregon, but as yet vineyard development on the Oregon side of the Columbia River is minimal.

Much of western Washington, east of the Cascade Range, is too cool for premium grape growing, and most of the wineries in this region use grapes grown in the Columbia Valley. More wineries and vineyards devoted to western Washington grapes are opening up, however, and cool climate white varieties have been produced successfully from grapes grown on such sites as the Nooksack, Carbon, and Puyallup River Valleys, and on Bainbridge Island in Puget Sound. Muller-Thurgau and Madeleine Angevine are the principal vinifera varieties. In southwest Washington, in what is essentially an extension of Oregon's Willamette Valley climate, Pinot Noir is very successful.

In the Columbia Valley, white wines, particularly Riesling, have been the foundation of the wine industry. Riesling is the most planted grape, and is likely to remain so for the forseeable future, but emphasis is gradually shifting toward dry white wines from traditional French varieties.

Chardonnays are good, if sometimes a bit short in the finish, but there have been some excellent examples, and recent vintages suggest that more winegrowers are finding the key to this grape. Sauvignon Blanc is very successful and, as in California, increasing in popularity and acreage. Semillon, a grape that yields indifferent wine in most of America, has found a home in Washington, producing wines similar in character to Sauvignon Blanc.

A quantitative mainstay, Chenin Blanc has gained recent acclaim, demonstrating more character and interest than usual for this grape. Gewurztraminer and Muscat Canelli, both very successful, are among the

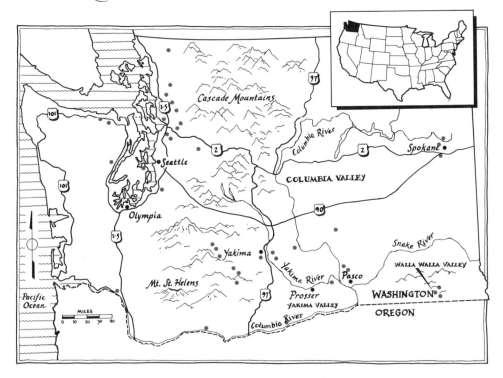

other principal white wine varieties. Virtually every year, though in very small quantities, late-harvest, ice, and botrytised wines are made from Riesling, Gewurztraminer, and sometimes Sauvignon Blanc.

Washington winegrowers have been longer in coming to terms with red wine grapes, but recent successes are stunning. Washington's best red wines have come from the smaller to medium-size producers. A reasonable argument can now be made that the very best Washington wines are red, although they are not nearly as uniformly successful as the whites. Cabernet Sauvignon is the premier red wine grape, followed by Merlot.

Vintage variation is greater in Washington than California, though less than Oregon or many of Europe's principal growing areas. In general, Washington red wines are more sensitive to vintage variations. Unless otherwise noted, the vintage remarks apply to Columbia Valley wines.

1980   The year Mount St. Helens erupted. A cool vintage, the wines are good overall, but sometimes lacking in concentration.

1981   Another cooler than average vintage, but a very warm late summer and early fall brought the acids in line with the sugars. The grapes showed fine varietal fruit.

1982   A warm growing season concluding with a highly unusual wet fall. Wine quality is very good but some wines, particularly the reds, are lacking in fruit intensity and extract.

1983   A moderately cool summer followed by an early frost in late September resulted in lower sugars and higher acids than the previous year, and the necessity for early picking in severely frosted vineyards.

W

The best of the red wines are especially fine with good acid structure.

1984   The September frost of the prior year followed by a damaging winter freeze substantially reduced the harvest. A cool spring and an early and cool fall reduced the growing season. The reduced crop and the smaller berries produced wines with concentrated fruit, balancing well with the vintage's slightly lower sugars and higher acids.

WEIBEL CHAMPAGNE CELLARS
Mission San Jose, San Francisco Bay South

The original Weibel winery was founded in 1945 on property that had seen vineyards planted by Franciscan missionaries as early as the 1780s.

Sparkling wines are Weibel's specialty and it is the largest bottler of private label sparkling wines in the United States, and the fifth largest producer of sparkling wines in the country. Bulk process sparkling wines are sold under other labels such as Napolean, Lafayette, and Jacques Reynaud, and most of the private label bottlings have also been made by this inexpensive method. All the sparkling wines under the Weibel label are bottle-fermented and spend little time on the yeast, resulting in light, fruity, slightly sweet wines. The extensive list of still wines is similarly light, simple, and economically priced.

Output: 1 million cases

Leading Wines:
Blanc de Blanc,
Blanc de Pinot Noir,
Brut, Chardonnay Brut,
Crackling Rosé,
Extra Dry,
Green Hungarian,
Pinot Noir Blanc,
Spumante, White
Cabernet Sauvignon,
White Zinfandel

WENTE BROS
Livermore, San Francisco Bay South

Now run by the fourth generation of Wentes, this winery has produced wines continuously at the same Livermore Valley site since 1883. At the end of Prohibition Wente was among the industry leaders working to revive the California wine industry.

In the Livermore Valley, which is fifteen miles long and ten miles wide, soils are gravelly, closely resembling those of Graves in Bordeaux, and growing season temperatures are cooled by the marine influence of San Francisco Bay. Perhaps more than any other winery, Wente has established the valley as one associated with white wines. Today, nearly its entire output is of white wines from their 680 Livermore acres and 600 acres they pioneered in the similarly cool and gravelly Arroyo Seco region of Monterey County.

Like Mirassou, their co-pioneers in Monterey, Wente was one of the first wineries to develop machine-harvesting and field-crushing to compensate for the distance between winery and vineyards. Cold fermentation in stainless steel and limited contact with oak produce light, fruity wines that characterize this 4.1 million-gallon winery. This style is reflected in one of their most popular and successful wines, the Blanc de Blancs blend of Chenin Blanc, with a little White Riesling and Ugni Blanc.

Output: 620,000 cases

Leading Wines:
Blanc de Blancs,
Blanc de Noir,
Cabernet Sauvignon,
Chablis, Chardonnay,
Chenin Blanc,
Gamay Beaujolais,
Gamay Beaujolais Blanc,
Grey Riesling,
Johannisberg Riesling,
Petite Sirah, Pinot Blanc,
Rosé Wente,
Sauvignon Blanc,
Dry Semillon, Zinfandel;
Brut sparkling wine

W

WESTON WINERY
Caldwell, Idaho

Output: 3,000 cases

Leading Wines:
Cabernet Sauvignon,
Chardonnay,
Gewurztraminer,
Riesling,
Semillon

Formerly crush foreman and vineyard manager for Ste. Chapelle Vineyards, Cheyne Weston began planting his own vineyards in 1979 and produced his first commercial vintage in 1982. The winery and some of its 15 acres of vineyards are in the Sunnyslope area of the Snake River Valley, near the Ste. Chapelle winery. Weston's other vineyard is farther up the valley, in a warm growing area near Hagerman, at an elevation of 2,800 feet.

Weston is working with several local vineyards, including a site just across the nearby Oregon border. Some of the new vineyards include experimental plantings of Zinfandel, Muscat Canelli, and Sauvignon Blanc, varieties that Weston believes will do well in Idaho but as yet are largely untested.

Riesling, more than half of Weston's production, is made in several styles from off-dry to sweet. When the Zinfandel vines mature, Weston will make a white wine from the grapes. Cabernet Sauvignon from Washington grapes is made into white and red wines. Weston's Chardonnay is barrel-fermented in French oak.

WESTWIND WINERY
Bernalillo, New Mexico

Output: 6,000 cases

Leading Wines:
Ruby Cabernet,
Vidal Blanc

With Westwind's first vintage in 1983, winegrowing in New Mexico resumed in earnest. This state was the site of America's first wine vineyards, at early 17th century Spanish missions. Small farm wineries rekindled New Mexico wine in the 1960s, but Westwind was the first major commercial venture, buying grapes from independent vineyards throughout the state. It makes dry varietal and blended table wines from vinifera and French-American hybrids. A 46-acre, all-vinifera estate vineyard was planted in 1985, but Westwind will continue to buy grapes and function as a clearinghouse for developing New Mexican wine styles.

WHALER WINERY
Ukiah, San Francisco Bay North

Output: 3,600 cases

Leading Wines:
Red Zinfandel,
White Zinfandel

This small winery has 24 acres of benchland overlooking the Russian River, all planted to Zinfandel. In 1981, when the vineyards matured, it began making small amounts of red and white Zinfandel from a 20,000-gallon winery.

WILLIAM WHEELER WINERY
Healdsburg, San Francisco Bay North

Output: 15,000 cases

Leading Wines:
Cabernet Sauvignon,

Wheeler winery was completed in 1981 after two earlier vintages of Cabernet Sauvignon and Chardonnay made in leased space had won widespread praise. The building stands in the midst of 32 acres of vineyards at elevations of 500 to 900 feet in Dry Creek Valley and is one of the highest in the Dry Creek area. Only Cabernet Sauvignon and Zinfandel are planted in the Wheeler vineyards. Grapes are purchased from other growers to produce Chardonnay, Sauvignon Blanc, and Pinot.

Wheeler's Chardonnay is produced with a Sonoma and a Monterey appellation in two styles. The Sonoma wine is partly barrel-fermented, whereas the Monterey version is fully barrel-fermented and goes through partial malolactic fermentation which reduces acidity and makes for a round, fuller style of Chardonnay. The Sauvignon Blanc is a blend of grapes grown in three vineyards in the Dry Creek and Alexander Valleys. Storage capacity is presently 60,000 gallons.

Chardonnay, Pinot Noir, Sauvignon Blanc

WHITE OAK VINEYARDS
Healdsburg, San Francisco Bay North

Founded in 1981, White Oak's six acres of vineyards, planted equally to Chardonnay and Cabernet Sauvignon, reflect the principal focus of this winery. The output of the small winery is supplemented with grapes purchased from Alexander, Russian River, and Dry Creek Valley locations.

Output: 8,000 cases

Leading Wines:
Cabernet Sauvignon,
Chardonnay,
Chenin Blanc,
Johannisberg Riesling,
Zinfandel

White Riesling

Often called Johannisberg Riesling, this German variety is planted to over 11,000 acres in California, most in the counties which surround San Francisco Bay. Formerly, most California Johannisberg Rieslings were made in the dry, alcoholic style of Alsace, where the grape is also grown. However, in recent years—late 1970s and early 1980s—there have been growing interest in and production of lighter, slightly sweet and fruity style of German Rieslings. In addition, several wineries have made excellent late-harvest wines from Riesling grapes which have been infected with botrytis mold.

WHITEHALL LANE WINERY
St. Helena, San Francisco Bay North

Whitehall Lane was founded in 1980 and produces mainly estate-bottled varietals from its 26-acre vineyard. Pinot Noir and some other grapes are purchased from selected vineyards. Whitehall's varietals are supplemented by two proprietary blends: Fleur d'Helene, primarily Pinot Noir that is meant to be drunk young; and Blanc d'Helene, an oak-aged blend of Chardonnay, Riesling, Sauvignon Blanc, and Chenin Blanc.

Output: 20,000 cases

Leading Wines:
Blanc d'Helene,
Blanc de Pinot Noir,
Cabernet Sauvignon,
Chardonnay,
Fleur d'Helene

W

WIDMER'S WINE CELLARS
Naples, Finger Lakes

Output: 450,000 cases

Leading Wines:
Cayuga White, Chablis,
Cream Sherry, Johannisberg
Riesling, Lake Niagara,
Marechal Foch, Sherry,
Sparkling Lake Niagara

1983 NOUVEAU
Finger Lakes
FOCH

A soft, fruity, red varietal wine with the distinctive bouquet of a Nouveau Beaujolais. Selected grapes were hand picked on September 30th at the Widmer's Vineyards. The old world method macération carbonique was employed for two weeks prior to pressing and fermentation. This traditional process produces an early maturing red wine intended for immediate consumption. Serve at cool room temperature with fine meats, fowl and cheeses.

PRODUCED AND BOTTLED BY WIDMER'S WINE CELLARS, INC.
NAPLES, NY · ALCOHOL 10.5% BY VOLUME

Widmer's centennary in 1988 belies its struggle to establish a clear identity. The winery began as one of the two wine-family dynasties on the Finger Lakes, the rival on Canandaigua Lake to the Taylors of Keuka Lake. In the 1940s, encouraged by Frank Schoonmaker, it was one of the first American wineries to market varietals, using old eastern wine grapes like Moore's Diamond and Vergennes. A sherry solera established at that time continues in operation to this day. Over the years the winery's trademark has become its roof of barrels, a dramatic display of cooperage atop the winecellar that is used to mature fortified wines through exposure to the elements.

After the Widmer family sold the winery in 1961, it passed through a number of owners, including the R.T. French Co., which tried unsuccessfully to link it with its vineyard in California's Alexander Valley. In 1983 the winery's managers bought out French, reversing an industry pattern of corporate acquisition.

Well over half the winery's production is Lake Niagara, both still and sparkling wines from the labrusca variety Niagara. Intensely grapey, semisweet but with a hint of tartness, Lake Niagara is perhaps the quintessential labrusca wine: fermented grape juice in its simplest form, bursting with fruit. Widmer was one of the first producers of two hybrid varietals—Marechal Foch and Cayuga White—consistently among the best examples of these varieties. Widmer's Rhine Wine is predominantly Cayuga and a good buy for a light, fruity, semidry quaffing wine.

Little or no sherry has been made in recent years because of large inventories, a marketing headache for the winery but a boon to consumers. Widmer's sherries on the market today have spent up to 20 years in barrel and bottle, giving them mellow, nutty character and a reputation, with one or two rivals, as the best in the East.

WIEDERKEHR WINE CELLARS
Altus, Arkansas

Output: 500,000 cases

Leading Wines:
Cabernet Sauvignon,
Chardonnay, Johannisberg
Riesling, Niagara, Rosé de
Cabernet Sauvignon,
Sauvignon Blanc, Di
Tanta Maria, Verdelet

The largest winery between the East and West Coasts is also one of the oldest, tracing back to Swiss immigrants in 1880. Wiederkehr was following a post-Prohibition market for fortified-wine when a new generation of family managers introduced French-American grapes to Arkansas in the early 1960s, followed by the Midwest's first vinifera. The hybrid Verdelet Blanc is a cold-sensitive vine that found the Ozark foothills to its liking, producing a delicate, floral wine. Niagara is handled well here, but Wiederkehr's principal achievement is a diverse line of vinifera varietals. Not surprisingly, warm climate varieties are the most successful: Sauvignon Blanc, Rosé de Cabernet, and a luscious, muscat-flavored Di Tanta Maria—wines that offset low acid levels with strong flavors or astringent edges.

HERMANN J. WIEMER VINEYARD
Dundee, Finger Lakes

After an erratic start, Wiemer has settled into a style of very clean, elegant, somewhat understated Riesling, usually a dry bottling (green label) and a riper version (brown label) that varies in sweetness according to the vintage. Wiemer's delicious sparkling Riesling was one of the first made in America. The Chardonnay has lately been shaking off the fragrant, fruity aura of Riesling that launched this winery, and developing its own lean, Chablis style. A first vintage of Pinot Noir in 1983 promised good, limited releases of this variety in a bright, forward style. Wiemer has earned a reputation for consistent quality.

Output: 4,000 cases

Leading Wines:
Chardonnay,
Pinot Noir,
Riesling

THE WINERY RUSHING
Merigold, Mississippi

In 1977, Sam and Diane Rushing started Mississippi's first winery since Prohibition to revive the region's traditional Muscadine wines using modern winemaking techniques. The Rushings use varieties bred for wine in southern experiment station nurseries to make a half dozen dry and sweet varietals and blends with strong, exotic flavors.

Output: 5,000 cases

Leading Wines:
Carlos Red, Noble White,
Rosé, Red Sweet Wine,
White Muscadine

WOLLERSHEIM WINERY
Prairie du Sac, Wisconsin

Wollersheim likens itself to a small Burgundian property, starting with well-matured fruit and using warm fermentation temperatures, plenty of wood, malolactic fermentations, and bottle-aging to produce full, round, complex wines. Domaine Reserve Red and Sugarloaf White are the principal wines, made from the French-American hybrids Marechal Foch and Leon Millot, and Seyval Blanc. Barrel-fermented and barrel-aged, these are adventurous wines, minimally processed, unafraid of racy flavors, a little volatile acidity, or oxidation. A dry, estate-bottled Riesling (in Wisconsin!), Chardonnay, and Ruby Nouveau are made in small quantities. River Country is a second label for semidry wines. Grapes from other midwestern and New York State vineyards supplement the 25-acre estate. The Wollersheim property was first planted by Agoston Haraszthy, who struggled against a few Wisconsin winters, dug a winecellar, then moved on to become the father of the California wine industry.

Output: 4,500 cases

Leading Wines:
Chardonnay,
Domaine Reserve,
Riesling,
River Country,
Ruby Nouveau,
Sugarloaf White

WOODBURY VINEYARDS
Dunkirk, Lake Erie

If one winery were chosen to represent the extraordinary diversity of wine types that is produced in the eastern United States, it would be Woodbury.

Output: 12,000 cases

Leading Wines:
Blanc de Blancs Brut,

W

*Cabernet Sauvignon,
Chardonnay, Dutchess,
Gewurztraminer, Glacier
Ridge white, red, rosé,
Johannisberg Riesling,
Johannisberg Riesling sekt,
Niagara, Seyval Blanc,
Spumante*

This New York winery offers a smorgasbord of sparkling and still table wines from vinifera, French-American, and labrusca grapes. Enveloping this diversity, however, is a style of clean, fruit flavors and relatively low alcohol (mostly 10-11.5 percent) designed to complement food.

The Woodbury farm was one of the first cooperators of Dr. Konstantin Frank, the viticultural pioneer of the Finger Lakes. Woodbury vinifera plantings introduced the classic European varietals to New York and remain the most extensive in the state. Its semi-dry Riesling and Gewurztraminer have had consistently full, fresh varietal character. A Riesling *sekt* was one of the first American sparkling wines from this variety. Blanc de Blancs Brut shows strong Chardonnay fruit with a hint of Pinot Noir structure. Woodbury's clean, firm fruit style comes through best in its sparkling wines.

Among its line of French-American hybrids, Seyval Blanc has excelled. Two varietal labrusca wines — Niagara and Dutchess — are well-made examples of wines at opposite ends of the native American flavor spectrum. Woodbury Glacier Ridge wines blend hybrid and native varieties to lighten the fresh grape flavors of labrusca.

WOODBURY WINERY
San Rafael, San Francisco Bay North

Output: 4,000 cases

*Leading Wines:
Alexander Valley Reserve,
Petite Sirah, Pinot Noir,
Vintage ports, Zinfandel*

Founded in 1977, to produce high quality dessert wines, Woodbury purchases grapes mainly from the Alexander Valley for a varied line of blends and varietals in a port style. The vintage ports are blends of Zinfandel, Petite Sirah, and Cabernet Sauvignon. But port-styled varietal wines are also made from Zinfandel, Petite Sirah, and Pinot Noir.

An unusual wine labeled Alexander Valley Reserve Dessert wine and blended from Pinot Noir with some Zinfandel and Petite Sirah, was released by this 60,000-gallon winery in 1984. It was made from 60 year-old vineyards in the Alexander Valley and was fortified with an aged brandy (rather than with the 192 proof neutral distillate commonly used in the production of dessert wines in California).

Y | Z

YORK MOUNTAIN WINERY
Templeton, Central Coast

York Mountain Winery has stood on the eastern slopes of the Santa Lucia Mountains in San Luis Obispo County since its founding in 1882. Its modern history began in 1970 when it was purchased from the grandson of the founder and modernized to 75,000-gallon capacity. Since then it has been noted primarily for robust Zinfandels. A dozen other wines are produced, including a bottle-fermented sparkling wine, but its reputation is chiefly for its rugged, earthy reds.

Output: 6,000 cases

Leading Wines:
Cabernet Sauvignon,
Chardonnay, Chenin
Blanc, French Colombard,
Merlot, Pinot Meunier,
Riesling, Zinfandel

ZACA MESA
Los Olivos, Central Coast

Founded in 1978, Zaca Mesa Winery was one of the pioneers in the Santa Ynez Valley in the northern portion of Santa Barbara County. Three hundred fifty winery-owned acres of grapes now supply most of Zaca Mesa's needs and wines are produced under three labels: Zaca Mesa; Toyon, a less expensive label for everyday varietals; and American Reserve, a limited bottling of wines given special care and longer aging.

Chardonnay and Cabernet Sauvignon have been its most consistent wines and the treatment they get in the American Reserve bottlings has only improved the winery's reputation. The American Reserve Chardonnay, made exclusively from estate-grown grapes, is entirely barrel-fermented and aged 5 to 6 months in French oak. Sixty percent of the 'regular' Chardonnay is barrel-fermented, with the balance being fermented in stainless steel. This wine, made from grapes grown in fifteen vineyards, is aged for 5 to 6 months in French oak barrels after completion of fermentation. The lighter and simpler Toyon Chardonnay is fermented entirely in stainless steel and receives only three months of wood development.

Zaca Mesa has continued to work with Pinot Noir, a difficult variety but with the winery's cool microclimates, one that has promise. While still waiting for a breakthrough, each vintage has been a marked improvement and refinement upon previous years.

Output: 55,000 cases

Leading Wines:
Cabernet Sauvignon,
Chardonnay, Pinot Noir,
Sauvignon Blanc, Syrah,
White Riesling

Z

ZD WINES
Napa, San Francisco Bay North

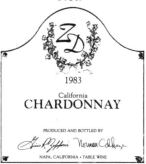

Originally started as a home-winemaking operation in Sonoma, ZD's early growth encouraged the partners to establish a winery in 1979. Winemaking at the 37,000-gallon winery, situated in the Napa Valley, is controlled by Norm deLeuze and until his death in 1985, Gino Zepponi, his partner, oversaw Domaine Chandon's sparkling wine production and participated in winemaking decisions at ZD.

ZD is best known for its full-flavored Burgundian varietals, robust Pinot Noirs, and full-bodied Chardonnays. Chardonnay accounts for half its output and is typically cold-fermented and aged in American oak for approximately 10 months. The Pinot Noir is fermented to extract maximum color and flavor and is aged in American oak for nearly two years.

STEPHEN ZELLERBACH WINERY
Healdsburg, San Francisco Bay North

From a 194,000-gallon ultra-modern winery built in 1981 in the Alexander Valley, Zellerbach continues a family tradition for winemaking. Cabernet Sauvignon and Merlot are estate-bottled. The Cabernet accounts for more than 75 percent of the winery's output, and Chardonnay grapes are purchased from neighboring vineyards. All wines are fermented in stainless steel, then transferred to small oak barrels to mature. The Zellerbach wines have received wide critical acclaim for their well-structured elegance and outstanding varietal definition.

Zinfandel

Long thought to have been brought to California by Agoston Haraszthy, the Hungarian immigrant who carried over 100,000 cuttings to California in the early 1860s, it now appears that this red vinifera was already growing in the vineyards at Buena Vista in Sonoma when Haraszthy bought his in 1857. (There is also evidence that Zinfandel is Italian in origin and may be the same grape variety as Primitivo.) Zinfandel is the most heavily planted red wine grape in California with 27,000 acres. Central Valley acreage accounts for 11,000 of this. Once used as a blending grape in red generics, Zinfandel is chiefly used now in varietal table wines.

A number of distinct styles have emerged. Just before the modern boom in Zinfandel, it was thought of as California's answer to Beaujolais, and grapey, sappy, light wine is still commonly made from the grape. A more serious style emerged from the Sierra Foothills in Amador County: dark, intense Zinfandels with strong pepper-berry-spice varietal character. In the late 1960s and early 1970s, this style was extended even further; and late-harvest Zinfandels, with 16 or 17 percent alcohol, gained popularity for some time. Perhaps as a reaction to this, a number of wineries began to make Zinfandels that could be described as claret-like: elegant, with more finesse than the varietal had ever shown before. Today, Zinfandel is achieving new life with the fad for White Zinfandel, so-called blush wines made by leaving the must on the skins for a short period of time. As California's "own" wine, Zinfandel remains an evolving delight, since there are no major international models to copy.

ACKNOWLEDGEMENTS

A book such as this could not have been possible without the cooperation and generous assistance of many people, particularly winemakers and their associates. It is not possible to list everyone who gave of their time and knowledge. But special thanks are due to: Zelma Long, Frances Mahoney, Caroline and Stan Anderson, Doug Meador, Merry Edwards, Terrance Leighton, Andy Quady, Paul Draper, Don Galleano, Warren Winiarski, Frank Cadenasso, Michael Martini, Phil Posson, Dawnine Dyer, J. Richard Sanford, James Lapsley, Holbrook Mitchell, and Klaus Mathes. Leigh Andriance, Millie Howie, and Sandra McIver shared their expert knowledge, while The Wine Institute and Phil Hiaring's Wines and Vines provided essential factual information.

In the East, Lucie Taylor Morton, Hudson Cattel, Linda McKee of Wine East, Bruce Zoecklin, and Craig Goldwyn of Beverage Testing Institute all contributed their time and knowledge to the text.

Smallwood & Stewart would like to thank: Bob Rogers, Mark Bregman, Sue Ewell, Joanne Green; Michelle Vidro for her tireless work on the layout of the book; David Rosengarten, who acted as associate editor on the California section; and Rory Callahan of The Wine Institute, who patiently gave his time to answer numerous questions about California wines and wineries.